SHAKESPEARE FOR THE PEOPLE

Beginning by mapping out an overview of the expansion of elementary education in Britain across the nineteenth century, Andrew Murphy explores, for the first time, the manner in which Shakespeare acquired a working-class readership. He traces developments in publishing which meant that editions of Shakespeare became ever cheaper as the century progressed. Drawing on more than a hundred published and manuscript autobiographical texts, the book examines the experiences of a wide range of working-class readers. Particular attention is focused on a set of radical readers for whom Shakespeare's work had a special political resonance. Murphy explores the reasons why the playwright's working-class readership began to fall away from the turn of the century, noting the competition he faced from professional sports, the cinema, radio and television. The book concludes by asking whether it matters that, in our own time, Shakespeare no longer commands a general popular audience.

ANDREW MURPHY is Professor of English at the University of St Andrews. His books include *Shakespeare in Print: A History and Chronology of Shakespeare Publishing* (Cambridge, 2003) and *But the Irish Sea Betwixt Us: Ireland, Colonialism, and Renaissance Literature* (1999), and he is the editor of *A Concise Companion to Shakespeare and the Text* (2007) and *The Renaissance Text: Theory, Editing, Textuality* (2000).

SHAKESPEARE FOR THE PEOPLE

Working-class Readers, 1800–1900

ANDREW MURPHY
University of St Andrews

CAMBRIDGE UNIVERSITY PRESS
Cambridge, New York, Melbourne, Madrid, Cape Town, Singapore,
São Paulo, Delhi, Dubai, Tokyo, Mexico City

Cambridge University Press
The Edinburgh Building, Cambridge CB2 8RU, UK

Published in the United States of America by Cambridge University Press, New York

www.cambridge.org
Information on this title: www.cambridge.org/9780521176552

© Andrew Murphy 2008

This publication is in copyright. Subject to statutory exception
and to the provisions of relevant collective licensing agreements,
no reproduction of any part may take place without the written
permission of Cambridge University Press.

First published 2008
First paperback edition 2010

A catalogue record for this publication is available from the British Library

Library of Congress Cataloguing in Publication Data

Murphy, Andrew.
Shakespeare for the people: working-class readers, 1800–1900 / Andrew Murphy.
p. cm.
Includes bibliographical references.
ISBN 978-0-521-86177-9
1. Shakespeare, William, 1564–1616 – Study and teaching – Great Britain. 2. Books and reading –
Great Britain – History – 19th century. 3. Shakespeare, William, 1564–1616 – Criticism
and interpretation. 4. Publishers and publishing – Great Britain – History –
19th century. 5. Shakespeare, William, 1564–1616 – Influence. 6. Literature and society –
Great Britain – History – 19th century. I. Title.
PR2987.M87 2008
822.3'3–dc22 2007043009

ISBN 978-0-521-86177-9 Hardback
ISBN 978-0-521-17655-2 Paperback

Cambridge University Press has no responsibility for the persistence or
accuracy of URLs for external or third-party internet websites referred to in
this publication, and does not guarantee that any content on such websites is,
or will remain, accurate or appropriate.

For Frank

Contents

List of illustrations — *page* viii
Acknowledgements — ix
List of abbreviations — xi

Introduction — 1
1 The educational context — 28
2 The publishing context — 58
3 Reading — 95
4 Political Shakespeare — 135
5 Decline and fall — 162

Afterword — 198

Appendix 1: Autobiographers by year of birth — 207
Appendix 2: Autobiographers listed alphabetically — 218
Bibliography — 221
Index — 237

Illustrations

1. The tercentenary celebrations at Stratford-on-Avon, from *Illustrated London News* page 2
2. The tercentenary tree-planting ceremony on Primrose Hill, from *Illustrated London News* 3
3. The monitorial system of teaching, from *Manual of the System of Teaching Reading, Writing, Arithmetic, and Needle-work* 36
4. A London street stationer, from Henry Mayhew, *London Labour and the London Poor*, vol. 1 74
5. Cover of John Dicks' shilling Shakespeare 84
6. Embossed presentation plate of the Chester Mechanics' Institute, included in a Shakespeare collected works edition 109

Acknowledgements

Shakespeare for the People could not have been written without the very generous support of the British Academy, and I am deeply grateful to the Academy for providing me with a Research Readership, a small research grant and funding to present material based on the book at the World Shakespeare Congress in Brisbane in 2006. Heartfelt thanks also go to Eric Langley, who served as my replacement during the course of my BA Readership.

As ever, I am grateful to my colleagues at St Andrews for their support and encouragement. In particular, I thank Neil Rhodes, who read the entire typescript of the book, Gill Plain, who looked over Chapter 5 and the Afterword and Nick Roe and Susan Manly, who advised on the project when it was at proposal stage. Thanks are also due to Richard Foulkes, who also read the entire book, and to Stuart Sillars, who read the material on Shakespeare and nineteenth-century publishing. All of these readers – and the anonymous press reviewers – provided invaluable feedback. The mistakes that remain are, sadly, all my own.

Anyone who works on nineteenth-century working-class culture owes an incalculable debt to John Burnett, whose own work in the field was groundbreaking in itself and also provided the tools and resources that have made other research possible. It was a pleasurable surprise to discover that this historian, from whose work I had been furiously taking page after page of notes, was, in fact, the father of a friend of long-standing: Mark Thornton Burnett. Mark was kind enough to ask his father to read the proposal for the book and the meticulous and incisive feedback that I received was enormously helpful. I am grateful to Mark for making this connection and for his own invaluable encouragement of the work. It was with great sadness that I learned of the death of John Burnett in November 2006. This book is, I hope, a small tribute to his scholarly legacy.

My work on this book has been greatly facilitated by the assistance I have received from a number of particularly helpful librarians. I especially thank: Penny Lyndon at Brunel University, who helped with accessing texts from the autobiographies archive at Brunel library; Niky Rathbone at the Birmingham Central Library, who arranged for a large number of Lemuel Matthews Griffiths' scrapbooks to be called up in advance of my visit to the library; Claire Drinkwater of the Institute of Education Library (University of London), who very kindly assembled a selection of nineteenth-century school textbooks for me to look at; and Georgianna Ziegler of the Folger Shakespeare Library, who helped to source the image reproduced as Fig. 6. My thanks also to Margaret Grundy and the staff of the interlibrary loans department of St Andrews University Library, who good humouredly fielded what must have seemed like an endless stream of requests for obscure nineteenth-century autobiographies to be summoned from the four corners of the UK.

The arguments of this book received their first outing at the 2004 Stratford Shakespeare conference. I am grateful to Russell Jackson and John Jowett for their kind invitation to speak at the event and to the various people who provided me with very helpful feedback on the paper. My thanks also to Peter Holland for accepting an article based on the Stratford paper for publication in *Shakespeare Survey*. I thank the participants in my 2007 Shakespeare Association of America seminar on 'Shakespeare and the Invention of a Mass Audience' for a stimulating discussion of many of the issues with which this book attempts to engage.

It has, once again, been a great pleasure to work with Sarah Stanton. Her intelligently probing questions when the book was at its earliest stage helped to shape and sharpen my thinking, and I am very grateful to her for the support and advice which she has provided throughout the whole process.

For friendship in troubled times, I thank: Julian Batts, Jim Burke, Vincent Durac, Eibhlín Evans, Camilla Hey, Sarah Hussain, Romney Johnstone, Chris Jones, Sally Kilmister, Neale Laker, James McKinna, Neil and Alice Pearson, Gill Plain, Rhiannon Purdie, Neil and Shirley Rhodes, Andrew Roberts, Amy Curtis Webber and Gene Webber. Once again I am deeply indebted to my brother, Gerard Murphy.

Shakespeare for the People is dedicated to Frank Hayes, in gratitude for more years of friendship than either of us might wish to count.

Abbreviations

BLA	*Bent's Literary Advertiser*
BS	*The Bookseller*
EUL	Edinburgh University Library
LMG	Lemuel Matthews Griffiths archive, Birmingham Central Library
NS	*The Northern Star*
PC	*The Publishers' Circular*
PMG	*The Poor Man's Guardian*
SRO	Stratford-on-Avon Records Office

Introduction

'SHAKSPEARE, THE POET OF THE PEOPLE.' So proclaimed the headlines of a poster distributed in Stratford-on-Avon in April 1864, in advance of the festival organised to celebrate the tercentenary of the playwright's birth.[1] The poster was addressed to the common people of Stratford and it asked them: 'Where are the seats reserved for YOU at the coming Festival? What part or lot have YOU, *who originated it*, in the coming Celebration?' The answer, the poster declared, was a resounding 'NONE!' The people were to be offered nothing more than 'cold "wittles" ' ' *after the swells have dined*' (Fig. 1). For this reason, the ordinary Stratfordians were enjoined to make their own festival and to let their watchword be 'SHAKSPEARE, the POET of the PEOPLE'.

In London, too, the tercentenary celebrations proved to be contentious. The official committee in charge of the affair had comprehensively failed in its mission, and its efforts were roundly attacked on all sides. *The Bookseller* observed that the committee had 'made a mess of their business' and that the whole affair had 'turned out to be a miserable failure'.[2] *Reynolds's Newspaper* offered an analysis of 'The Shaksperian Commemoration – Its Blunders and Its Failures', and it concluded that 'Had it not been for the once despised working man there would have been no London commemoration at all!'[3] The paper was referring here to the efforts of the Working Men's Committee, which organised a procession to Primrose Hill, where an oak sapling was planted in Shakespeare's honour (Fig. 2). The Committee called on 'the workmen and operatives of the United Kingdom' to attend the ceremony, and a crowd somewhere in the region of 100,000 strong assembled.[4] *The Times* was sarcastically dismissive of the affair, observing of the procession that 'Altogether it formed an assemblage which might be fairly classed as among those with which Falstaff would have avoided Coventry.'[5] Other papers were, however, more positive in their coverage of the event. *The Observer* commented that the demonstration

Figure 1. The tercentenary celebrations at Stratford-on-Avon, from *Illustrated London News* (reproduced by kind permission of Birmingham Library and Information Services).

bore ample testimony to the rapid strides which education and intelligence have made, when certainly, at least one hundred thousand people could assemble, not for any political or party purpose, but to pay a debt of gratitude and admiration to that man who has done more to humanise the feelings of our race, and for the pure literature of his country than any poet who had gone before or who has ever succeeded him.[6]

The Daily News mirrored *The Observer*'s comments on education by noting that, while the two hundredth anniversary of Shakespeare's birth 'shone on the chill reflection of restricted education', the Tercentenary 'beams in the light of a people growing to know their strength, and with their strength their duties and their destinies'. The same article in *The Daily News* celebrated also the ready availability of Shakespeare's plays in a great multiplicity of editions:

Figure 2. The tercentenary tree-planting ceremony on Primrose Hill, from *Illustrated London News* (reproduced by kind permission of Birmingham Library and Information Services).

every year sees now three or four fresh impressions of his works. They are of all sorts and sizes and prices, with notes and without notes, with illustrations and without illustrations, reproductions of old and scarce copies for the luxurious student, penny a week issues for the apprentice or artisan. And they all sell. No book that ever was printed – save one – has had a circulation so enormous, so increasing, so real.[7]

The same theme is picked up by *The Morning Star*, in an article which asserts that

We should be afraid to hazard a guess with regard to the number of editions of his works which have issued from the press since the commencement of the present century. But their name is legion, and they are adapted to every purse – ranging from the luxuriously got up and richly illustrated octavo to the single plays at a penny, and even at a halfpenny, the market for which cannot be a very aristocratic one.[8]

The events in Stratford and London serve to indicate the extent to which Shakespeare had become intertwined with issues of class by the middle decades of the nineteenth century and also, more specifically, the extent to which the working class really had taken possession of Shakespeare.[9] The coverage in *The Observer*, *The Daily News* and *The Morning Star* helps to provide some indication of how, exactly, Shakespeare's following among the working class had been established. Education had expanded considerably over the course of the nineteenth century, with increasing numbers of the poorest members of society being granted access to basic schooling for the first time ever from the earliest decades of the century. In his autobiography, published in 1898, the union leader Joseph Arch (1826–1919) registers the importance of the struggle for education in the period: 'Over and over again I used to say, "If you want your dear children to have a fair chance of rising, of bettering themselves and enabling them to better their surroundings in time, you must see that they are educated" '. He provides a strikingly vivid picture of his own efforts to ensure that working-class children gained access to education:

> Sometimes I used to feel as if I was on a bank I had climbed up, and was pulling other labourers and their wives and children out of a Slough of Despond, till my arms ached fit to drop off, and my head was swimming, and my legs were shaking under me. But I, and my mates standing by me, kept pulling and tugging with might and main; we did not stop longer than to fetch our breath, and then we set to work pulling and tugging again.[10]

As the century progressed, the struggle gradually became easier, as the school network expanded and, in time, the government came to accept direct responsibility for education. By the end of the century, the illiteracy rate had been reduced almost to zero.

The journalist Thomas Frost noted in *Forty Years' Recollections* (1880) that the expansion of the educational franchise prompted publishers to think in terms of serving an expanding market for cheap literature: 'Enterprising publishers began to dream of standard works issued at prices within the means of every one, and therefore to be sold by tens of thousands.'[11] By the mid-point of the century, books had become cheap enough and the reading habit had become sufficiently well established among the working class that F. Mayne, writing in the *Englishwoman's Magazine*, felt moved to declare that it would be

> found on inquiry, that in most cases the minds of the working classes are by no means allowed to lie fallow after the period of quitting school. Nay, I know for certain, that the working-classes of the country, both in agricultural and manufacturing districts, are, to a great extent, a *reading people; a reading* and a *thinking people!*[12]

By 1868, Thomas Wright observed approvingly that 'the books necessary for a complete course of self-education can be obtained for a few shillings.

"Shakespeare's Complete Works" are advertised for sale for one shilling; and a really handsome, useful, and well-edited copy of these matchless works may be had for three shillings and sixpence.'[13] Even four years prior to this, as we have seen *The Morning Star* note, individual Shakespeare plays could be had for as little as ½d. each.

The purpose of this book is to map out the history of these developments in detail. It offers an account of working-class education over the course of the nineteenth century, and it traces developments in publishing to indicate the manner in which, by the middle decades of the century, editions of Shakespeare became affordable to those of even the most modest means. Having outlined this contextual background, the study then goes on to examine the actual experience of working-class readers as they came to encounter Shakespeare, and it also details the ways in which the playwright gained a political value for a particular subset of these readers, namely, those who were involved in the various radical, reform and labour movements during the course of the century. I conclude the book by looking forward to the twentieth century, to suggest some reasons why, having gained a working-class readership in the 1800s, Shakespeare began to lose that popular readership over the course of the new century.

The central resource for this study is a set of autobiographies written (at least for the most part) over the course of the nineteenth century. In using this material, I am following in the footsteps of Jonathan Rose, whose extraordinarily rich and engaging *The Intellectual Life of the British Working Classes* draws on the same resource to map out a large-scale history of working-class culture in the nineteenth century.[14] It is a striking feature of working-class life in this period that so many people felt motivated to record the details of their lives. Pioneering work in the field of working-class autobiography has been carried out by the historians John Burnett, David Vincent and David Mayall. In their impressively extensive annotated critical bibliography of such texts, they note that the 'trickle of works which began to appear in the 1790s was to develop into a remarkably diverse and fertile genre whose existence reflected a major transformation in the way in which the labouring poor regarded themselves'.[15] Burnett and his colleagues see the nineteenth-century texts as being a secular extension of the Puritan tradition of the confessional autobiography: 'In their different ways all the working class autobiographers were building upon puritan assumptions about the significance of the inner lives of ordinary men and women, and about the necessity of understanding human identity in the dimension of time.' They note, however, that most of the nineteenth-century writers depart from the spiritual autobiographers' ultimate disregard for the affairs of this world, and base their accounts on an essentially secular view of the times they have witnessed. For them, the social, economic and political events which they seek to describe have an importance in themselves, irrespective of the ultimate destination of the writer's soul.[16]

The autobiographers themselves frequently address the question of why they feel the need to tell their life stories. Robert Lowery (1809–63), the Chartist activist, was motivated largely by political considerations, noting that he had often been urged to write his autobiography by 'many of my friends who are labouring to elevate the working classes' and 'who think that my life would be interesting and instructive in incidents and events connected with those movements which have engaged the attention of these classes for these last twenty years'.[17] George Elson (b. 1833), by contrast, had a much simpler aim: he wanted to tell the story of a chimney-sweep's life at first hand for the first time. He writes: 'I should never have attempted so presumptuous a task as to write my own biography, only that I believe there never was a book written and published by a genuine sweep-lad before me'.[18] Hannah Mitchell (1872–1956) also had endearingly modest ambitions for her work, as she observed of her autobiography: 'My readers may not find it a very thrilling story, but I hope it will reveal to them the early dreams, secret hopes and half-realized ambitions of one very ordinary woman.'[19]

There was some resistance in establishment circles to the idea of members of the working class setting out their life stories. In 1827, the *Quarterly Review* complained that the expansion of literacy had the 'disgusting effect' of emboldening 'beings who, at any period, would have been mean and base in all their objects and desires, to demand with hardihood the attention and the sympathy of mankind, for thoughts and deeds that, in any period but the present, must have been as obscure as dirty'.[20] Eight years later, Francis Place testified before a Select Committee on Education. He discussed the particulars of his own life in some detail and his observations on his life were subsequently included in the Committee's report. *The Times*, commenting on this development under the heading 'Autobiography of Francis Place', dismissed Place's recollections as 'miserable and vulgar twaddle' and 'mere trash'.[21] By the middle of the century, however, Charles Manby Smith was able to observe in his autobiography, *The Working Man's Way in the World*, that

The time has been when an apology would have been thought necessary for obtruding on the notice of the public these passages in the life of a Working Man: that time is however past, and there are now an abundance of precedents to keep any man in countenance who, for reasons good, bad or indifferent, may choose to draw aside the veil from his personal history, and publish it to the world.[22]

A central set of about one hundred of these autobiographical texts provides much of the evidence presented in this study.[23] For the most part, they are printed texts, published in a variety of different ways – some serialised in newspapers, others produced by the authors themselves, some published by provincial presses, others brought to print by mainstream London publishers. About 10% of the sample is made up of unpublished manuscript and typescript autobiographies, mostly drawn from an archival collection established by John Burnett at Brunel University Library.[24] This latter set of texts is particularly valuable in giving an insight into the lives of those who had very little in the way of a public profile and who recorded the details of their lives, oftentimes, simply to pass them on to members of their own immediate families.

There are certain limitations to the autobiographies as a source of evidence, and I will come on to discuss these presently. First, however, I attend to a fundamental issue of definition of central importance to my study. The meaning and utility of the term 'working class' has been much discussed and disputed in recent years. In part, the reaction against the term has been prompted by a desire to interrogate and re-evaluate E. P. Thompson's classic study, *The Making of the English Working Class*, now seen by some historians as offering an unhelpfully totalising narrative in its efforts to track the emergence of class consciousness over the course of the nineteenth century. Patrick Joyce, for example, has argued of this period that 'British political development was about a good deal more than the growth of a class-conscious proletariat' and he observes that 'however broadly class is defined it is still only one among many understandings of the social order held by people'.[25] The desire to investigate a wider range of possible fields of identity has had the effect of undermining class as an analytical category. Thus, Peter Bailey has observed that

Sapped by gender and race, class now seems about to collapse into mere difference, a master (*sic*) category on its last legs. Social identity, we are now told, starts with the self, a multiple subject constructed by language, culture and the symbolic system, a self for whom class may be one narrative thread among many, for whom work and material existence may be less significant than consumption and life style. Class is an imagined community competing with other collective identities for the allegiance of an overdetermined subject.

Bailey himself has offered some resistance to the tendency to see class as just one element of identity for the fractured self called to subjecthood through language and the symbolic order. He observes, for example, that 'the mark of class sticks like a burr in nineteenth-century society and remains among the more potent vectors of difference, however indeterminate or relativised'.[26] David Cannadine has also tried to reclaim class as a useful analytical concept, defending it on what amount to positivistic empirical grounds:

> Whatever the devotees of the 'linguistic turn' may claim, class is not *just* about language. There is reality as well as representation. Go to Toxteth, go to Wandsworth, go to Tynecastle, go to Balsall Heath, and tell the people who live in the slums and the council estates and the high-rise ghettoes that their sense of social structure and social identity is no more than a subjective rhetorical construction, that it is nothing beyond a collection of individual self-categorisations. It seems unlikely that they will agree.[27]

Most theoretically informed critics and historians are, of course, unlikely to find Cannadine's argument satisfactory, since it represents an essentialist appeal to a reality that is presented as uncomplicatedly sitting outside any kind of analytical framework: it just *is*. This is a fair point but, at the same time, it is hard not to feel that there is, nevertheless, a certain force to what Cannadine has to say here. There *are* divisions of wealth within society, and those with the least resources surely have a different experience of the world from those who enjoy real prosperity. And postmodern concepts of subjecthood provide scant consolation to those who must struggle on a day-to-day basis through a life of poverty and deprivation.

Cannadine usefully invokes a division, which he takes from Marx, between class 'in itself' and class 'for itself', the former being 'no more (and no less) than an objective social category, which grouped individuals together on the basis of their shared economic characteristics: the source of their income, the extent of their wealth, and the nature of their occupation'. Class 'for itself', by contrast, is connected with the emergence of a sense of class consciousness – 'a shared process of self-discovery and self-realisation', which must lead ultimately, for Marx, to conflict between the classes.[28] The emergence of a sense of class 'for itself' might be said to be the organising principle of Thompson's *Making of the English Working Class* – and it is the construction of that kind of grand narrative that historians such as Joyce find problematic. For the purpose of this study, however, I wish to deploy the term 'working class' primarily as a form of social description rather than necessarily thinking of it as a form of highly self-conscious social identity (though the question of class identity is of some importance to one element of the argument I put forward in Chapter 5 of this book). In this sense, my concern can be said to be largely with class 'in itself' rather than 'for itself'.

Debates over the meaning of the term 'working class' are not new. This was as much a live issue in the nineteenth century as it is in our own time. Thomas Wright offered a crude but effective definition in his *Habits and Customs of the Working Classes* (1867), where he observes that the working class 'comprises all, who, in the literal sense, earn their bread by the sweat of their brow, and, to use their own phrase, "have black hands to earn white money." '[29] In the same year, in their *Progress of the Working Class, 1832–1867*, J. M. Ludlow and Lloyd Jones offered a rather more nuanced view, noting that, in their work, the terms 'working class' and 'working man' would be taken

in their every-day acceptation, as meaning those who work, chiefly with their muscles, for wages, and maintain themselves thereby. The phrase, 'we are all working men,' as used by the brain-worker, has a truth to it, but becomes a cant when carried too far. It is not, indeed, intended to deal with 'the poor,' – *i.e.* those who may work, but cannot thereby habitually maintain themselves, otherwise than by an occasional glimpse at some of their efforts to raise themselves into the true working class.[30]

Taken together, Wright and Ludlow and Jones provide the rough outlines of a definition of the term 'working class' which fits reasonably well with my own use of the phrase in this study. 'Working class', for my purposes, serves to describe those who grew up in a certain set of circumstances, and whose lives conformed to the same broad, general trajectory. To be a little more precise: the vast majority of the autobiographers considered here are the sons and daughters of tradesmen or unskilled workers (where their mothers have worked they have generally been servants); virtually all of them have received, during their childhood, no more than the very basic education that was generally available to the children of the poor (largely in dame schools and church schools); with a small number of exceptions, the typical autobiographer considered here worked in a trade of some sort and, while some achieved significant success in their trade (the tailor Francis Place being a notable example), most lived modest lives, often struggling to get by, especially if they were heavily burdened with family responsibilities. The range of occupations of the autobiographers considered includes baker, basketmaker, blacksmith, bricklayer, cabinetmaker, chimneysweep, dressmaker, housepainter, maid, miner, navvy, printer, ropemaker, servant, shoemaker, soldier, stonemason, tailor, waterman, weaver, whitesmith. Some autobiographers combined a number of different occupations over the course of their lives. Betsy Cadwaladyr was a servant, a ship's steward and a nurse; George Elson was a hawker, then a chimneysweep, ultimately becoming a swimming instructor, shampooer and masseur at a Turkish baths; John Bedford Leno notes that he specialised in 'p' occupations, having been a 'Pieman, Pastrycook, Printer, Publisher, Politician and Poetaster'.[31] A few of the autobiographers did achieve some degree of eminence in life, principally in the fields of education and politics. Henry Jones became a professor at the University of St Andrews, where he taught (among other things) English literature. A fairly modest degree of eminence this, to be sure, but, nonetheless, it meant that he moved in a rather different world from that of his original trade of shoemaker. Similarly, a number of autobiographers born later in the century entered parliament as Labour MPs and achieved cabinet positions when the Labour party finally came to power. J. R. Clynes falls into this category; he served, at various times, as Lord Privy Seal, Deputy Leader of the House of Commons and Home Secretary. Taking my sample as a whole, however, Jones and Clynes are the exceptions rather than the rule. Most of the autobiographers drawn on here worked steadily at their trades and lived fairly modest lives.[32]

As already noted, there are various important limitations to the evidence provided by the autobiographies, most notably in terms of the nature of the sample of working-class opinion which they provide. The first thing to register is that the size of the sample relative to the general working-class population should not be overestimated, nor should these writers' views necessarily be taken as fully representative of their community as a whole. Thomas Wright noted, in *Our New Masters* (1873), that 'Individual instances of well-educated working men are tolerably numerous, but compared with the vastness of the general body they are exceptional, are by others regarded as exceptional, and not always as favourably exceptional'.[33] John Burnett and his colleagues have also observed that

> it will never be possible to approach the autobiographies as a statistically accurate cross-section of all, or any part of the population. They remain pieces of literature, their content shaped not only by the intentions of the writers and the traditions within which they were working, but also by the mode in which they were recorded.[34]

From the specific perspective of the current project, it should also be noted that it is an inevitable effect of the particular focus of this study that Shakespeare will seem to be a significant centre of interest for the writers quoted throughout. In some cases, this is an entirely accurate reflection of the autobiographers' preoccupations. Thus, for example, Thomas Cooper refers extensively to Shakespeare throughout his work, as he tells us of his reading of the plays, of memorising them, lecturing on them, performing the lead role in *Hamlet*, re-reading the plays in prison and visiting Stratford-on-Avon. In other cases, however, what amount to fleeting references to Shakespeare run the risk of being excessively magnified in the context of a study of this kind. A nice example of this is provided by Thomas Carter, author of a two-volume autobiography, the first volume of which was issued by Charles Knight, the publisher and renowned Shakespeare editor. Carter's programme of reading is quite extraordinary. One of his favourite books was Burton's *Anatomy of Melancholy* and the point of attraction of Burton for Carter is precisely 'the extensive and widely varied reading of the author'.[35] Carter does indeed read Shakespeare, but the playwright's works are merely one item in a miscellaneous list of other books:

In my leisure-hours during this year, and the years 1838 and 1839, I read the whole of Shakspere's dramatic works, Mr. Sharon Turner's 'Sacred History of the Creation,' the 'Memoirs of Mr. Samuel Drew,' and Dr. Stilling's 'Theory of Pneumatology,' together with some odd volumes of the Edinburgh and Quarterly Reviews.[36]

In the *Continuation* volume of his memoirs Carter quotes from *Hamlet* 'There is a Providence [*sic*] that shapes our ends, / Rough-hew them how we will' and he then adds a footnote, reading: 'I know not where to look for this quotation; but if it be in one of Shakspeare's plays, which I think it is, I cannot verify it, as I do not possess his works, nor are they readily within my reach.'[37]

It is not, in fact, uncommon for the autobiographers to include quotations or half-quotations from Shakespeare in their work, oftentimes without identifying Shakespeare as the source of the quote, and sometimes without making any substantial reference to the playwright elsewhere in their texts. In many cases these are simply stock phrases, such as 'conscience doth make cowards of us all', 'age cannot wither her', 'there are more things in heaven and earth ... Than are dreamt of in your philosophy' or 'all the world's a stage'. A nice example of this kind of deployment of Shakespeare is provided by Henry Broadhurst (1840–1911), whose autobiography *Henry Broadhurst, M. P.: The Story of his Life from a Stonemason's Bench to the Treasury Bench* was published in 1901. Writing of the Factory and Workshop Amendment Bill, Broadhurst observes of its author that he 'is no longer found in the Lower Chamber; he has gone to that "other place" whence no traveller returns to the House of Commons'.[38] He makes no other direct or indirect reference to Shakespeare.

It should also be noted here that some working-class autobiographers were, in fact, either indifferent to Shakespeare or even actively disliked him. Samuel Bamford (1788–1872) observed that

Some of Shakespear's works having fallen in my way, I read them with avidity, as I did almost every other book, and though deeply interested by his historical characters and passages, I never either then or since relished his blank verse, or that of any other poet. I never, as it were, could get the knack of it and as compared with rhymed poetry, it has always seemed to me, indeed,
 'Like the forc'd gait of a shuffling nag.'[39]

The quotation is, of course, from Hotspur, in *1 Henry IV*, with Bamford rather neatly using Shakespeare's poetry as a way of providing a negative comment on Shakespeare's poetry. Sarah Martin (1791–1843) read Shakespeare with some pleasure, but religious conviction eventually turned her against the playwright's work: 'with eagerness I read Shakspere's Plays, and other dramatic works; Addison's Spectator, the Guardian, &c.; the works of Johnson, and others, and the British Poets. Still however, when a ray of gospel light came across my mind in any way, I turned from it as from a reptile.'[40] Joseph Barker (1806–75) writes that, while he 'often read Shakespeare ... and never without pleasure', he was 'far from regarding him, as some do, as one of the first of moral teachers'.[41] Likewise, James Bonwick (1817–1906), who read through the collected plays during the course of a 116 day sea voyage, found that there was 'some barbarism' in Shakespeare and he 'was rather shocked at some parts' of the plays. He concluded, however (writing in the shadow of the authorship controversy), that '*Hamlet*, by whomsoever written, must be classed among the noblest illustrations of human genius'.[42] Broadly speaking, then, it should not be taken for granted that all of the autobiographers invoked in this study are in every instance positive Shakespeare enthusiasts.

A further – and very important – limitation of the autobiographies made use of here is the gender breakdown of the sample. In volume one of their *Autobiography of the Working Class: An Annotated, Critical Bibliography*, John Burnett and his colleagues log a total of 1,028 biographical texts of all kinds (books, articles, manuscripts, diaries, oral sources, extracts, compilations, etc.) for the period 1790–1900. Of their main group of 783 autobiographies, they note that 'just seventy, less than one in ten, record the lives of daughters, wives and mothers from their own point of view. Few of these were actually published in the nineteenth century, and over half of this meagre collection are still in manuscript'.[43] Several commentators have speculated as to why there is such a dearth of women's autobiography in this period. In his introduction to Elizabeth Ham's autobiographical texts, published in 1945 (Ham herself was born in 1783 and died in 1859), Eric Gillett writes that: 'Most women talk their autobiographies. Very few have had the patience to write them. This may be due to modesty, discretion, or shyness. More probably it is because their sex has a notable dislike for direct expression, except in intimate conversation.'[44] Gillett seems to feel that there is something, well, *constitutional* in women that makes them less likely to write and publish the story of their lives. It seems rather more plausible, however, that there may have been practical reasons for the relative silence of working-class women in the nineteenth century. Nan Hackett, for example, seems much closer to the mark when she observes: 'When we consider what we know about the lives of working-class women, the hard work, disease and obscurity, it is surprising that any women found the time to write.'[45] Joseph Terry (b. 1816) gives us some indication of the difficulties faced by women when he observes of his wife, who shared his love of reading:

I have often seen of an evening when the elder ones have got safely lodged for the night, Mrs. Terry my beloved little wife, sit down to her worktable with one child on her knee, one in the cradle, and some interesting book, for she always contrived to do some reading, propped up before her on the table, when she would nurse, rock, read and knit, all at the same time.[46]

And Mrs Terry was, of course, fortunate in having a husband who supported her in her intellectual activities. The vast majority of working-class women, it seems reasonable to say, would have been more likely to have had husbands who expected them to concentrate their energies on their nursing, rocking and knitting, together with their cooking and their cleaning. One woman, Elizabeth Andrews (1882–1960), gave her autobiography the title *A Woman's Work is Never Done* – a cliché, of course, but none the less true for all that. Andrews recalled that, having left school when she was thirteen, she began to attend evening classes two years later and 'At the end of the session I carried away two first prizes for the best essay and for the best pie!'[47]

One other problem that may have faced women in the period is that, by contrast with men, they did not often find their own experience reflected in print. Mary Ann Hearn (1834–1909), who wrote under the name Marianne Farningham, recalled the sense of disappointment she felt at the gender bias in some of her childhood reading matter:

My father gave us two monthly magazines published by the Sunday School Union, the 'Teacher's Offering,' and the 'Child's Companion.' In one of these was a series of descriptive articles on men who had been poor boys, and risen to be rich and great. Every month I hoped to find the story of some poor ignorant *girl*, who, beginning life as handicapped as I, had yet been able by her own efforts and the blessing of God upon them to live a life of usefulness, if not of greatness. But I believe there was not a woman in the whole series.[48]

Even when women did find the time, energy and inspiration to write down their life stories, they often then found it difficult to get their autobiographies published (as Burnett and his colleagues note, more than half the small number of women's texts they log are in manuscript form only). Hannah Mitchell's autobiography was actually brought to print by her grandson, twelve years after her death. In his introduction to the text, Geoffrey Mitchell observes:

The fate of the manuscript is ... not without interest, for although she was not unpushing in trying to get a publisher to accept it, at the time none found it interesting enough to undertake. During her lifetime she had to be content to see short extracts published in interested journals and to accept praise and admiration from a few friends to whom she sent the work.[49]

Some efforts have been made, since the publication of the Burnett, Vincent and Mayall bibliographies, to identify a greater number of working-class women's autobiographical texts. Julia Swindells challenges the taxonomic bases specifically of David Vincent's work in her study *Victorian Writing and Working Women: The Other Side of Silence*. She registers that Vincent's intention, in his *Bread, Knowledge and Freedom: A Study of Nineteenth-century Working Class Autobiography*, is 'to study only those autobiographies where the autobiographer is the child of a working man and has "remained a member of the working class until the composition of his memoirs"' and observes that 'For a variety of reasons, these kinds of classification are unlikely to lead Vincent to women's texts'.[50] However, it is notable that Swindells' own rather looser taxonomies do not really enable her to unearth much in the way of genuinely new material. Despite including work by women of middle-class origin who have undergone the experience of 'losing caste' and becoming 'working women', her study is substantially based on a set of just ten texts, spanning a very wide chronological stretch.[51] The fundamental problem remains unchanged (and probably, in truth, unchangeable): the *sample size* for women is cripplingly small by comparison with what is available for men.

In the context of a project such as *Shakespeare for the People*, one of the particular problems of having just a small sample of texts to draw on is that the number of essentially irrelevant texts diminishes the sample still

Introduction

further; with the much larger overall pool of male autobiographers this is much less important. So, for example, while Jane Andrew's autobiography, *Recorded Mercies*, might well be of real interest to someone working in the field of general working-class history, it is of no assistance to the current study, since she has nothing to say about education, reading or Shakespeare, the central topics of this project.[52] Likewise, while Margaret Bondfield (1873–1953) is a thoroughly impressive figure, with an extraordinary catalogue of 'firsts' to her name (first woman elected to the TUC executive, one of the first three women Labour MPs, first woman government minister, first woman cabinet member and privy councillor), nevertheless, apart from some passing comments on her education, her autobiography, again, contains very little that is of relevance to this study.[53]

There are, however, some exceptions to this rather gloomy picture, and some of the exceptions are notable. One of the writers I draw on in this book is Mary Smith (1822–89), whose autobiography appeared in 1892. Smith was 'a vehement champion of ... efforts to improve the condition of women's lives' and believed that 'society as a whole would remain degraded until women were given full civil rights'.[54] She helped to establish a women's suffrage society in Carlisle, campaigned in favour of the Married Women's Property Bill and agitated against the Contagious Diseases Acts. Her views, as expressed in her *Autobiography*, are often trenchant and incisive. After recounting her own early educational experiences, she observes: 'For long years Englishwomen's souls were almost as sorely crippled and cramped by the devices of the school room, as the Chinese women's feet by their shoes.'[55] Smith turned down an offer of marriage rather than compromise her own intellectual independence. When the proposal was mooted to her at secondhand, she responded: '"No, it's no use. I cannot do that." I could see all my intellectual castles falling with a crash, to rise no more. And, moreover, I had formed the opinion, that to marry for earthly advantage, without one's affections being intertwined, was a foul blot which nothing could justify.' Of her intended partner, she observes: 'He's not intellectual. What is marriage *without* happiness! The bare idea of it is dreadful to contemplate.'[56] Smith was a keen Shakespeare enthusiast, having begun to read the plays as a young girl. She visited the Shakespeare monument at Westminster Abbey and delivered a lecture on the playwright as part of the Tercentenary celebrations in Carlisle. It must be acknowledged, however, that Smith's voice is one of a small number of exceptional women to be discussed in this book; *Shakespeare for the People* therefore necessarily reflects the experience specifically of male readers much better than it does that of female readers.

While recognising the limitations of the autobiographical evidence, it is also necessary to acknowledge its real value and importance. Patricia Anderson, in *The Printed Image and the Transformation of Popular Culture 1790–1860*, has registered the problematics of working with autobiographical material, noting that 'by the very fact of having written a book, the autobiographers were not typical of working people, and we must be cautious about generalizing from their experience'. But she also notes, crucially, that 'culture emanates from both producers and consumers; and if we are to recognize adequately the role of the latter, then we must use available evidence, however fragmentary. The alternative is our own silence'.[57] The great value of the autobiographies is that they enable us, in some measure at least, to break the silence of working-class readers with regard to their educational and reading experiences and their experience, specifically, of encountering Shakespeare. Breaking this silence is important more generally, since, as John Carey has observed, 'The history of audiences and readerships is largely a blank' and he argues that 'Arts research needs to change direction, to look outwards, and ... investigate the audience not the texts'.[58] This book seeks, in some measure at least, to respond to the challenge that Carey poses here.

In addition to issues relating specifically to the autobiographies as a source of evidence, it is also necessary to note some limitations specific to the nature and parameters of this particular project. For example, the geographical limitations of my study should be registered here. A central element of my argument is that church organisations such as the Sunday School Society (founded in 1786), the British and Foreign School Society (1807) and the National Society for the Education of the Poor in the Principles of the Established Church (1811) raised the literacy rate by providing basic educational facilities for the children of the poor. This, in turn, led to an increase in reading among the working class, with a significant number of working-class literates ultimately becoming Shakespeare enthusiasts. It should be noted, however, that the developments in education on which my argument rests were largely specific to England and Wales, and that Scotland and Ireland in this period had their own particular educational arrangements (and, indeed, Scotland and, now, Northern Ireland, continue to do so).[59] Robert Lowery provides some indication of the differences in the educational systems between the two sides of the Scottish border. Born in North Shields in 1809, his family moved for a spell to Peterhead, north of Aberdeen, while he was still a child. Lowery noted that, in sharp contrast with English schools, in Scotland 'There were no strictly religious books read during the week except on Saturday, which was especially devoted to religious instruction, when the Scriptures were read, and either the Scotch or English cateschism [*sic*] taught the children according to the request of their parents'. Because of this difference in emphasis, Lowery encountered secular literature in the classroom much more readily than he would have done had his education taken place exclusively south of the border, where religious material (and, specifically, Bible reading) dominated the curriculum.[60] As he observes:

> I trace my desire for reading to the class-book we used, which was called the 'Scotch Beauties,' being composed of extracts from the chief historians, poets, and didactic writers of Great Britain, and I remember the strong desire I felt to be able to get the books from which these extracts were quoted.[61]

Because of the differences in the structure and nature of education provided in the different parts of the United Kingdom, I have concentrated my attention specifically on England and Wales and, for this reason, my conclusions should be taken to apply to these territories only. On the other hand, the great strength of the autobiographies as a research resource is that, taking England and Wales as the exclusive area of focus, they actually do represent a widely dispersed sample, including writers born in Allerton, near Bradford (John Wood), Barnwell, Cambridgeshire (John Brown), Coventry (Joseph Gutteridge), Donnington Wood, Shropshire (Emmanuel Lovekin), Edwinstone, Sherwood Forest (Fred Kitchen), Farningham, Kent (Mary Anne Hearn), on to Llangernyw, Denbighshire (Henry Jones), Maesteg, Glamorgan (Philip Boswood Ballard), Newlyn, Cornwall (William Lovett), and Toxteth Park, Liverpool (Daisy Cowper), Uxbridge, Middlesex (John Bedford Leno) and Whitechapel, London (Frederick Rogers) and many other places besides.

There is one further self-imposed restriction on this project which should also be noted here. Shakespeare was not known to a working-class audience solely through the printed word. In a much-quoted observation, John Clare noted that the 'common people' were familiar with 'the name of Shakspeare as a great play writer, because they have seen him nominated as such in the bills of strolling-players, who make shift with barns for theatres'.[62] In some cases, these performances were burlesques or other forms of adapted or reduced productions, such as the 1833 bill at a Leicester theatre which included, consecutively, the second act of *Romeo and Juliet*, the third acts of *Macbeth*, *Hamlet* and *Othello* and the fifth act of '*King Richard*' (a fascinating combination when imagined as a complete performance). Also included on the bill was 'Signor Martini, the celebrated

Man Monkey from the Theatre Royal, Drury Lane, whose astonishing performances have created a doubt in thousands whether he is really a Monkey or of the Human Species'.[63] At the same time, Shakespeare was also available in essentially orthodox productions, both before and after the abolition of the patent theatres monopoly in 1843.[64] Certainly, after this date, Richard Foulkes has registered 'an explosion of Shakespeare from lowly suburban theatres such as Sadler's Wells and Shoreditch to the West End and the Court itself', so that during 'the two decades leading up to the tercentenary of his birth ... Shakespeare had achieved unprecedented status and popularity on the English stage'.[65]

There is much evidence in the autobiographies of frequent theatre attendance, and even of involvement in productions of one sort or another. Christopher Thomson registers his sense of utter wonderment on attending the theatre for the first time (at the age of seventeen) to see a production of *King John*: 'So enwrapped was I in the business, that at the fall of "the drop" at the end of the first act I felt bewildered, and almost doubted my existence, I was so struck "By the very cunning of the scene."'[66] Seeing the play provided the impetus for Thomson to go and read it: 'So intensely was my mind riveted to that play, that as soon afterwards as I could raise a sixpence I purchased a copy of it'.[67] Thomson eventually became a supernumerary at his local theatre, where he found a visiting Edmund Kean good-humoured and affable, though very serious about his craft.[68] He also had a spell on the road with a travelling company, including playing Capulet in *Romeo and Juliet*.

It is striking how many of the autobiographers report seeing Shakespeare performed by the leading actors of the day. J. Passmore Edwards saw Macready play Hamlet and W. E. Adams saw Phelps in *Timon of Athens*.[69] Frederick Rogers saw

many Hamlets: some of them great. Miss Marriott made a great Hamlet. Barry Sullivan and T. C. King were actors whose artistic ideas were conscientious and commanded respect, and the Hamlets of Forbes Robertson and the younger Irving dwell long in the memory. But no Hamlet I ever saw left in my mind such a sense of intellectual greatness, and of artistic completeness, as did the Hamlet of Henry Irving.[70]

Philip Boswood Ballard also had a keen appreciation of Henry Irving, of whom he says that he 'never saw him take a character which he did not make sympathetic' (including Shylock).[71] Edward Brown saw Herbert Beerbohm Tree in various productions, including performing as Cardinal Wolsey in *Henry VIII*.[72]

Theatre clearly, then, forms an important element of working-class appreciation of Shakespeare over the course of the nineteenth century. However, an adequate treatment of this strand of the playwright's working-class reception lies outside the scope of this volume. The topic is, in fact, taken up at various points in this book, particularly in Chapter 5, where I draw on the work of Richard Foulkes to discuss the issue of a late nineteenth-century shift in theatrical values which served partly to facilitate the emergence of a distinctive elite culture which defined itself specifically against the popular. For the most part, however, since this is a book about Shakespeare's working-class *readers*, his working-class *spectators* must, I am afraid, wait for another scholar to tell their story in full.[73]

There is also one logistical issue which I should just briefly touch on in this introduction. By relying on the autobiographical texts as my central evidential resource in this study, I draw on the testimony of about one hundred 'witnesses' (if that is not too pretentious a term) during the course of the book, with some being called to give evidence on more than one occasion. This presents something of a problem, from a rhetorical or presentational point of view. For each autobiographer, it is generally useful to establish dates of birth and death, place of birth, the details of occupation(s) and, perhaps, a little family background as well. However, repeating this information in a formulaic way can have the effect of making the text of the book numbingly repetitive. It can also reduce the narrative to an endless parade of fundamentally interchangeable individuals. I have tried to avoid this as best I can by not necessarily always providing the same range of information when I introduce a new autobiographer (and by not always repeating information about an autobiographer when I refer to him or her more than once). However, this has its own perils, in that the text may, as a result, sometimes appear vague and imprecise. To counter these problems, I have included a simple appendix at the end of the book. This appendix lists the autobiographers chronologically, by date of birth, and it provides details of place of birth; parent(s) primary occupation; the autobiographer's own primary occupation(s) and the year in which the writer's autobiography was published (together with an indication of the nature of the text – for example, printed book, manuscript, series of newspaper articles). It also indicates for each autobiographer whether he or she is included in the *Dictionary of National Biography*. I also provide an alphabetical list of the autobiographers, together with details of their year of birth; this is intended, quite simply, as a finding aid for the chronological listing. My hope is that the appendix will allow the reader easily to place all of the autobiographers chronologically and geographically (and also to gain something of an overview of the complete range of individuals and texts deployed in these pages).

The Working Men's Shakespeare Committee disbanded after the celebrations on Primrose Hill, noting with some satisfaction that the event they had organised 'not only redeemed the metropolis from a charge of utter indifference to the interest of the day, but must ever be memorable as the first open act of homage paid by the English people to a purely poetical idea'. Before winding up their affairs completely, however, they set in train a further scheme. Noting the failure of the official Tercentenary Committee in their objective of raising a national monument to Shakespeare, the Working Men's Committee proposed that

> The Tercentenary year of the Poet ought to be marked by some effort, however humble, to honour his memory; and it remains for the People of England, who claim him as their own, to take the matter in hand, and erect in this island the first National Statue to a great National Poet.

The plan was a simple one, and the Committee set out the details:

> It has been ascertained that a Statue, ten or eleven feet high, in marble, mounted on a pedestal proportionate in height, can be procured for the moderate sum of about £1,500, and that an ornamental Shrine of iron and glass, to enclose it, (hereafter to become a Temple of Poesy, and receive the Statues of other eminent English bards), will cost about £1,200 or £1,500 more. A sum, therefore, of, say, £3,000, or in other words, a little more than 50,000 shillings, 100,000 sixpences, or 500,000 pence, will be amply sufficient to place an elegant and imposing structure and work of art on Primrose Hill, or in such other part of the metropolis as may be deemed desirable.[74]

The financial breakdown here provides an indication of how the Committee envisaged raising the necessary funds. Writing to the celebrated Shakespearean J. O. Halliwell-Phillipps, the Honorary Secretary, John Bainbridge, observed that the intention of the Committee was 'as far as possible, to confine themselves to penny subscription amongst the working classes; at the same time they are anxious to secure the sympathy of gentlemen who represent the world of letters'.[75] Towards the close of the year, a series of events was held at the Theatre Royal, Drury Lane, 'in aid of the People's Shakspeare Memorial Fund'. On the night of 6 December, James Bruton read a poem, which concluded:

> Then, as the THAMES holds many a limpid rill,
> And countless atoms build up Primrose Hill,
> So may the Pence of fair and horny hand
> Set up a Statue to adorn the land;

Introduction 21

> And, wide as are the Poles apart, proclaim
> The People's reverence of SHAKSPEARE'S name!

On the following night, William Sawyer delivered another poem, declaring Shakespeare 'The People's Poet' and concluding, of the 'working sons' of the country:

> Strong in their numbers, stronger in their cause,
> All hindrance, all impediments they dare –
> Hold difficulties 'trifles, light as air,'
> And picturing what the Future must unfold
> The People's Shakespeare Monument behold![76]

Sadly, the People's Shakespeare Monument never was beheld by Britain's working sons or daughters or anyone else. Like the official Tercentenary committee, the Workingmen's Committee also failed to bring their plan to fruition. The level of working-class investment in Shakespeare which prompted the various activities of the committee is, however, striking. And, in any case, the working class had already been spending their pennies on Shakespeare during the course of the Tercentenary year. In April 1864, John Dicks began issuing the plays at the rate of two a penny. He found such a ready sale that it prompted him to publish a 2s. complete works, which he subsequently reduced in price to just 1s. Within the space of a short few years, he had sold nearly 1,000,000 copies of the complete works.[77] Had everyone who bought a copy of Dicks' editions of the complete works contributed the penny asked for by the Workingmen's Committee, they would, of course, have had enough money in hand to erect not one shrine, but two. But, then, reading Shakespeare was surely a much more worthwhile way of commemorating the playwright than erecting any number of statues.

NOTES

1 A copy of the poster is included in Stratford Records Office (hereafter SRO) file ER1/58, vol. 2. An image of the poster is included as Fig. 1 in Werner Habicht, 'Shakespeare Celebrations in Times of War', *Shakespeare Quarterly*, 52:4 (2001), pp. 441–5.
2 *Bookseller*, 30 April 1864, p. 241.
3 'The Shaksperian Commemoration – Its Blunders and Its Failures', *Reynolds's Newspaper*, 716 (1 May 1864), p. 4.
4 See the Working Men's Committee, address 'To the Workmen and Operatives of the United Kingdom', included in SRO file ER 1/107.
5 *The Times*, 25 April 1864, p. 7. Cutting included in SRO file DR330.

6 *The Observer*, 24 April 1864, p. 5, included in SRO file DR330.
7 *The Daily News*, 26 April 1864, included in SRO file ER1/58, vol. 1.
8 *The Morning Star*, 23 April 1864, included in SRO file ER1/58, vol. 1.
9 It was not just in Stratford and London that the Tercentenary had a working-class dimension. In Liverpool, the mayor 'expressed his intention of throwing open the theatres free to the working classes on the evening of the Shakspeare tercentenary': 'The Shakspeare Tercentenary', *Illustrated London News*, 16 April 1864, included in Lemuel Matthews Griffiths, *Newspaper Cuttings Relating to Shakespeare* at the Birmingham Central Library, vol. 4, p. 24. In Dudley, the local Garrick Club honoured the Tercentenary by presenting a copy of one of Knight's editions of Shakespeare and a copy of Mary Cowden Clarke's *Shakespeare Concordance* to the local Mechanics' Institute – see 'The Tercentenary Celebrations at Dudley', *The Birmingham Daily Post*, 26 April 1864, included in Birmingham Central Library *Tercentenary Shakespeare Scrapbook*, vol. 1, p. 104.
10 Joseph Arch, *The Autobiography of Joseph Arch*, ed. John Gerald O'Leary (London: MacGibbon & Kee, 1966; originally published London: Hutchinson, 1898), pp. 90, 93–4.
11 Thomas Frost, *Forty Years' Recollections: Literary and Political* (London: Sampson Low, Marston, Searle, and Rivington, 1880), p. 79.
12 F. M[ayne], 'The Literature of the Working Classes', the *Englishwoman's Magazine and Christian Mother's Miscellany*, N.S., V (October 1850), p. 619.
13 Thomas Wright (originally published under 'The Journeyman Engineer'), *The Great Unwashed* (New York: Augustus M. Kelley, 1970; originally published London: Tinsley Brother, 1868), pp. 217–18.
14 Jonathan Rose, *The Intellectual Life of the British Working Classes* (New Haven: Yale University Press, 2002).
15 John Burnett et al., *The Autobiography of the Working Class: An Annotated, Critical Bibliography*, 3 vols. (Brighton: Harvester, 1984), vol. 1, p. xiii.
16 *Ibid.*, vol. 1, pp. xiii, xiii–xiv.
17 Robert Lowery, *Robert Lowery: Radical and Chartist*, Brian Harrison and Patricia Hollis (eds) (London: Europa, 1979) (originally published anonymously as a series of 33 articles in the *Weekly Record of the Temperance Movement*. Publication at irregular intervals between 15 April 1856 and 23 May 1857), p. 39.
18 George Elson, *The Last of the Climbing Boys, an Autobiography* (London: John Long, 1900), p. 287.
19 Hannah Mitchell, *The Hard Way Up: The Autobiography of Hannah Mitchell, Suffragette and Rebel*, ed. Geoffrey Mitchell, preface by George Ewart Evans (London: Faber & Faber, 1968), p. 239.
20 'Autobiography', *Quarterly Review*, 35 (1827), p. 164.
21 'Autobiography of Francis Place', *The Times*, 23 December 1835, p. 3.
22 Charles Manby Smith, *The Working Man's Way in the World* (London: Printing Historical Society, 1967; originally published serially in *Tait's Edinburgh Magazine*, March 1851–May 1852; published in book form London: William and Frederick G. Cash, 1853), p. v.

23 I should perhaps say a word about how this particular set of texts was selected. I began, in the time-honoured fashion, by raiding the bibliographies of critical work by other scholars, including John Burnett, Jonathan Rose and David Vincent. I then made a more systematic search through the Burnett, Vincent and Mayall *Bibliography* and Nan Hackett's much shorter *XIX Century British Working-class Autobiographies* (New York: AMS, 1985) – both of which are very helpfully annotated – looking for material that seemed as if it might fit with my project. One consideration I kept in mind in trawling for relevant texts was to establish a representative sample, spanning the period covered by my study, beginning with autobiographers born in the final decades of the nineteenth century and moving forward, decade by decade, through that century. In an attempt to redress the gender imbalance (discussed at a later point in this introduction), I paid particular attention to women's autobiographies and I also looked at some of the texts included in Julia Swindells, *Victorian Writing and Working Women: The Other Side of Silence* (Cambridge: Polity Press, 1985). My total working sample ran to about 150 texts. Of these, 108 texts detailing the lives of 101 individuals provided material which has, in one way or another, been directly used in *Shakespeare for the People*.

24 Information on the collection is available at www.brunel.ac.uk/depts/lib/brio/collections/autobiographies.html (accessed 8 January 2007), which includes a link to a complete list of the texts held at the library.

25 Patrick Joyce, *Visions of the People: Industrial England and the Question of Class 1848–1914* (Cambridge: Cambridge University Press, 1991), pp. 74, 337.

26 Peter Bailey, *Popular Culture and Performance in the Victorian City* (Cambridge: Cambridge University Press, 1998), p. 5.

27 David Cannadine, *Class in Britain* (New Haven: Yale University Press, 1998), p. 17.

28 *Ibid.*, pp. 3–4.

29 Thomas Wright (originally published under 'The Journeyman Engineer'), *Some Habits and Customs of the Working Classes* (New York: Augustus M. Kelley, 1967; originally published London: Tinsley Brothers, 1867), p. 109.

30 J. M. Ludlow and Lloyd Jones, *Progress of the Working Class, 1832–1867* (London: Alexander Strahan, 1867), p. 3.

31 John Bedford Leno, *The Aftermath: With Autobiography of the Author* (London: Reeves & Turner, 1892), p. 22.

32 It might also be noted here that there are a number of working-class figures who attained a certain profile specifically as writers (usually poets) in this period. These writers include John Clare, Eliza Cook, Ebenezer Elliott, Joseph Skipsey and (rather earlier) Robert Bloomfield. Many of these writers had strong Shakespearean connections. For the most part, however, while this study does draw on the writings of some these figures, I try to avoid placing them too much at the very centre of my narrative, since the point of the book is, as far as possible, to focus on the experience of a general working-class readership, rather than the experience of exceptional figures who were allowed (if only to a limited extent) to enter the fringes of the cultural elite.

33 Thomas Wright (originally published under 'The Journeyman Engineer'), *Our New Masters* (New York: Augustus M. Kelley, 1969; originally published London: Strahan & Co., 1873), p. 114.
34 Burnett *et al.*, *Autobiography*, vol. I, p. xix.
35 [Thomas Carter], *A Continuation of the Memoirs of a Working Man; Illustrated by Some Original Sketches of Character* (London: Charles Cox, 1850), p. 170.
36 [Thomas Carter], *Memoirs of a Working Man* (London: Charles Knight & Co., 1845), p. 232.
37 Carter, *Continuation*, p. 32.
38 Henry Broadhurst, *Henry Broadhurst, M.P.: The Story of his Life from a Stonemason's Bench to the Treasury Bench* (London: Hutchinson, 1901), p. 254.
39 Samuel Bamford, *Passages in the Life of a Radical*, in W. H. Chaloner, ed., *The Autobiography of Samuel Bamford*, 2 vols. (London: Frank Cass, 1967), vol. I, p. 209. Bamford did not particularly care for the theatre either: 'That sort of thing did not please me; there was too much of tinsel and clap-trap – too little reality – of thorough natural freshness for my taste' (vol. I, p. 211). Stratford-on-Avon fared no better: 'we arrived at Stratford-on-Avon ... I [went to see] the house in which the poet resided – a dilapidated place' (vol. II, p. 32).
40 Sarah Martin, *A Brief Sketch of the Life of the Late Miss Sarah Martin* (Yarmouth: C. Barber, 1845; originally published Yarmouth, 1844), p. 2.
41 Joseph Barker, *The Life of Joseph Barker. Written by Himself*, ed. John Thomas Barker (London: Hodder & Stoughton, 1880; originally published London: Chapman Brothers, 1846), p. 71.
42 James Bonwick, *An Octogenarian's Reminiscences* (London: James Nichols, 1902), p. 256.
43 Burnett *et al.*, *Autobiography*, vol. I, p. xviii.
44 Eric Gillett, 'Introduction' to Elizabeth Ham, *Elizabeth Ham by Herself, 1783–1820* (London: Faber & Faber, 1945), p. 7.
45 Nan Hackett, *XIX Century*, p. 7.
46 Joseph Terry, 'Recollections of My Life', typescript, Brunel University Library, 1:693, p. 78.
47 Elizabeth Andrews, *A Woman's Work is Never Done* (Ystrad Rhondda: The Cymric Democrat Publishing Society, 1949?), p. 2.
48 Marianne Farningham (pseud. of Mary Anne Hearn), *A Working Woman's Life: An Autobiography* (London: James Clarke, [1907]), p. 44.
49 Geoffrey Mitchell, 'Introduction' to Mitchell, *Hard Way*, p. 32.
50 Julia Swindells, *Victorian Writing*, p. 123. Vincent examines a total of 136 published autobiographical texts of various kinds from the period 1790–1850. Of these, six (just over 4%) are by women. My own bibliography includes 108 texts relating to the lives of 101 individuals, 17 of whom are women. This, too, is an unsatisfactory figure, but it is hard to see how it could be much improved upon.
51 *Ibid.*, p. 127. As an example of the kind of autobiographer that Swindells' taxonomy might retrieve, we might note M. A. S. Barber's account of her own

class location, in *Bread-winning; Or, the Ledger and the Lute. An Auto-biography* (London: William Macintosh, [1865]). Barber observes that her family suffered 'poverty of a peculiar kind; not that which hides in the dark narrow street, the hovel, the cabin, or the cellar, but poverty of the middling classes, the intellectual, the educated, the refined; the poverty which springs from the desire of great things in this world, and the vain struggle to obtain them' (p. 4). This kind of background makes writers such as Barber less useful for the present study. It is also worth pointing out that one of Swindells' texts – Rose Allen, *The Autobiography of Rose Allen. Edited by a Lady* (London: Longman, Brown, Green, and Longmans, 1847) – is, as Swindells herself acknowledges, almost certainly a work of fiction. Neither Barber nor Allen have been included in the autobiographical section of my bibliography or in my appendix.

52 Jane Andrew, *Recorded Mercies: Being the Autobiography of Jane Andrew* (London: E. Wilmhurst; Cranbrook: Miss A. Smart, [1889]).
53 Margaret Bondfield, *A Life's Work* (London: Hutchinson, [1949]).
54 Quoted from Kathryn Gleadle's *DNB* entry for Smith, www.oxforddnb.com/view/article/48577 (accessed 27 October 2004).
55 Mary Smith, *The Autobiography of Mary Smith, Schoolmistress and Nonconformist. A Fragment of a Life* (London: Bemrose & Sons, 1892), p. 32.
56 *Ibid.*, p. 136.
57 Patricia Anderson, *The Printed Image and the Transformation of Popular Culture 1790–1860* (Oxford: Clarendon, 1991), pp. 13–14.
58 John Carey, *What Good are the Arts?* (London: Faber & Faber, 2005), p. 167.
59 Ireland does factor into the equation in the sense that developments in Irish education sometimes served as a model for the English system. A central figure here is Thomas Wyse. Born in co. Waterford in 1791, Wyse was the author of *Education Reform, or, the Necessity of a National System of Education* (1836) and he was closely involved in the Central Society for Education (CSE). In his CSE paper 'Education in the United Kingdom, – its Progress and Prospects', Wyse lamented the fact that, unlike Ireland, England did not have a central Board of Education. He asserts that 'There is no possible reason why Government, in the case of England, should not act as in the case of Ireland. Is a Home Secretary here, of shorter arm and poorer courage than a Chief Secretary there? a "Letter of Instructions" may fairly anticipate an "Act of Parliament." What we want is the organisation. We will take it even as an experiment, and for the legislative sanction consent to wait' – Central Society of Education, *Papers*, vol. 1 (London: Taylor and Walton, 1837), p. 63. On the Irish context of developments in English education (including the use of Irish textbooks by English schools), see J. M. Goldstrom, *The Social Content of Education, 1808–1870: A Study of the Working Class School Reader in England and Ireland* (Shannon, Ireland: Irish University Press, 1972).
60 See Chapter 1, pp. 46–8.
61 Lowery, *Robert Lowery*, pp. 43, 43–4. Given that Lowery seems to indicate that the writers included in the volume were British rather than necessarily

narrowly Scottish, it would be interesting to know whether the book included any passages from Shakespeare. I have, however, been unable to trace the volume. Searches of the National Library of Scotland, British Library and COPAC (a consortium of British and Irish academic libraries, including Cambridge University and Trinity College Dublin) catalogues failed to return any hits for either 'Scotch Beauties' or 'Scots Beauties'.

62 John Clare, 'Popularity in Authorship', *European Magazine*, November 1825, reprinted in J. W. and Anne Tibble, eds, *The Prose of John Clare* (London: Routledge & Kegan Paul, [1951]), p. 256.

63 Charles James Billson, *Leicester Memories* (Leicester: Edgar Backus, 1924), p. 113.

64 On Shakespeare's broad popularity in advance of 1843, see Jane Moody, *Illegitimate Theatre in London, 1770–1840* (Cambridge: Cambridge University Press, 2000), esp. pp. 130–5. For Shakespeare's audience in the cheap London theatres, see Jim Davis and Victor Emeljanow, 'New Views of Cheap Theatres: Reconstructing the Nineteenth-century Theatre Audience', *Theatre Survey*, 39:2 (November 1998), pp. 53–72.

65 Richard Foulkes, *Performing Shakespeare in the Age of Empire* (Cambridge: Cambridge University Press, 2002), pp. 2, 57.

66 Christopher Thomson, *The Autobiography of an Artisan* (London: J. Chapman; Nottingham: J. Shaw & Sons, 1847), p. 98.

67 *Ibid.*, p. 101.

68 See *ibid.*, p. 103.

69 See J. Passmore Edwards, *A Few Footprints* (London: np, 1905), p. 22 and W. E. Adams, *Memoirs of a Social Atom*, 2 vols. (London: Hutchinson, 1903), vol. 1, p. 77.

70 Frederick Rogers, *Labour, Life and Literature: Some Memories of Sixty Years*, ed. and intro. David Rubinstein (Brighton: Harvester, 1973; first published London: Smith, Elder, 1913), p. 133.

71 Philip Boswood Ballard, *Things I Cannot Forget* (London: University of London Press, 1937), pp. 101–2.

72 Edward Brown, untitled manuscript, Brunel University Library, 1:93, pp. 178–9.

73 Particularly important work on this topic is currently being undertaken by Richard Schoch.

74 Working Men's Shakespeare Committee, 'Shakespeare Celebration. Address of the Working Men's Shakespeare Committee', dated 7 June 1864, included in Birmingham Central Library *Tercentenary Shakespeare Scrap Book*, vol. 1, item number 207.

75 Letter from J. Bainbridge to J. O. Halliwell-Phillipps, dated September 1864, University of Edinburgh Library, James Orchard Halliwell-Phillipps Collection, L.O.A. vol. 7. Halliwell-Phillipps promised 'to subscribe my mite, say two guineas', but declined an invitation to join the Honourary Council, on the basis of 'a long established rule not to join any sort of C^e in

which I could not take a working part' – see his reply, dated 3 September, drafted on the verso of Bainbridge's letter.
76 Both poems are included in *Addresses Delivered at the Theatre Royal, Drury Lane, in Aid of the People's Shakspeare Memorial Fund. December 5th, 6th, 8th, 9th, 10th, 1864* (London: Thomas Hailes Lacy, [1864]), unpaged.
77 For Dicks' editions, see Chapter 2, pp. 81–6.

CHAPTER I

The educational context

Betsy Cadwaladyr was born in Pen Rhiw in Wales in 1789. She was sent by her parents to a small-scale local school in Bala. Her father well understood the value of education, as he himself had received no formal schooling. A small farmer and sometime Methodist preacher, Dafydd Cadwaladyr had taught himself to read his native Welsh in the most extraordinary manner. Tending sheep on a mountain, he learned much of the alphabet from the owners' initials tarred on the sides of the various flocks grazing on the hillside. Afterwards, leafing through the pages of the Llyfr Gweddi Gyffredin (the Book of Common Prayer), he recognised some of the letters, and 'finding out their sounds in combination, he taught himself to read in the course of two months'.[1] After hoarding every penny he could lay his hands on, he was eventually able, following two years' saving, to purchase a Bible. Later in his life, hearing a rumour that the Pope had determined to deprive him of his textual liberties by setting in train a secret plan to burn all Bibles, he embarked – successfully – on the task of memorising the whole of the New Testament and a substantial portion of the Old.

Extraordinary though Cadwaladyr's story is, it is by no means exceptional for the time. Allen Davenport, the farm worker, horse breaker, soldier, shoemaker, poet and radical activist, was born in Ewen, near Cirencester, in 1775, one of ten children of a hand-loom weaver. Writing of his education, he tells us in his autobiography: 'I never was in any school, for the purpose of instruction, in all my life' and he explains the novel way in which he taught himself to read:

I learnt, as most children do, a number of songs by heart, and having acquired, as best I could, a knowledge of all the letters in the alphabet, I saved all my halfpence and bought up all the printed songs that I could sing, and began with those that appeared the most easy, my new process of education. I proceeded to match all the words in my printed songs, with those I had previously stored in my mind, and by remembering the words thus learnt, by comparing notes, I knew them again whenever they met my eye.[2]

While Cadwaladyr and Davenport acquired literacy exclusively through their own efforts, others relied on chance kindness to gain the power of reading. Henry Hetherington (1792–1849), the radical publisher from Soho, was only able to train as a compositor because his master, Luke Hansard (publisher of the House of Commons reports which still bear his name), 'determined to teach him to read; and while Mr. Hansard was being shaved every morning outside his country house door, young Hetherington was posted by his side to read to him, and subjected to the criticism of a pert, ignorant talkative barber'.[3]

The experiences of Cadwaladyr, Davenport and Hetherington point to a general lack of educational opportunity for children of the poorest backgrounds born in the eighteenth century. Cadwaladyr's daughter Betsy was lucky that there was a local school available to her, but, even here, her experience was not wholly satisfactory, as she herself writes: 'I was quick and sharp, and liked to learn to read and write, but the writing-master himself spoiled my progress. It seemed that he was not pleased that I got on so fast.'[4] Betsy Cadwaladyr's educational advancement was, then, hindered specifically by the grudging unhelpfulness of a particular teacher. But, more generally, the informal schools available to the children of the poor at this time and on through much of the nineteenth century were of, at best, an indifferent, and, at worst, an extremely low standard. In 1835, the Committee of the Manchester Statistical Society published a report on the state of education in that city. It noted of the casual schools serving Manchester's poorest districts that 'they are generally in the most deplorable condition. The greater part of them are kept by females, but some by old men, whose only qualification for this employment seems to be their unfitness for every other.' One of the best schools, they noted, was 'kept by a blind man, who hears his scholars their lessons, and explains them with great simplicity, he is however liable to interruption in his academic labours, as his wife keeps a mangle, and he is obliged to turn it for her'.[5] A similarly grim picture emerged in a report into educational provision in Liverpool, where one school was described as being located in 'a garret, up three pairs of dark broken stairs ... with forty children in the compass of ten feet by nine'. In the room itself, 'on a perch, forming a triangle with the corner'

> sat a cock and two hens; under a stump-bed, immediately beneath, was a dog-kennel in the occupation of three black terriers, whose barking, added to the noise of the children and the cackling of the fowls on the approach of a stranger, were almost deafening. There was only one small window, at which sat the master, obstructing three-fourths of the light it was capable of admitting.[6]

The testimony of many autobiographers serves to confirm the reports of the quasi-official bodies who investigated educational provision in the first third of the nineteenth century. Joseph Terry, born in Mirfield in Yorkshire in 1816, recalled of his first school, run by 'Old Dame Blackburn' that it was in a house 'which was part of an old barn at one end, and there was a kind of loft open at one side, or a half-chamber where the dame kept hens, which hens had a free passage through the midst of the seminary'. It was not uncommon, he writes, for the hens 'in their ascent and descent from the loft to do a kind of business, and drop something amongst our ranks not the most agreeable'.[7] Mary Smith (1822–89), who later ran a school herself, observes of her experience at 'Dame Garner's' in her native Oxfordshire: 'I have an impression that I learnt nothing or next to nothing during that time.' Of Garner herself, she comments that her face was 'as dark as the darkest day in winter. No smile was ever seen to illuminate her stern countenance, from the time of our arrival at school, to the time we made our curtsies and hurried out of it.'[8] Others, however, were appreciative of the efforts of their dame school and other casual teachers, despite their shortcomings. The silk weaver Joseph Gutteridge (1816–99) was taught by an old Quaker woman, who had just a 'limited stock of general knowledge'. For all that, close to his eightieth year, he writes of her fondly: 'Even now as age advances I recall her gentle, placid face and her motherly kindness in dealing with the rough untutored natures committed to her care.'[9] Likewise, Charles Shaw (1832–1906), writing under the name 'An Old Potter' in *When I Was a Child*, observes of his teacher 'Poor old Betty' that she 'was, perhaps, above the average of her class who taught the children of England in those days for a mere pittance, when our rulers were squandering the resources of the nation in less useful ways, and were blind to the wisdom of educating the children of the country'.[10]

It would be some ways into the nineteenth century before the rulers of the country opened their eyes even slightly to the wisdom of educating the children of the poor. However, non-governmental initiatives began to take shape as early as the 1780s, when the newspaper publisher Robert Raikes set in train a scheme for establishing a network of church-based Sunday schools to provide basic educational facilities for children from poor families. Raikes concentrated his activities largely in his own immediate area (Gloucester), but his efforts prompted William Fox to establish the Sunday School Society in September of 1786. Ann Yearsley, the 'milkwoman poet' of Bristol assured Raikes that, as a result of his work, 'when trembling worlds expire' his acts would 'resound, supported in the blast / By grateful Infants, and by ripen'd Man, / To whom you gave perfection'.[11] More prosaically, Joseph Barker, the Methodist minister and politico-religious controversialist (born in Bramley, near Leeds in 1806) neatly indicated why the Sunday School system represented a vital educational connection for himself and for many others like him: 'When we had work, we had not time to go to school; and when we had not work, we had nothing with which to pay school wages, so that a Sunday-School was our only resource.'[12]

Writing in his *Memoirs* (which first appeared in 1791), the publisher James Lackington noted that 'The *Sunday-Schools* are spreading very fast in most parts of England' and he confidently predicted that this would 'accelerate the diffusion of knowledge among the lower classes of the community' (this was a welcome development for the publishing industry, Lackington felt, because it would 'in a very few years exceedingly increase the sale of books').[13] It is certainly true that the movement expanded rapidly and extensively: by 1833 there were 1,550,000 pupils attending 16,828 schools, rising to 1,800,000 in attendance (with a total of 2,400,000 on the registers) by 1851, and the schools continued to prosper throughout the remainder of the century.[14] Whether the church schools genuinely served to extend literacy among the children of the poor is, however, another matter. Some certainly felt that they did. For example, the activist weaver, Samuel Bamford, writing of the period running up to 1815, observed that 'the Sunday Schools of the preceding thirty years ... produced many working men of sufficient talent to become readers, writers, and speakers in the village meetings for parliamentary reform'.[15] Christopher Thomson (b. 1799) went further than this in his *Autobiography of an Artisan* and celebrated 'the memories of those philanthropists who, in the dark morning of our history, laboured to establish Sunday Schools, and, on our one day of rest from labour, let in a ray of civilization upon the degraded children of toil'. For Thomson, the Sunday School teachers 'were the pioneers, cutting down the cumbrous forests of degradation – paring down the baleful weeds of ignorance, and preparing the soil of humanity for the seeds of intellectuality'.[16] Others, however, offered a less positive assessment. The author of an 1838 report on the 'Present State of Education Among the Working People of England' for the Central Society of Education (an organisation dedicated 'to searching out the means of affording to the poor an Education suited to their wants and their duties') concluded that the possibility 'that Sunday school instruction alone is generally efficient for teaching the art of reading, excepting in comparatively rare instances ... may be reasonably doubted'. The writer of the report notes that interviews with many agricultural labourers revealed that 'although they were once taught to read a little at a Sunday school, they never learnt to read with ease or satisfaction ... and had now entirely lost the little they had acquired'.[17]

While the church schools may very well have been a good first step on the road to literacy for some, the amount of instruction that could be provided during a relatively short teaching session one day a week was very limited. In addition, the curriculum was highly restricted. The schools concentrated on Bible reading and the majority did not teach writing, as it was considered by many to be a desecration of the Sabbath. John James Bezer (b. 1816) greatly enjoyed his Sunday school experience, but noted that, even after fifteen years of attendance (during the course of which he himself became head teacher at the school), he 'knew nothing of arithmetic, and could scarcely write [his] own name', and he concluded 'I learnt more in Newgate than at my Sunday school'.[18] However, as John Burnett has noted, the broader significance of the movement may be said to lie in the fact that it provided a model for a national system of free (or very cheap) education, targeted specifically at the children of the poorest class.[19] In this sense, it laid the groundwork for other, more ambitious initiatives, which began to emerge from the turn of the century.

If the Sunday schools can be said to have provided only a very limited education to those children who attended them, there were some for whom the provision of even this minimal service was a troubling and dangerous innovation. Writing in *The Gentleman's Magazine* in October 1797, 'Eusebius'[20] observed that

> the Sunday-school is so far from being a wise, useful, or prudential institution, that it is in reality productive of no valuable advantage; but, on the contrary, subversive of that order, that industry, that peace and tranquillity, which constitute the happiness of society; and that, so far from deserving encouragement and applause, it merits our contempt.

Eusebius' reason for damning the movement so absolutely was that, since the 'laborious occupations of life must be performed by those who have been born in the lowest stations', and since the uneducated man 'can discharge his duty in the most sordid employment without the smallest views of raising himself to a higher station', the poor had best be left uneducated in order that they may fulfil their appointed menial role in society. Furthermore, Eusebius notes, a 'man of no literature will seldom attempt to form insurrections, or plan an idle scheme for the reformation of the State'.[21] Education here becomes enmeshed with politics and, in the background, of course (with Eusebius writing in 1797), are developments that had occurred across the channel during the previous decade. As J. M. Goldstrom has noted,

English society had been shaken by the events in France and not a few Englishmen feared there might be revolution in their own country next. They looked nervously at the working classes for signs that they might be proving receptive to Jacobin ideas and wondered how best to cope with such an eventuality.[22]

That Eusebius had indeed the possibility of a literate working class 'proving receptive to Jacobin ideas' on his mind is confirmed by a further letter of his, published in the January 1798 edition of *The Gentleman's Magazine*, where he writes with heavy-handed sarcasm:

It is a well-attested fact, that no less than 400 copies of Paine's Age of Reason were, on one market day, distributed *gratis*, among the ordinary farmers, servants, and labourers, at York, in a cheap and commodious edition, in order to disseminate its principles, and extend its *illuminating* influence among the vulgar. Those, who have received a tincture of scholarship at a Sunday-school, without any regular discipline for the rest of the week, will be proper subjects for their purpose, and, no doubt, will be the first to derive instruction from the luminous pages of this precious reformer. It would have been useless, it would have been throwing their pearls before swine, to have *stuffed* these edifying publications into the pockets of illiterate rusticks.[23]

For Eusebius, then, ignorance and lack of education provide a necessary barrier against the spread of radical ideas. For some of his contemporaries, however, precisely the opposite was true: education offered the possibility of inculcating establishment values in the children of the poor, thereby fashioning them into compliant subjects, content with the prevailing order of society. Within this paradigm, to withhold education was to risk breeding a dangerous ignorance. This was exactly the argument advanced by Herbert Marsh, Lady Margaret Professor of Divinity at Cambridge, in a sermon preached at St Paul's in June 1810. For Marsh, if the foundation of 'moral and religious habits' is not 'deeply laid' by the time a child is ten years old, 'it is much to be feared, that it will rarely be laid, to any useful purpose, afterwards'. But, if the foundation *is* laid before this age, the child will 'be strongly impressed with a sense of the immutable difference between good and evil, between idleness and useful industry'.[24] Marsh further suggested, in what amounts effectively to an inversion of Eusebius' argument, that 'an uneducated, unemployed poor, not only must be liable to fall into a variety of temptations, but they will, at times unavoidably prove restless, dissatisfied, perverse, and seditious'. To fail to educate the children of the poor finally risks the consequence 'that the property of those who have anything to lose, and even their lives, will become insecure, precarious possessions'.[25] Working-class education, from this viewpoint, is a vital necessity to the continued existence of a stable social order and the security of property.

Marsh preached a further sermon at St Paul's in the following year, in which he called for a new body to be established to provide a national network of day schools, aiming primarily to serve the children of the poor. This sermon proved to be a rallying call to the national church and, specifically, to the Society for Promoting Christian Knowledge. The sermon prompted the Society to convene a meeting of its members, with the Archbishop of Canterbury in the chair, and a new organisation was created, taking as its title the rather cumbersome 'National Society for the Education of the Poor in the Principles of the Established Church throughout England and Wales'. The aims of the Society were 'to instruct and educate the poor in suitable learning, works of industry, and the principles of Christian Religion, according to the Established Church, and the Liturgy and Catechism provided for that purpose'.[26] Children were also 'to be brought as much as possible to the parish-church on the Lord's day'.[27] A public appeal for support raised an initial sum of £20,000, with pledges for subscriptions amounting to £1,500.[28]

We have seen that there was a political element to the position which Marsh adopted on education. There was also a religious dimension to his suggestion that a national organisation be set up under the auspices specifically of the established church. There already was, in fact, a national organisation in existence, dedicated to affording educational provision to the poor. This was the British and Foreign School Society (BFSS), which had been created in 1808. Nominally, the BFSS was non-denominational and, indeed, Article IV of its 'Rules and Regulations' stated that 'All Schools which shall be supplied with Teachers at the expense of this Institution, shall be open to the children of parents of all religious denominations' and that 'no catechism or peculiar religious tenets shall be taught in the Schools, but every child shall be enjoined to attend regularly the place of worship to which their parents belong'.[29] In practice, however, the Society had strong connections with the nonconformist churches and it was viewed with grave suspicion by the Anglicans. In 1809, Thomas Bernard, Chancellor to the Diocese of Durham, anxiously noted that the labours of the dissenters of the BFSS were 'not confined to their own members, but are extended to other societies of Christians, not excluding the poor of the established church' and he registered the fact that there were 'some persons, who now dread their active zeal, their indefatigable industry, and their unceasing activity'. 'If this is a time for apprehension', he asked, 'what must we look forward to, if we do not now supply all our own poor with the inestimable benefit of education?' In the absence of such an educational initiative, he predicted a bleak future for the established church:

> What must be the effect, when in a very few years, myriads of our children, indebted to sectaries for the advantages of education, shall enter on the stage of life; – more instructed, more informed, and more animated by religious zeal and ardour, than the ignorant and untaught members of our own church! If the outworks of the establishment appear to the timid mind to be now in danger, what arms will then be found to defend the citadel against such numerous and powerful assailants?[30]

A decade into the new century, then, two societies dedicated to providing day schools for the children of the poor had been established and a state of (often antagonistic) rivalry existed between them. In 1845 Frederich Engels observed sharply in *The Condition of the Working Class in England* that the two societies had been founded 'simply and solely in order to bring up children of their members in their particular faiths; and, if possible, now and again to filch the soul of some poor little child from a rival religious body'.[31] Certainly, the competition between the two societies could have a pernicious effect. Mary Anne Hearn (1834–1909) was born into a Baptist family and, in *A Working Woman's Life* (published under the pseudonym Marianne Farningham), she noted that there had been a National Society school in her village when she was a child, but that it was 'a Nonconformist principle not to allow Chapel children to learn the Church Catechism, and whatever might have been my father's opinion, his fellow-members considered it a far greater sin to send children to the National school than to let them remain uneducated'.[32] Luckily for Hearn, a BFSS school was opened in her area when she was still a child and she and her younger sister were among the first pupils to be enrolled (she subsequently went on to become herself headmistress of the infants' department of a BFSS school in Northampton). The rivalry between the two societies did, however, have its positive effects, in that it drove both organisations competitively to expand their provision, so that, as Thomas Frost nicely puts it, 'the National and British School Societies began to dot the darkened land with schools'.[33] By 1854, the National Society reported that 10,191 schools were formally attached to its organisation, with a total enrolment of 937,129 pupils.[34] The BFSS never came close to matching these numbers; by mid-century, when 76% of pupils at public elementary schools were being

Figure 3. The monitorial system of teaching, from *Manual of the System of Teaching Reading, Writing, Arithmetic, and Needle-work* (reproduced by kind permission of the Trustees of the National Library of Scotland).

educated by the Anglicans, British Society provision accounted for only 10% of pupils.[35] Thus, Thomas Bernard's 1809 fears for the citadel of the established church were ultimately unrealised, but we can say that those fears did positively spur the national church to a radical expansion of its educational work among the poor, with the result that many more schools became available to working-class children, and these schools were certainly of a higher quality than the common run of dame schools.

Though the two educational societies competed with each other for pupils, they both relied on essentially the same methods in their classrooms. The British Society emerged in the first instance from the Royal Lancastrian Society. This organisation had been formed to carry forward the work of Joseph Lancaster, who had set up a free school for poor children in Borough Road in Southwark in 1801 (this school would ultimately become a BFSS model institution and training centre). To cope with the numbers of pupils who came to avail of the school, Lancaster instituted a 'monitorial' system of teaching, whereby the older students were given the task of teaching the younger ones, under the supervision of the master (Fig. 3). In setting up his school in this way, Lancaster was drawing on the work of Andrew Bell, a native of St Andrews, whose long and varied career included a spell running a male orphanage at Egmore Redoubt, Madras, for the East India Company.[36] Bell had seen older Malabar children teaching younger ones the alphabet by drawing letters in the sand and this gave him the idea both of incorporating the Madras children themselves into the teaching process at the orphanage and of using the simplest, cheapest materials in the classroom. In 1797 he published *An Experiment in Education Made at the Male Asylum at Madras* and this account of his work in India influenced Lancaster in his own undertaking at Borough Road. By the time the second, expanded, edition of the *Experiment* appeared in 1805, Bell had met with Lancaster in London and he sent him fifty complimentary copies of the new edition.[37]

When the Anglicans set their sights on providing an alternative to the BFSS, they too drew on the work of Bell, and Bell himself became energetically involved in the process of promoting the new schools of the established church. The oppositional relationship between the British and National societies contributed to a break in the friendly personal relations between Lancaster and Bell (though, in fact, both being rather egotistical figures, they could as likely have managed to fall out entirely on their own initiative). The systems which Bell and Lancaster evolved had certain differences of emphasis: Lancaster's was the more highly regimented and, unlike Bell, he relied as much on punishments as rewards; he was also something of a martinet (both in and out of the classroom). Nevertheless, the basic structure of the two systems was the same. Each allowed for as many as a thousand pupils to be educated in a single school by a single master, with the bulk of the teaching being carried out by the children themselves. Indeed, Lancaster typically accepted about a thousand students at Borough Road, serving himself as the sole teacher and making use of between sixty and seventy monitors.[38]

The monitorial system seemed to offer itself as a model of early nineteenth-century proto-industrial efficiency. As the historian John Burnett has noted, it appeared to exhibit 'the division of labour applied to educational purposes':

The material to be taught was subdivided in such a way that each section was completely simple: the monitors taught from cards on which each lesson was reduced to components which could be learned by heart, and were not allowed to go beyond what was on the card. Indeed, it was claimed as one of the merits of the system that as the monitors themselves knew no more, they could not digress or waste time. As children learned the work of one 'draft', they were promoted to the next, and the principle of dividing pupils into groups or Standards according to ability was an important innovation in English education.[39]

The system was much praised in its time. For Thomas Bernard 'The discovery of Dr. BELL is not less the production of a philosophic mind, or less the effect of science working by experiment, than that of Mr. DAVY on alkalies, or Dr. JENNER on vaccination.'[40] Wordsworth included a note on 'the discovery of Dr. Bell' in *The Excursion* (1814), in which he observed that 'it is impossible to overrate the benefit which might accrue to humanity from the universal application of this simple engine under an enlightened and conscientious government'.[41] Ebenezer Elliott, the 'Corn-law Rhymer', born in 1781, looked ruefully back at his own inadequate education at the hands of Dame Nanny Sykes, and at another school presided over by a master who could do little on his own to advance the learning of his 150 students, and he regretted the fact that 'In those days the science of monitorship was undiscovered.'[42]

The new schools were not, of course, without their problems. John Bedford Leno, born in Uxbridge in 1826, is tersely dismissive of the education he received at his local National school: 'I made no headway whatever, nor is this to be wondered at, when the slovenly system then in vogue there is remembered.'[43] Thomas Dunning is more specific in his criticism. He too attended a National school and, like Leno, he felt that he learnt 'but very little'. The problem, he explains, lay in the requirements of the monitorial system itself: 'The boys who could read moderately well were appointed to teach the younger or lower classes. I was one of these and I had very little time allowed me for either writing or arithmetic, and none for grammar or geography.'[44] Others, however, could see clear benefits in the system. Francis Place (1771–1854), the illegitimate son of a drunken baker, experienced the usual dreary dame school education, of which he concluded that 'it can scarcely be said that I learned any thing, all I knew, when I left it, was how to read in Dilworths Spelling Book and that too badly'. In addition to being involved with the London Corresponding Society and other radical organisations, Place became an active supporter and promoter of the Lancastrian movement. In a section of his autobiographical writings dated 1823 he registered the real significance of the initiative, celebrating the 'desire which the general movement produced in all below the very rich to give their children a much better education than they themselves received'.[45] At around the time when Place was writing this, James Bonwick (1817–1906) was just beginning to experience the benefits of the BFSS programme. Bonwick was a thorough-going product of the monitorial system: though he was born in Surrey, his father had to move to London to find work as a carpenter, and the young Bonwick was enrolled at Borough Road. He trained as a teacher with the British Society and taught at schools in Hemel Hempstead, Bexley, Liverpool and London, while also spending several extended spells in Australia. Drawing on his own experience, he writes in *An Octogenarian's Reminiscences*:

Without a doubt, this system revolutionized Public Instruction in England. The dense darkness which brooded over this land, when George III. was King, was lifted from the mass of the people. The great difficulty had been the expense of educating poor little ones. The Monitorial System let in the sunshine of hope by relieving the expenditure.

Bonwick lived long enough to see the dawn of a new century and to witness great changes in the educational system – specifically, increased funding and extensive government intervention. But, writing from a different world at the very beginning of the twentieth century, he is able still to see the merits of the old system as he had known it: 'Now ... with our great staff of Teachers, on good pay, we can afford to smile at Monitors. Yet these, in the old times of the neglect of the poor by the State and the rich, did excellent service, and proved a strong moral force.'[46]

What Place and Bonwick stress in their memoirs is the extent to which the British and National schools represented a genuine advance in the field of working-class education.[47] From the first decade of the nineteenth century forward, it became increasingly possible for children from the poorest backgrounds to gain access at least to some basic form of schooling. The education they received at the church schools was often rough and ready – particularly in the earliest days before the societies formalised their systems of teacher training. Often enough, too, such education was short-lived, as many children were taken out of school at an early age and sent to work to supplement the family income. But the British and National schools did help, we might say, to bring an end to the days when the alphabet had to be learned from the tarred backs of sheep, and when schools consisted of crowded menageries offering little more than glorified day care. These schools did make a real contribution to raising standards of literacy among the poorest children and, just as importantly, they served to create a nationwide network of schools which could be built on as the government slowly began to acknowledge its responsibility for the education of its people. As the church societies' programmes developed, then, a genuine school *system* began to emerge and, as a result, working-class children learned to read in ever greater numbers.

Increasing levels of government funding and intervention are, in fact, the signal characteristic of the history of education in England and Wales throughout the remainder of the nineteenth century. Christopher Thomson, who was born on the cusp of a new century, on Christmas day, 1799, and who published his autobiography just short of the middle of that new century, in 1847, welcomed 'the recognition by Government, of the necessity of extending the means of education amongst the people' and he hoped 'through God's blessing, to live to see the education of our common country universal and free'.[48] He would have needed to have lived on into the beginning of yet another new century to see his ultimate wish come true, but some progress had, indeed, been made by the middle of the nineteenth century and much more would be achieved before that century's end.

The government began providing central funding for education in 1833. Looking back from seven decades later, James Bonwick observes that 'We cannot, with our annual Bill of a dozen millions now, avoid a smile at the modest [first] Grant of £20,000.' Bonwick notes that, of this initial grant, £13,200 went to the National Society, while the BFSS was offered £6,800, which was declined on grounds of principle – a position he feels contributed to the gradual demise of the British Society.[49] The grant did not remain at a modest level for very long. The education budget rose steadily year by year and in 1839 the government established the Committee of Council on Education to ensure that school funding was being spent effectively. As part of this process, the Committee set up a system of schools inspection. By the mid-century the grant had increased almost ten-fold, to just under £200,000 and, by 1858, it had climbed to over £700,000.[50] At this point, the government instituted a Royal Commission (the Newcastle Commission) which presented its findings in 1861. At the time of the Commission's report, it was calculated that if every school took advantage of every grant to which it was entitled, the total cost to the government would have been over £2,000,000 a year, with the possibility of costs rising to as much as £5,000,000 per annum within just a few more years.[51] Among the proposals advanced by the Newcastle Commission was a suggestion that the government should introduce a 'Revised Code' for schools and that, as part of this new code, a system of 'payment by results' should be instituted, which would tie the size of the grant paid to any given school directly to student performance. This suggestion was enthusiastically taken up by the government, who saw it as a convenient mechanism for controlling costs. Robert Lowe, who bore responsibility for implementing the new system, (in)famously observed in parliament of government-funded education that 'If it is not cheap, it shall be efficient; if it is not efficient, it shall be cheap.'[52]

Under the terms of the 'payment by results' system, all pupils in grant-receiving schools were to be tested in the 'three Rs' on an annual basis. Each child in regular attendance (which is to say, attending on more than 200 mornings or afternoons a year) would earn a standard payment for the school of 8s., with 2s. 8d. deducted for every failure in one of the three core subjects.[53] Children were also to be sorted into a hierarchy of six standards, with the requirements for each standard being stipulated by the government. For reading, the requirements were as follows:

Standard I Narrative in monosyllables.
   II One of the narratives next in order after monosyllables in an elementary reading book used in the school.
   III A short paragraph from an elementary reading book used in the school.
   IV A short paragraph from a more advanced reading book used in the school.
   V A few lines of poetry from a reading book used in the first class of the school.
   VI A short ordinary paragraph in a newspaper or other modern narrative.

The effects of the assessment regime were felt by many to be extremely oppressive. Thomas Jones, born in Rhymney, Monmouthshire, in 1870, and later a civil servant and educational activist, experienced the rigours of the system as a child, and he wrote in his memoirs:

No one who was present can forget the examination day; it was like a funeral and the Judgement Day rolled into one. The hectic preparation at home, the girls in their spotless pinafores, the boys doubly brushed and scrubbed; the arrival of that terrifying ogre, Her Majesty's Inspector, with his strange English name.

Jones provides a sample entry from the headmaster's diary at his old school:

May 25. Day of Examination of H.M.I. and his assistants. Many of the children assembled shortly after 8 a.m. Mr. Waddington kept the infants waiting for him until after one o'clock and consequently they were tired and restless. A very wet day and hence some absenteeism amounting to £6 8s.[54]

Philip Boswood Ballard (1865–1950), who – like James Bonwick before him – trained at Borough Road, experienced, as a teacher, the final stages of the payment by results system, and he observed that 'The grind of the annual examination drove all humane culture out of the school. There was no belief in the goal and no joy in the pursuit.'[55]

The most narrowly constraining version of payment by results, with its exclusive focus on the 'three Rs', was, in fact, relatively short-lived. As Alec Ellis has noted, 'the Code was gradually liberalized ... so that from 1868 grants were extended to one extra subject' in addition to reading, writing and arithmetic. By 1871, the subjects for which additional grants could be awarded included history, geography, geometry, natural sciences and English literature. By 1890, the annual examinations had become less important, with only a selection of students being put through the experience and, in 1895, the examinations were replaced by a simple inspection.[56] Ballard, for one, was happy to have seen the final end of the system, as he picturesquely observes: 'These things have passed away, never to return. The school itself no longer has a frown upon its face.'[57]

John Burnett concisely summarises the negative consequences of payment by results:

The effects on children were to emphasize mechanical drilling of the three Rs, to restrict the curriculum, and, often, to vitiate relationships between teachers and pupils since teachers had little choice but to try to earn the maximum grant – by threat, by punishment, even by bringing sick children into school on examination day if they were likely to win points.[58]

The faults of the system were certainly considerable and, at its very worst, it turned the classroom into the kind of joyless, grant-earning forcing shop of which Thomas Gradgrind might well have served as patron saint. The weakest students were often excluded from the examination process and the brightest often went unchallenged, as teachers concentrated on getting the maximum number of pupils successfully through the grant-earning procedure. Alternatively, in a new twist on monitorialism, the energies of the brightest students might be directed not towards their own intellectual advancement, but towards coaching their weaker classmates. Thomas Okey (1852–1935), who progressed from being a basket-maker to becoming the first holder of the Serena Chair of Italian at Cambridge, recalled of his time at school: 'Those were [the] days of payment by results, and shortly before the Government inspection was due the brighter and more advanced boys were set to coach the dull and backward that the grant might not suffer.'[59]

If something positive can be salvaged from the history of the payment by results scheme, it might be said that the new code at least brought some element of rigour and accountability to the education sector. As we have seen, the expansion of basic school provision for the poorest children in England and Wales over the course of the nineteenth century occurred as a result of the well-intentioned efforts of religiously based, non-governmental agencies. The increasing reliance of the church schools on government subsidy led to the requirement that schools demonstrate that they were fulfilling the core educational mission for which they were being funded. The methods of assessment were certainly crude, had many negative consequences, and were driven as much by governmental penny-pinching as by clear educational goals, but they did at least have the effect of imposing some formal controls and standardised requirements on a school system that had hitherto developed in a rather haphazard and uncoordinated manner.

If the government's aim in the 1860s was to bring some element of accountability to the education sector, in the final three decades of the century it turned its attention to the question of expanding provision. The first step in this direction was the 1870 Education Act, which sought to fill in the gaps in what was, as J. S. Hurt has nicely put it, 'a geographical and pedagogic mosaic, the uncoordinated creation of countless individuals, albeit with some central encouragement from the National Society and other concerned bodies'.[60] Under the provisions of the act, the country was divided into a set of some 2,500 school districts. Each district was to elect a school board that was to determine what additional provision might be required in the area, with the board having the power to fund the building and maintenance of new schools from the local rates.[61] Enough descendants of *The Gentleman's Magazine*'s Eusebius survived for there to be some resistance to the act's instituting a system of mass education (and at the ratepayer's expense, no less), but the legislation was widely welcomed among those who understood its true value. Joseph Lawson, looking back, in 1887, over social developments in the previous six decades, noted the past 'lamentable state of the people of this country as regards education' and offered high praise for the 1870 legislation, observing that it had 'already proved one of the greatest measures ever passed by the British Parliament'. Registering the limitations of 'voluntaryism', he concludes, 'what was proved impossible to accomplish by individual action, is now being done by the united efforts of the nation.'[62] Likewise, Frederick Rogers (1846–1915), a bookbinder and trade unionist, who had ended his own formal education at the age of ten, following stints at a dame school and a BFSS school, writes in his *Labour, Life and Literature: Some Memories of Sixty Years*:

The passing of the Elementary Education Act of 1870 was one of the greatest pieces of social legislation that my life has seen. It was the public – and unconscious – recognition of a principle ... that voluntary effort on the part of well-disposed groups of people, however strenuous and sincere it might be, is not sufficient to solve any social problem of magnitude, and that it is the duty of the State to step in where individual effort fails.[63]

Lawson and Rogers both stress here the fact that the 1870 Act signalled the end of well-meaning voluntarism in the education sector. Henceforth, working-class children would not need to rely on the good efforts of local religiously minded activists to provide them with some form of schooling. Indeed, many voluntary schools were happy enough, in the wake of the act, to move themselves wholly under the jurisdiction of the local board. Thomas Raymont, born 1864, in Tavistock, notes that his local 'school was of the "British" variety', that it has been 'provided by the Duke of Bedford, the great Whig landowner who owned most of Tavistock' and that it 'became a Board School when [he] was in [his] tenth year'.[64] Thomas Jones tells us that the British Society schools in Rhymney underwent a similar transition, and he explains: 'The nonconformist ministers were in the forefront of the demand for a change. They had been managers and examiners of the British Schools and were probably glad to be rid of the financial anxiety attached to them.'[65]

If the 1870 Act signalled the end of 'voluntarism' in the setting up and running of schools, it might also be said to have pointed towards the ending of voluntarism in another sense as well. The act allowed for the possibility that local boards might wish to make school attendance compulsory, rather than continuing with its being a matter of voluntary choice for parents. The idea of compulsory attendance met resistance from various quarters. On the one hand, some rate-payers were opposed to making ever-increasing contributions to the cost of educating those who received their schooling for free. On the other hand, those impoverished parents who were not able to secure free schooling for their children resented the added burden of imposed school fees, not to mention the loss of income involved in having children in school when they could have been out working. Thus, Mrs Wrigley, a plate-layer's wife, born in Cefn Mawr in 1857, indicates clearly the impact which even the small amounts of money earned by children had on the household. When she had her fifth child, she tells us, her husband was earning £1 6s. 6d. and she recalls times when her 'white tablecloth and clean empty pots were waiting for father to bring his wages, before we could have something to eat'. The family's situation improved incrementally as each child grew to be old enough to gain employment: 'I was feeling myself after my eldest boy began to work for 5/- per week. When the next came to work for another 5/-, and the next went out with newspapers, while the fourth boy, only young, delivered milk, I began to get on my feet.'[66] For these reasons, and more generally because of the bureaucratic complexity of the school board system nationally, the imposition of compulsory attendance was a gradual process. In 1873, 'attendance became mandatory for children whose parents received the payment of school fees as part of their outdoor relief'; three years later, attendance up to the age of ten was nominally compulsory, but there were still loopholes in the law and these were not finally closed until 1880.[67] The leaving age was extended to eleven in 1893 and to twelve in 1899.[68]

Joseph Stamper, born in 1886 in St Helens, Lancashire, the son of an iron foundry worker, recalled the compulsory schooling regime with some element of mirth, in his autobiography *So Long Ago . . . .* He was due to start school as a five-year-old in the autumn of 1891, but his soft-hearted mother observed to his father 'I think it a shame, a child of five having to trail to and from school just when winter is coming on. It's better for them to start in the spring, when you can expect the weather to get warmer.' Stamper's father 'wagged his whiskers and made acquiescent noises' and so the child was allowed to skip the first half year's schooling. But he was warned by his mother to be on the look out for the 'School Board Man', whom she discreetly pointed out to the child:

He had a sallow face, a tufted moustache, and sideboards, that is whiskers down to the joint of his lower jawbone, but none on his chin. He wore a dark blue frock-coat and a flat cap with a peak. The underside of the peak was glazed, grass-green, which reflected a greenish glow downward and, by accident or design, gave his eyes a vicious and malignant aspect.

Stamper regarded the attendance officer 'in fear and loathing', becoming 'a Lone Ranger in our streets; whenever I ventured out in school hours my eyes were continuously roving from left to right, then right to left, alert for the first glimpse of the enemy'.[69] There were many, like Stamper, who scrambled away from the School Board Man, and for many he was to be avoided for much longer than just the first half of the first school year.[70] But the final decades of the century are remarkable for the increases which were achieved in the numbers of children attending school and for the ever-lengthening span of their education. In the first decade following the 1870 Education Act, the size of the school population rose from roughly 1,500,000 to almost 4,000,000, with the average length of school life increasing year on year as well, from 2.55 years in 1870 to 5.19 in 1880, 6.13 in 1890 and 7.05 in 1897.[71] By the end of the century, then, from humble beginnings in dame schools, Sunday schools and the voluntary agencies of the churches, a genuine nationwide system of mass education had been forged and universal literacy had, in essence, been achieved.

The first long section of this chapter has concerned itself with the history of working-class education in the nineteenth century, tracking developments from the earliest attempt at creating a network of institutions by the Sunday School Society, through to increasing government intervention and the advent of compulsory schooling by the end of the century. In the final section, I wish to turn my attention to the question of exactly what it was that the children of the poor learned when they attended the schools that were available to them in this period and, more specifically, what reading matter they were exposed to at school.

In the earliest decades of the century, school books of any kind were a rare commodity, particularly in the case of the dame schools and their equivalents. An analysis of the work of the Manchester Statistical Society in relation to Manchester, Liverpool, Salford and Bury published in 1837 noted that very few such schools 'were found to possess more than fragments of books, and in many cases no books were to be seen; the children depending for their instruction on the chance of some one of them bringing a book or a part of one from home'. In Salford, 'one mistress stated that she had expended no less than 10s. in the purchase of books only three years ago, but that they were now lost, or so dirty and torn as to be utterly useless'. Of sixty-five Salford dame schools and equivalents visited, only five (less than 8%) appeared 'to be tolerably well provided' with books; three had no books at all, and in nineteen schools 'the supply was wretched'.[72] Thomas Wood, born in 1822 in Bingley, Yorkshire, confirms this picture. He attended a casual school run by a local man called Jim Lister. The school met in Lister's living room and Wood observes that he remembers only 'one book in the room ... It was a big Bible, bound in leather. The little ones learnt letters out of it. Bigger ones learnt to read'. Looking back, Wood recalls that he is 'not quite sure we ever read anything but the first chapter of St. John'. His final observation on his master is that he has 'a notion he thought he had acquitted himself of his duties by taking care of us and the 1st of John was thrown in to the bargain'.[73]

In the Lancastrian schools the situation, at least in the early days, was not much better. Lancaster himself thought the book an inefficient piece of educational technology:

It will be remembered, that the usual mode of teaching requires every boy, to have a book; yet each boy can only read or spell one lesson at a time, in that book. Now, all the other parts of the book are in wear, and liable to be *thumbed* to pieces; and, while a child is learning a lesson in one part of the book, the other parts are useless.[74]

The obvious solution was to take the book apart, setting the individual lessons on cards for the use of whole groups of students. Beyond this, Lancaster began printing up his own large reading sheets. As J. M. Goldstrom observes, it eventually became possible 'in Lancastrian schools for a child to learn to read without ever touching a book'.[75]

When children attending BFSS schools encountered books, their experience was often akin to that of Thomas Wood. Mary Ann Hearn looks back on the BFSS system from the perspective of the opening decade of the twentieth century and notes just how much it diverged from current practice:

Sixty years ago the elementary education of the British schools was carried on by very different methods from those of the Council schools of the present day. The great book of the school was the Bible. The teachers were not obliged to pass government examinations, but they were required to be members of some Christian Church, and to love, revere, and teach the Book of books.[76]

The Bible was not, however, the only book in use at British schools. Ingram Cobbin, who served for some time as Secretary to the British Society, published an *Instructive Reader ... Designed to Teach Reading, and to Inform and Develop the Powers of the Infant Mind* in 1831. In it, he states that he 'has a strong aversion to making the Scriptures *a task-book*', feeling it better that 'children be allured to read them voluntarily'.[77] But the reading book that he offers as a substitute is also heavily freighted with religious matter. The first lesson in the book reads as follows:

1. God is. God is not as man.
2. God is not to die as man.
3. God can not die.
4. God can see me.
5. God can see all men.
6. God can do as no man can do.[78]

By lesson XII, the sentences become more complicated, but the basic thrust of the material is the same:

1. When time shall end, then the dead shall all rise from the grave.
2. God shall then *judge* all that have been in this world.
3. If we love God's dear Son, and have done as God has told us to do, he will give us rest and joy with him.[79]

The final division of the book includes sections 'On Natural History', 'On Trades and Manufactures' and 'On British History', but even here a religious mindset intrudes. Of Queen Mary, Cobbin writes, 'When her excellent young brother, Edward, died, she had the next legal right to the crown; but as he was a Protestant, and knew her to be a very bigoted Papist, he made a will, and left the crown to Lady Jane Grey'; 'big'-ot-ed' is defined here as 'Hating all who do not think with us on matters of religion.'[80]

The situation at National Society schools was little different, not least because of the strong links that existed between the National Society and the Society for Promoting Christian Knowledge (SPCK), of which, as we have seen, it was essentially an outgrowth. National schools tended to rely heavily on the SPCK for their books and, even as, over time, the National Society relaxed its requirements that books be purchased through the SPCK, schools nevertheless tended to continue to rely on it for their supply of materials, not least because of the heavy discount which the SPCK offered. SPCK publications had much the same cast to them as the

British Society's. For example, George Ludlow's *Class Reading Book*, published for the SPCK by J. W. Parker in 1836, provides a selection of 'Poetical Pieces' for students and the opening set of titles gives a flavour of the volume as a whole:

> The All-seeing God
> Early Piety
> Gratitude to Parents
> To a Redbreast that flew in at the Window
> A Kind and Gentle Temper of great importance[81]

An advertisement placed in the *Publishers' Circular* in January of 1851 by Thomas Varty of the 'Educational Depository' in the Strand serves nicely to illustrate the extent to which the field of education was dominated by religiously orientated texts in the first half of the century. Under the heading 'Reading & Elementary Books', Varty lists some twenty-five titles. With just a handful of exceptions, almost all the books have some religious element to them. The list ranges from 'Abridgement of the Bible, by Ostervald. Bible-Class Book, with Notes & Poems. Book of Bible History, in 3 gradations' at one end to 'Watts' Divine Songs. Watts' First Catechisms. Wyld's Sketches of Religious Communities' at the other.[82]

In fact, however, by the mid-century, Varty's list would have been starting to look just a little old-fashioned. By this point, secular reading books (or readers with at least a strong secular component) were beginning to proliferate in the educational publishing trade. It is difficult to say to what extent these readers found their way into the schools of the religious societies, but we can say that, with the advent of 'payment by results', the question of what children read in school became more pressing, since, as we have seen, under the terms of the Revised Code, the government laid down guidelines for what children at each one of the defined set of 'standards' should be capable of reading. In the wake of this, educational publishers turned their attention specifically to producing texts that were designed to meet the requirements of the code. Thus, in May 1863, Longmans, Green & Co. advertised a new series – Stevens and Hole's Grade Lesson Books – which were aimed squarely at the Revised Code market, 'no suitable work having hitherto been in use'. The series provided an individual volume for each standard and the publishers claimed that the books contained all the material required for achieving a pass in each of the three examinations. It is clear that the books were aimed at the widest possible market, since the advert indicates that 'they are published at a price which places them within the reach of almost the poorest child'.[83] The 'almost' is not without its significance here, since part one sold at 9d. and part two at 1s. and this may well have been enough to place the books outside the easy reach of many working-class families. But the fact that the poorest child was coming within the sights of commercial educational publishers is noteworthy. Within four years of placing this advert, the same publisher was offering an alternative set of readers – The Class and Standard Series of Reading Books, compiled by Charles Bilton – again 'Adapted to the requirements of the Revised Code', with the prices of at least the early standard volumes being pitched much lower (though, admittedly, these volumes provided material specifically for the reading examination only). The Standard I reader cost just 4d. Standard II, 6d. Standard III, 9d.[84]

The quality of the new reading books varied considerably. Matthew Arnold had been appointed as a schools inspector in 1851 and he served in this role for a total of thirty-five years. His reports are particularly valuable for the light which they shed on the quality of the material available in government-aided schools. In 1860 he complained that the common reading books too often presented the student with 'bad literature instead of good – with the writing of second or third-rate authors, feeble, incorrect, and colourless'. Arnold observed that he had

seen school-books belonging to the cheapest, and therefore most popular series in use in our primary schools, in which far more than half of the poetical extracts were the composition either of the anonymous compilers themselves, or of American writers of the second or third order; and these books were to be some poor child's Anthology of a literature so varied and so powerful as the English![85]

However, where the compilers of the readers did manage to avoid second-rate writers and Americans of the third order, they often included in their volumes authors precisely of the kind Arnold would have appreciated – stalwarts of the English canon – and in many cases, this included Shakespeare. Book 5 in Laurie's Graduated Series of Reading Lesson Books included Wolsey's 'Farewell, a long farewell to all my greatness' from act 2, scene 3 of *Henry VIII* and also Mark Antony's 'Friends, Romans, countrymen' – both passages destined to be repeated many times over in many different readers. Book 6 in Laurie's series reproduces sonnet 73 ('That time of year thou mayst in me behold').[86] In Charles Bilton's series mentioned above, book 5 includes the trial scene from *Merchant of Venice*, supplemented by an 'accompanying abridgment of Lamb's Essay on the Play, by which means the connecting links of the story are supplied'.[87] The volume also provides 'Selections from *Richard II*' and various shorter quotations from Shakespeare, as, for example, in a section on 'Insects', where we learn that 'Shakespeare has a famous passage on the honey bees, in which they are represented as teaching the "act of order to a peopled kingdom."' There then follows Canterbury's 'They have a king and officers of sorts' from act 1, scene 2 of *Henry V*.[88]

From the 1860s forward, quotations from Shakespeare become a standard element of the reading books, with certain passages establishing themselves as absolute staples of the schoolbook repertoire. Whether working-class children encountered such material at school is, however, difficult to say. It is worth noting here that the Shakespeare material tended to appear only in the advanced readers – those for Standards V and VI in the original Revised Code scheme. In fact, however, before the closing decades of the century, very few of the poorest children would have stayed in school long enough to reach these standards (though some undoubtedly did).[89] The number of students in each band tailed off quite considerably across the six standards. In his report for 1871, for instance, Matthew Arnold noted that '39.20[%] of the examinees were in Standard I., 23.44 were in Standard II., 17.66 were in Standard III., 10.93 were in Standard IV., 6.15 were in Standard V., 2.61 were in Standard VI'.[90] Thus, less than 10% of Arnold's total group of examinees (not all of whom, of course, were working class) were studying in the standards where they would have been most likely to encounter Shakespeare in their reading books.

Shakespeare was, in fact, directly incorporated into the school requirements in 1882, when, in a revision of the Code, the Standard VI reading requirement became 'Read a passage from one of Shakespeare's historical plays or from some other standard author, or from a history of England' and a new Standard VII was added, being effectively a somewhat more open version of the revised Standard VI, in that it required that students 'Read a passage from Shakespeare or Milton, or from some other standard author, or from a history of England.'[91] The revision to the Code prompted one enterprising publisher to produce an edition of *King John* which included in its preliminaries the Code requirements which the edition served to satisfy.[92] Again, however, it is unlikely that very many working-class children would have found themselves attempting a pass in these standards. David Vincent notes that, in 1882, a total of just over 3,500,000 children presented themselves for inspection and that, of these students, only 1.9% passed the requirements for reading at Standard VI. In the following year 'fewer than one child in six hundred even attempted the newly introduced Standard VII'.[93] Charles Morley, in *Studies in Board Schools*, published in 1897, noted that when he asked one London Board School teacher 'how many boys out of a thousand get to the very top', the teacher 'shook his head. "No; very few in proportion to the multitude we deal with in a dozen years, say." '[94]

As the century drew to a close, and as compulsory attendance kept children in school for ever longer periods, Shakespeare finally did become a meaningful part of the curriculum for many students from working-class backgrounds. Daisy Cowper, for example, born in Liverpool in 1890, the daughter of a sailor who was lost at sea when she was just five, progressed through seven standards at her local board school and remained an extra year as part of the 'ex-VII' group (like many other of the women autobiographers drawn upon in this study, Cowper herself became a teacher). She had clear memories of reading Shakespeare all through the later years of her schooling. At Standard VI (by which point her class was shrinking because 'a few older members who were nearing fourteen ... were allowed to leave, if leaving was essential to their home circumstances') she studied *The Merchant of Venice* and she recalls acting the play out with school friends 'in our back yards, with all the exaggerations and gesticulations we liked. How we laughed and applauded our own skill.'[95] At Standard VII, she read *As You Like It* 'with plenty of memorising', which led to her later being selected to play the part of Rosalind in a production at her teacher training college, as she 'already knew the words, without a book, and our happy, backyard "acting" may possibly have made me a shade less "wooden" than some of the aspirants'.[96] Cowper's schooling spanned the century's end and her Shakespearean encounters would be much more characteristic of the twentieth-century classroom experience. For the vast bulk of working-class children throughout almost the entire nineteenth century, however, the classroom was a place where, at best, the basics of literacy were to be picked up during a few short years of indifferent schooling. Reading Shakespeare – or, indeed, other canonical writers more generally – was something that typically happened outside rather than inside the classroom. But that extramural reading was only possible because of what happened within the walls of the available schools – flawed and ramshackle though they undoubtedly were during the greater part of the century.

NOTES

1 Betsy Cadwaladyr [Elizabeth Davis], *The Autobiography of Elizabeth Davis*, ed. Jane Williams (Cardiff: Honno, 1987; originally published London: Hurst & Blackett, 1857), p. xxv.
2 Allen Davenport, *The Life and Literary Pursuits of Allen Davenport* (New York: Garland, 1986; originally published London: for the author by G. Hancock, 1845), pp. 9, 12.

3 Transcription of a biographical fragment, Holyoake Collection, Bishopsgate Institute, London; original held in the Holyoake Collection, Manchester. A note from Holyoake states the manuscript was signed 'J. W.' (possibly James Watson?), but that the handwriting seems to be Hetherington's own.
4 Cadwaladyr, *Autobiography*, p. 7.
5 *Report of a Committee of the Manchester Statistical Society on the State of Education in the Borough of Manchester, in 1834* (London: James Ridgway & Son; Manchester: Bancks & Co., 1835), pp. 7, 9.
6 Editor, 'Analysis of the Reports of the Committee of the Manchester Statistical Society on the State of Education in the Boroughs of Manchester, Liverpool, Salford, and Bury', Central Society of Education, *Papers*, vol. 1 (London: Taylor and Walton, 1837), p. 298.
7 Joseph Terry, 'Recollections of My Life', typescript, Brunel University Library, 1:693, p. 8.
8 Mary Smith, *The Autobiography of Mary Smith, Schoolmistress and Nonconformist. A Fragment of a Life* (London: Bemrose & Sons, 1892), pp. 17–18.
9 Joseph Gutteridge, 'The Autobiography of Joseph Gutteridge', in Valerie E. Chancellor, ed. & intro., *Master and Artisan in Victorian England: The Diary of William Andrews and the Autobiography of Joseph Gutteridge* (London: Evelyn, Adams & Mackay, 1969; Originally published as *Lights and Shadows in the Life of an Artisan* Coventry: Curtis Beamish, 1893), p. 84.
10 Charles Shaw, *When I Was a Child* (Firle, Sussex: Caliban, 1977; originally published serially in *The Staffordshire Sentinel*, December 1892–May 1893, author identified as 'An Old Potter'), p. 5.
11 Ann Yearsley, 'To Mr. R——, on his Benevolent Scheme for rescuing Poor Children from Vice and Misery, by promoting Sunday Schools', in *Poems on Several Occasions* (London: T. Cadell, 1785), p. 50.
12 Joseph Barker, *The Life of Joseph Barker. Written by Himself*, ed. John Thomas Barker (London: Hodder & Stoughton, 1880; originally published London: Chapman Brothers, 1846), pp. 34–5.
13 James Lackington, *Memoirs of the Forty-Five First Years of the Life of James Lackington* (London: for the author, 1794; originally published 1791), pp. 243–4. Since Lackington falls outside my sample of working-class auto-biographers, his text is listed in my general bibliography and I have not included him in the appendix.
14 For these figures, see John Burnett, ed., *Destiny Obscure: Autobiographies of Childhood, Education and Family from the 1820s to the 1920s* (London: Allen Lane, 1982), p. 141.
15 Samuel Bamford, 'Passages in the Life of a Radical'. in W. H. Chaloner, ed., *The Autobiography of Samuel Bamford*, 2 vols. (London: Frank Cass, 1967), vol. 2, pp. 7–8.
16 Christopher Thomson, *The Autobiography of an Artisan* (London: J. Chapman; Nottingham: J. Shaw and Sons, 1847), pp. 19, 19–20.

17 'Prospectus for the Society', p. xi and 'Schools for the Industrious Classes', p. 349, Central Society of Education, *Papers*, vol. 2 (London: Taylor and Walton, 1838).
18 John James Bezer, 'Autobiography of one of the Chartist Rebels of 1848', in David Vincent, ed., *Testaments of Radicalism: Memoirs of Working Class Politicians, 1790–1885* (London: Europa, 1977), p. 157. Originally published serially in *The Christian Socialist*, 6 September–13 December 1851.
19 See Burnett, *Destiny Obscure*, pp. 140–1.
20 The original Eusebius, who lived *c*. 275–339, was bishop of Caesarea and is regarded as the father of church history.
21 Eusebius, letter to *The Gentleman's Magazine*, 67 (October 1797), p. 820 (all quotations). He also offers the intriguing argument that 'There are, perhaps, more criminals among that class of men who have had a superficial education than among those who have never been taught either to write or read.'
22 J. M. Goldstrom, *The Social Content of Education, 1808–70. A Study of the Working-class School Reader in England and Ireland* (Shannon, Ireland: Irish University Press, 1972), p. 8.
23 Eusebius, letter to *The Gentleman's Magazine*, 67 (January 1798), pp. 33–4.
24 [Herbert Marsh], *A Sermon Preached in the Cathedral Church of St. Paul, London: On Thursday, June 7, 1810* (London: for the Society for Promoting Christian Knowledge, 1810), p. 5.
25 *Ibid.*, pp. 13–14.
26 Thomas Boyles Murray, *National Education Promoted. An Account of the Efforts of the Society for Promoting Christian Knowledge, in Behalf of National Education: Together with a Notice of the Anniversaries of the Assembled Charity Schools* (London: Society for Promoting Christian Knowledge, 1848), p. 49.
27 National Society for Promoting the Education of the Poor in the Principles of the Established Church, *A Brief Account of the National Society* ... (London: National Society ..., 1854), p. 2.
28 Murray, *National Education*, p. 49.
29 *Report of the British and Foreign School Society, M.DCCC.XV with an Appendix and a List of Subscribers and Benefactors* (London: Printed by Richard and Arthur Taylor, 1815), p. xii.
30 Thomas Bernard, *Of the Education of the Poor; Being the first part of a digest of the reports of the society for bettering the condition of the poor: and containing a selection of those articles which have a reference to education* (London: for the Society, 1809), p. 40 (all quotations).
31 Frederich Engels, *The Condition of the Working Class in England*, trans. and ed. W. O. Henderson and W. H. Chaloner (Oxford: Blackwell, 1958; German first edition, 1845), p. 125.
32 Marianne Farningham (pseud. of Mary Anne Hearn), *A Working Woman's Life: An Autobiography* (London: James Clarke, [1907]), p. 17.
33 Thomas Frost, *Forty Years' Recollections: Literary and Political* (London: Sampson Low, Marston, Searle, and Rivington, 1880), p. 7.
34 National Society, *Brief Account*, p. 2.

35 See W. B. Stephens, *Education, Literacy and Society, 1830–1870* (Manchester: Manchester University Press, 1987), pp. 44–5.
36 Bell left money in his will for the setting up of a school in St Andrews. The school, named 'Madras College' in honour of his work in India, still exists (and 'Bell Street' is just across the road from its current main site).
37 See Jane Blackie's *DNB* entry for Bell, www.oxforddnb.com/view/article/1995 (accessed 11 November 2004).
38 See Burnett, *Destiny Obscure*, pp. 147–8.
39 *Ibid.*, p. 148.
40 Bernard, *Education*, p. 36.
41 William Wordsworth, *The Excursion, 1814* (Oxford & New York: Woodstock, 1991 (facsimile reprint); originally published London: Longman, Hurst, Rees, Orme, and Brown, 1814), p. 447.
42 John Watkins, *Life, Poetry, and Letters of Ebenezer Elliott. The Corn-Law Rhymer. With an Abstract of his Politics* (London: John Mortimer, 1850), pp. 5–6. Watkins was Elliott's son-in-law. The first chapter of the volume is an autobiographical text written by Elliott himself – it is from this that I quote.
43 John Bedford Leno, *The Aftermath: With Autobiography of the Author* (London: Reeves & Turner, 1892), p. 4.
44 Thomas Dunning, 'Reminiscences of Thomas Dunning', in David Vincent, ed., *Testaments of Radicalism: Memoirs of Working Class Politicians, 1790–1885* (London: Europa, 1977), pp. 119–20.
45 Francis Place, *The Autobiography of Francis Place*, ed. Mary Thale (Cambridge: Cambridge University Press, 1972), pp. 15, 30.
46 James Bonwick, *An Octogenarian's Reminiscences* (London: James Nichols, 1902), p. 7.
47 Given the space available in this chapter, I have necessarily provided a somewhat streamlined account of developments in working-class education in the first long stretch of the nineteenth century. There were other schools available to the children of the poor in addition to those provided by the National and British societies, though the numbers attending them were small. I have noted above, drawing on Stephens, *Education*, pp. 44–5, that, at the point when the National Society was responsible for educating 76% of students at public elementary schools, the British Society was responsible for 10% of such students. Stephens gives the following figures for other religious bodies: Roman Catholic, 5.5%, Wesleyan 4%, Congregational, 2%. Dame schools – as quotations from the autobiographers used throughout the chapter make clear – continued in existence until the final decades of the century when, as Jonathan Rose indicates, increasingly rigorous government regulations 'swiftly harried them out of existence' – *The Intellectual Life of the British Working Classes* (Yale: Yale University Press, 2002), p. 152. The 'Ragged Schools' also provided a resource for those who could not afford even the nominal fees of the British and National schools, particularly in the period from the mid 1840s to the late 1860s – see J. S. Hurt, *Elementary Schooling and the Working Classes, 1860–1918* (London: Routledge & Kegan Paul, 1979), pp. 56–7.

48 Thomson, *Autobiography*, pp. viii–ix.
49 Bonwick, *Reminiscences*, p. 79.
50 See Goldstrom, *Social Content*, Appendix I (pp. 193–4).
51 *Ibid.*, p. 156.
52 Quoted in Burnett, *Destiny Obscure*, p. 150, from *Hansard* vol. LXV (1862), col. 229.
53 For children under six years of age, the school received 6s. 6d. if they were in regular attendance and the inspector was satisfied that they were being provided with suitable instruction.
54 Thomas Jones, *Rhymney Memories* (Newtown: The Welsh Outlook Press, 1938), p. 49.
55 Philip Boswood Ballard, *Things I Cannot Forget* (London: University of London Press, 1937), p. 67.
56 Alec Ellis, *Educating Our Masters: Influences on the Growth of Literacy in Victorian Working Class Children* (Aldershot: Gower, 1985), p. 94.
57 Ballard, *Things*, p. 67.
58 Burnett, *Destiny Obscure*, p. 150.
59 Thomas Okey, *A Basketful of Memories: An Autobiographical Sketch* (London: Dent, 1930), p. 14.
60 Hurt, *Elementary Schooling*, p. 59.
61 Maud Clarke – a healthy 91-year-old, living in Tipton in 1978 – wrote out the details of her life in a 'Big Value Exercise Book' and recalled the early days of the local boards and the schools they helped establish: the new 'schools were called Board schools, as they were managed by a Board of local important men, who set up the schools, raised rates to help meet the cost, and appointed teachers, whilst attending to all other duties concerning education'. She herself was a student at a complex of new schools built in her area and was impressed that 'The schools, being newly built, were very clean and airy. They were also well lighted by having a high ceiling and well ventilated windows. The large playgrounds were completely paved and very large' – untitled manuscript, Brunel University Library, 1:156, no page numbers. Clarke herself became a school teacher and qualified as a headmistress, though she left the profession in 1913, on marrying her husband.
62 Joseph Lawson, *Letters to the Young on Progress in Pudsey during the Last Sixty Years* (Firle, Sussex: Caliban, 1978; originally published Stanningley: J. W. Birdsall, 1887), pp. 62–3.
63 Frederick Rogers, *Labour, Life and Literature: Some Memories of Sixty Years*, ed. David Rubinstein (Brighton: Harvester, 1973; first published London: Smith, Elder, 1913), pp. 53–4.
64 Thomas Raymont, 'Memoirs of an Octogenarian, 1864–1949', typescript, Brunel University Library, 1:571, p. 4.
65 Jones, *Rhymney Memories*, p. 43.
66 Mrs. Wrigley, 'A Plate-layer's Wife', in Margaret Llewelyn Davies, ed., *Life as We Have Known It*, Anna Davin (intro.) (London: Virago, 1977; first published London: Hogarth Press, 1931), p. 63.

67 Hurt, *Elementary Schooling*, p. 189.
68 Louise Jermy, in *The Memories of a Working Woman* (Norwich: Goose & Son, 1934), writes bitterly of being forced to end her schooling because her mother took in washing and she was needed to work a mangle. The effort, at such a young age and in such conditions, cost her her health and she observes 'all I ever say when people grumble about the school age being raised is, "Oh well, good job for the children, they can't be driven beyond their strength like I was"' (p. 29).
69 Joseph Stamper, *So Long Ago . . .* (London: Hutchinson, 1960), p. 87.
70 W. E. Adams recalls 'accompanying an antiquarian friend on a visit to some historic buildings in the neighbourhood of Tuthill Stairs, Newcastle. We were surprised to notice the effect of our appearance – women hurrying their children into the houses, or hiding them in other ways. When we came to inquire the cause of the commotion, we were told that we were thought to be officers of the School Board!' – *Memoirs of a Social Atom* (London: Hutchinson, 1903), vol. 2, pp. 373–4.
71 See Alec Ellis, *Books in Victorian Elementary Schools* (London: Library Association Pamphlet no. 34, 1971), p. 24 and Ellis, *Educating*, p. 28.
72 Editor, 'Analysis', p. 296.
73 Thomas Wood, autobiography, published serially in *Keighly News*, 3, 10, 17, 24 March and 7, 14 April, 1956. Quotations from the issue of 10 March, p. 5.
74 Joseph Lancaster, *Improvements in Education*, quoted from an abridged edition lacking a title page, c. 1807, National Library of Scotland shelfmark ABS.2.97.44(16), p. 30.
75 Goldstrom, *Social Content*, pp. 36–7.
76 Farningham, *Working Woman's Life*, p. 45.
77 Ingram Cobbin, *The Instructive Reader. Containing Lessons on Religion, Morals, and General Knowledge; in Easy Gradations. Illustrated by Instructive Cuts on an Original Plan; with Questions for Examination, and Elliptical Recapitulations: Designed to Teach Reading, and to Inform and Develop the Powers of the Infant Mind* (London: Frederick Westley and A. H. Davis, 1831), p. v.
78 *Ibid.*, p. 1.
79 *Ibid.*, p. 8.
80 *Ibid.*, pp. 93–4.
81 George Ludlow, *The Class Reading Book: Adapted for Schools, and particularly designed to furnish youth with practical information on a variety of interesting subjects* (London: J. W. Parker, 1836), contents page. The title page notes: 'Published under the direction of the committee of general literature and education, appointed by the Society for Promoting Christian Knowledge.'
82 *PC*, 14:320 (16 January 1851), p. 36, advert number 90. I quote extensively from adverts in *The Publishers' Circular, Bent's Literary Advertiser* and *The Bookseller*, particularly in Chapter 2. This material is not included in my bibliography.
83 *PC*, 26:616 (15 May 1863), p. 257, advert number 356.
84 Charles Bilton, *The Class and Standard Series of Reading Books Adapted to the Requirements of the Revised Code* (London: Longmans & Co., 1876–70). These

prices are stamped on the covers of the respective volumes. The British Library holds Books 1 through 5 – shelfmark 12985.bbb.37.
85 Matthew Arnold, 'General Report for the Year 1860', in Francis Sandford, ed., *Reports on Elementary Schools, 1852–1882* (London: Macmillan, 1889), pp. 87, 87–8. Three years later, however, Arnold was beginning to feel that the Revised Code had 'already had the happiest effect in improving the quality of school reading books': 'General Report for the Year 1863', same volume, p. 104.
86 James Stuart Laurie, *Laurie's Graduated Series of Reading Lesson Books* (London: Longmans, Green, & Co., 1866). The book 5 selections are at pp. 203–4 and 204–5 and sonnet 73 is at p. 12 of book 6.
87 Bilton, *Class and Standard*, Book 5, p. vi. The *Merchant of Venice* segment is at pp. 104–18.
88 The *Richard II* selections run from p. 119 to p. 133. Other selections are at pp. 136, 172, 185 and 188 ('honey bees').
89 Joseph Keating, born in Mountain Ash in south Wales in 1871, successfully passed through the first five standards, but his objective in passing Standard V was practical, rather than educational: 'I had worked diligently to reach this height, because failure at the last examination meant that Parliament would force me to remain at school another year – that is, till my age was thirteen. I was nearly twelve. By passing the fifth standard I was independent of Parliament, free to leave school and go into the mines as soon as I was actually twelve': Joseph Keating, *My Struggle for Life* (London: Simpkin, Marshall, Hamilton, Kent & Co., 1916), p. 37.
90 Arnold, 'General Report for the year 1871' in *Reports*, p. 155.
91 Quoted from Ellis, *Educating*, Appendix 1, p. 177. Ellis provides the text of all the reading requirements by standard from 1862 to 1890.
92 William Shakespeare *King John* (Manchester: J. B. Ledsham; London: Simpkin, Marshall, & Co., 1883).
93 David Vincent, *Literacy and Popular Culture: England 1750–1914* (Cambridge: Cambridge University Press, 1989), p. 90.
94 Charles Morley, *Studies in Board Schools* (London: Smith, Elder, & Co., 1897), p. 89.
95 Daisy Cowper, 'De Nobis', typescript, Brunel University Library, 1:182, pp. 84, 84–5.
96 *Ibid.*, p. 87.

CHAPTER 2

The publishing context

We have seen in the Chapter 1 that, as the nineteenth century began, initiatives for expanding educational provision were undertaken in a context of deep-seated anxiety with regard to the political upheavals of the final decade of the eighteenth century. Eusebius, in the *Gentleman's Magazine*, argued that basic literacy should not be extended to the masses, because it would leave them vulnerable to the propagandistic efforts of native radicals drawing inspiration from continental revolutionaries. Herbert Marsh, by contrast, felt that education could, in itself, serve as a weapon in the battle against such radicalism, helping to counter the threat it posed to the fundamental stability of British society. For Marsh, mass education provided an opportunity for inculcating establishment values in working-class children from an early age.

If the turn-of-the-century debates over literacy and education policy were shot through with the political concerns of the times, so too were those contemporary popular publishing initiatives which tapped into a gradually expanding reading public. It is telling that Eusebius' fears concerning literacy find their point of focus specifically in the work of Thomas Paine, since Paine's *Rights of Man* serves, in many respects, as the starting point for a set of publishing initiatives directed towards a broad readership which included a high proportion of working-class literates. Paine's work was produced, of course, as an immediate response to Edmund Burke's *Reflections on the Revolution in France* (1790). The *Reflections* sold a very respectable 19,000 copies in its first six months, but Paine's answering text ultimately reached a far greater audience. There has been some dispute over the exact number of sales generated individually by parts one and two of the *Rights of Man* and by subsequent complete editions. A claim that part two alone had reached a total circulation of 1,500,000 copies by 1809 has been much repeated, but William St Clair indicates that such claims 'defy credibility when seen in the publishing circumstances of the time as revealed in the archival record'.[1] St Clair's command of the history of publishing in this period is such that his reservations must be taken seriously. At the same time, however, it should also be noted that, even if the extent of Paine's success has been exaggerated, it is nevertheless true that his work enjoyed popularity of a kind that was unprecedented in British publishing history. In his biography of Paine, John Keane logs the impressive reprint record of part two of the *Rights*: the second edition appeared just three days after the first and sold out within hours; a third edition followed within weeks; a fortnight later, a fourth edition was published and, in the next month, two further editions appeared.[2] As St Clair himself notes, Paine refused a personal fortune in declining to sell the copyright in his work for the astonishing sum of a thousand guineas. Additionally, he agreed to the price of the work being reduced from 3s. 6d. to just 6d., thereby massively increasing its potential circulation.[3] Keane notes that within weeks of the work's first appearance 'requests to print popular editions poured in from all over Britain – from Sheffield, Rotherham, Chester, Leicester, several towns in Scotland' and that 'Paine consented to every request, waiving royalties without exception'.[4]

As editions of Paine's work spread throughout the country, his textual presence was certainly thought of as being ubiquitous and as extending particularly into the poorest sectors of society. The reprint editions of the *Rights of Man* triggered a trial for seditious libel (in Paine's absence, as he was by then in France) in 1792. The Attorney General, prosecuting, acknowledged that the central problem with the work was precisely its cheapness. The original edition, he observes, 'was ushered into the world under circumstances that led me to conceive that it would be confined to the judicious reader, and when confined to the judicious reader, it appeared to me that such a man would refute it as he went along'. In the wake of the original full-price edition, however, 'in all shapes, in all sizes, with an industry incredible, it was either totally or partially thrust into the hands of all persons in this country, of subjects of every description [with] even children's sweetmeats [being] wrapped up with parts of it.'[5] T. J. Mathias, in his *Pursuits of Literature* (1797) confirmed this sense of the widespread dissemination of the work, observing that 'Our peasantry now read the *Rights of Man* on mountains, and moors, and by the way side'.[6] Similarly, in his autobiography published at the mid-century, the printer Charles Manby Smith (1804–80), looking back to the days of his youth, comments that the 'works of Tom Paine . . . were read with an avidity of which we can now scarcely form an idea'.[7]

Louis James has observed of Paine that he 'wrote in a simple, direct style with which the common man could identify [and] skilfully played off against the refulgent rhetoric of Burke'.[8] Certainly, the 'common men' of the autobiographical tradition identified strongly with Paine, and his whole body of work had a real impact from the first, and right throughout the nineteenth century.[9] Thomas Hardy, founder of the London Corresponding Society, observed that Paine's work 'seemed to electrify the nation'.[10] In a remarkable passage in his autobiography, Francis Place (1771–1854) writes of being invited to sit in one of his landlady's rooms while she was assisting his wife in giving birth to their second child. He continues:

In this room was a number of books, and among them everything which had been published by Thomas Paine, all these I had read and cheap editions were in my possession; but here was one which I had not seen, namely 'the Age of Reason Part 1.['] I read it with delight.

Place makes no reference to his newborn child, but he does note how pleased he was to make the acquaintance of his landlady's husband, the owner of the books: 'He was an Irishman from the County of Antrim, a cabinet maker by trade [and] a mild quiet benevolent man'.[11]

Samuel Bamford (1788–1872) recalled that, in his childhood growing up in Middleton, Lancashire, his father was a member of a 'band of thinkers' who included 'Edmund Johnson, a druggist and apothecary; Jacob Johnson, his brother, a weaver and herb doctor; Simeon Johnson, another brother, weaver; Samuel Ogden, shoemaker, Thomas Bamford my uncle'. All were devotees of Paine, though their views were not shared by all of their neighbours. Bamford recalls that one Middleton wakes featured a cart, on which was placed

the figure of a man, which I thought was a real living being. A rabble which followed the cart, kept throwing stones at the figure, and shouting – 'Tum Pain a Jacobin' – 'Tum Pain a thief' – 'Deawn wi' o'th'Jacobins' – 'Deawn wi'th'Painites,' – whilst others with guns and pistols kept discharging them at the figure. They took care when they came to the residence of a reformer; the shouting and the firing were renewed and then they moved on.

'Poor Pain', Bamford writes, 'was thus shot in effigy on Saturday; repaired, re-embellished, and again set upright on Sunday; and "murdered out-and-out" on Monday'. 'I, of course', he observes, 'became a friend of Tom Pain's'.[12]

Opposition to Paine and his widely disseminated works extended beyond the elemental hatred expressed by Middleton rustics. Paine's views and his methods prompted real anxiety in establishment circles. He seems himself to have had a clear understanding of the value of cut-price political literature aimed at the poorest sectors of society and he wrote to one correspondent (Thomas Walker), 'As we have now got the stone to roll, it must be kept going by cheap publications. This will embarrass the Court gentry more than anything else, because it is a ground they are not used to'.[13] In fact, the opposition soon learned to meet Paine precisely on his own terms. A condemnatory *Life of Pain* by George Chalmers (published under the pseudonym Francis Oldys) was put into circulation from 1791 in several cheap editions. The pamphlet bore the instruction: 'Read this, and then hand it to others, who are requested to do likewise'.[14] Chalmers' *Life* was recommended to the writer Hannah More by the bishop of London, who thought it the best antidote to what he considered to be the poison of Paine's own publications.[15] More soon entered the battle in her own right with the anti-Painite *Village Politics: Addressed to All the Mechanics, Journeymen, and Day Labourers, in Great Britain*, conceived as a political dialogue between Jack Anvil, a blacksmith, and Tom Hod, a mason. Tom has been reading the *Rights of Man* and Jack warns him of the dire consequences that would follow should Paine's ideas ever be put into practice. For Jack, the issue of rights is a very straightforward matter:

I have got the use of my limbs, of my liberty, of the laws, and of my bible. The two first I take to be my *natural* rights; the two last, my *civil* and *religious*; these, I take it, are the *true Rights of Man*; and all the rest is nothing but nonsense, and madness, and wickedness.[16]

In addition to *Village Politics*, More (in conjunction with her sisters Sarah and Martha) also produced a large number of loyalist tales aimed at working class readers and priced at just ½d. or 1d. The sales figures for the tracts were every bit as impressive as those for Paine's works: within four months, 700,000 tracts had been sold and, within a year, the figure had exceeded 2,000,000.[17] Louis James notes that More's 'methods were followed by the Religious Tract Society (1799), which also used the chapbook format, and in 1812 formed the Hawkers Tract Society to supplement their other means of distribution'.[18]

What we witness, then, at the turn of the century is a dynamic whereby continental radicalism prompts political divisions in Britain, which are then played out in the arena of print. Radicals and conservatives alike quickly come to understand the power of cheap publications in disseminating their views to the mass of the people. This outpouring of cheap literature coincides with the earliest attempts to provide at least a basic education for the children of the poor (an enterprise which is itself, of course, partly motivated by political concerns). Thus, literacy and the availability of cheap publications advanced, we might say, hand-in-hand. As Ian Haywood has observed, at the turn of the century, the political situation 'made a vital and indelible contribution to the evolution of cheap literature and the idea of the common reader.'[19]

The dynamic which we see at play here continued throughout the first half of the century, intensifying at times of high political tension (such as during the height of the Chartist agitation). One of the most long-lived journals of the time was William Cobbett's *Political Register*, published weekly from 1802 until Cobbett's death in 1835. Though initially staunchly anti-Painite, Cobbett became a convert to radicalism (or, at least, his own particular version of radicalism) and he would eventually bring Paine's bones back from America, intending to provide a grand funeral and a fitting memorial for the radical.[20] In November 1816, Cobbett reproduced the leading article from the *Register* as a separate publication priced at just 2d. (the standard price of the *Register* was 1s. ½d.). The 'tuppeny trash' (a name which Cobbett himself enthusiastically embraced) was a great success and it served considerably to expand Cobbett's audience.[21] In one issue of the *Register*, Cobbett offered a powerful dismissal of Shakespeare, observing:

I ask you what it is that can make *a nation* admire Shakespear? What is it that can make them call him a 'Divine Bard,' nine-tenths of whose works are made up of such trash as no decent man, now-a-days, would not be ashamed, and even afraid, to put his name to? What can make an audience in London sit and hear and even applaud, under the name of Shakespear, what they would hoot off the stage in a moment, if it came forth under any other name?

This criticism does, however, need to be seen in context. It appears in a humourous piece about potatoes, in which Cobbett complains that 'It has become, of late years, *the fashion* to extol the virtues of potatoes, as it has been to admire the writings of Milton and Shakespear'.[22] Cobbett carries the joke forward by publishing letters from both Shakespeare and Milton in the next issue of the *Register*, with Shakespeare writing: 'I plead guilty to Mr. Cobbett's charge. But pray, Master William Cobbett, why so hard upon one who, like you, is a self-taught writer, and had only his mother-wit and honest heart to guide him'.[23] In fact, Cobbett was a great admirer of Shakespeare (and, indeed, of Milton) and quoted from him more frequently than from any other writer.

Like Paine, Cobbett deployed a natural style that was direct, vigorous and engaging, and he developed an appreciative and admiring audience among working-class readers. Samuel Bamford encountered Cobbett's work while he was working in a warehouse in Manchester. He writes of the *Political Register* that he 'found within its pages far more matter for reflection than, from its unattractive title and appearance, I had expected to find there. The nervous and unmistakeable English of that work there was no withstanding.' He immediately became a regular reader of Cobbett's writing and an 'ardent admirer of his doctrines'.[24] Thomas Carter (b. 1792) indicates that Cobbett was a substantial figure even among those who did not necessarily read him themselves. In his *Memoirs*, Carter notes that, when working in a tailoring business in Grosvenor Square, his shopmates

> were much pleased at the extent and variety of the intelligence which I was able to give them about public affairs; and they were the more pleased because I often told them about the contents of Mr. Cobbett's 'Political Register,' as they were warm admirers of that clever and very intelligible writer.[25]

The shipwright, housepainter and sometime actor Christopher Thomson, born in 1799, also registers how he was indebted to Cobbett from a young age. 'In early life', he writes,

> my attention was turned to politics. . . . 'Cobbett's Register,' and 'Wooler's Black Dwarf,' were the first works I purchased and studied on political economy. It was my custom every Saturday evening, after my work was over, to go to the Market Place, and from a stall there, to purchase the breathings of those men of mind. How, at the early age of sixteen, my attention was turned to 'that side of the question,' I know not; doubtless an undiscovered influence, working through those forcible common-sense writers, was directing me in spite of myself.[26]

Thomson's crediting of both Cobbett's *Political Register* and Thomas Wooler's *Black Dwarf* as foundational texts in his political education indicates the extent to which the early decades of the century were marked by a substantial culture of cheap radical publishing. The *Black Dwarf* ran from 1817 to 1824 and, during that time, it sat side-by-side with a range of similar journals, such as William T. Sherwin's *Political Register* (1817–19) and Richard Carlile's *Republican* (1819–26). The government tried to constrain these papers through the provisions of the Seditious Publications Act, one of the notoriously illiberal and proscriptive 'Six Acts' of 1819 (passed in the aftermath of Peterloo). The act imposed a 4d. tax on periodicals which included news or comment, which were published more frequently than every twenty-eight days and which cost less than 6d. The aim was to push the price of the radical journals beyond what the ordinary working-class reader could easily afford. In his *Sixty Years of an Agitator's Life*, George Jacob Holyoake nicely characterised the government's position as follows: 'Type was in their opinion the most serious form lead could take'; the stamp duty 'put money into the Crown's purse and limited news. It robbed the reader by making him pay exorbitantly for his paper, and kept the poorer classes ignorant'.[27]

For about a decade, the government's strategy was broadly successful. Both Cobbett's *Register* and Carlile's *Republican*, for example, lengthened their publication intervals (to qualify as 'pamphlets' rather than newspapers) and doubled their price. By 1830, however, radical publishers were beginning to push back against the restrictions imposed upon them. Henry Hetherington launched his *Penny Papers for the People* in 1830 and, in the following year, he turned this venture into *The Poor Man's Guardian* (1831–5), which proclaimed its position boldly on its masthead: '*The Poor Man's Guardian, a Weekly Paper for the People.* Published in defiance of "Law", to try the power of "Right" against "Might". "Taxation without representation is tyranny, and ought to be resisted."' The front page of the journal featured the device of a printing press, with 'Liberty of the Press' emblazoned on the sheet being printed. Around the press was a banner proclaiming 'Knowledge is Power'.[28] The paper sold for 1d. and Hetherington resolutely refused to pay the required tax.

In his struggle against the stamp duty, Hetherington achieved a near-legendary status. The Chartist leader Thomas Cooper admired the 'deliciously provoking coolness' which was his signature characteristic and Henry Vizetelly (1820–94), the London-born journalist and publisher (co-founder of the *Illustrated London News* and other publications) provides an account of Hetherington's career in which the publisher of the *Poor Man's Guardian* appears as a romantic cross between the Scarlet Pimpernel and Robin Hood.[29] Summoned to appear on charges of publishing a newspaper without a stamp, 'Hetherington sent a note to the magistrates informing them that he could not have the pleasure of the proposed interview, as he was going out of town'. A second summons was issued and Hetherington 'was apprized that if he failed to attend, the court would proceed *ex parte*. To this he responded by a chaffing note asking the magistrates the meaning of the phrase, and why the English language, which he could understand, was not made use of.' Bow-street runners were despatched to arrest the publisher at a political meeting in Manchester, but Hetherington was forewarned 'and as the officers made their entrance at the door of his lodgings, he sprang out of the window'. He was eventually drawn back to London owing to his mother's being seriously ill 'but spies were on the watch, and he was seized the very moment he laid his hands on the door knocker'.[30] In total, he would serve three terms in prison for defying the law.

Hetherington was not the only one to end up in jail in the cause of the *Poor Man's Guardian*. Anyone who sold the paper was also liable to prosecution and at least 500 (and possibly as many as 750) were committed to prison for selling unstamped publications.[31] Securing distribution became itself a kind of bravura game of outwitting flatfooted dull authority. At Hetherington's funeral in 1849, Thomas Cooper recalled that the publisher's agents carried the journal

> in their hats, in their pockets: they left them in sure places 'to be called for;' and when, for a few weeks, government actually empowered officers to seize parcels, open them in the streets, and take out any unstamped publications ... Hetherington ... made up 'dummy' parcels, directed them, sent off a lad with them one way, with instructions to make a noise, attract a crowd, and delay the officers, if they seized him: meanwhile, the *real* parcel for the country agent was sent off another way![32]

At its peak, the *Poor Man's Guardian* achieved a circulation of as many as 15,000 copies, with a readership estimated at twenty times that number. But its influence was much wider than this, in that Hetherington's career inspired others to join in the great game of the unstamped. Between 1830 and 1836 (when the government finally admitted defeat by reducing the newspaper tax to 1d.), more than 560 unstamped periodicals were launched.[33] Robert Lowery (1809–63), the Chartist and temperance activist, observes in his autobiography that 'the whole multitude seemed to be roused to interest themselves in the matter of the unstamped papers and their collateral subjects. Even those who could not read themselves often became subscribers with others who would read to them'.[34]

Just as the wildfire popularity of Paine's works was a matter of concern at the turn of the century, so too did the success of the unstamped evoke a sense of anxiety within the establishment. Hannah More and the other purveyors of religious tracts had, as we have seen, ridden out to do battle with Paine. Hetherington and his fellows in the ranks of the unstamped were met by opponents of a rather different kind. The utilitarian activist Henry Brougham served in several Whig administrations (becoming, late in his career, Lord Chancellor) and was a member of the Royal Lancastrian Society and a vice-president of the British and Foreign School Society. His educational initiatives extended beyond the basic provisions of the BFSS and he was closely involved in setting up mechanics institutes and in the founding of University College London. In 1825, in a pamphlet entitled *Practical Observations upon the Education of the People, Addressed to the Working Classes and their Employers*, he argued that the best method 'for promoting knowledge among the poor, is the encouragement of cheap publications', observing that 'in no country is this more wanted than in Great Britain, where ... we have never succeeded in printing books at so little as double the price required by our neighbours on the continent'.[35] Brougham and his utilitarian colleagues took practical steps towards achieving the goal of circulating cheap literature by founding, in the following year, the Society for the Diffusion of Useful Knowledge (SDUK). Charles Knight, the noted Shakespeare editor, served as publisher to the Society, which, as its initial programme, issued two series of books: the Library of Useful Knowledge (from 1827, in 6d. fortnightly parts) and the Library of Entertaining Knowledge (from 1829, in 2s. parts or at 4s. 6d. per volume). Knight himself observed of the SDUK titles that they 'were to be manuals for self-education – clear, accurate, but not to be mastered without diligence and perseverance'.[36] Diligence and perseverance aplenty were certainly required to make much headway with many of the titles published, as the Library of Entertaining Knowledge ran to such engrossing volumes as *Secret Societies of the Middle Ages*. As Richard Altick has observed, the series demonstrated 'that "entertaining" is a relative term'.[37]

While the Libraries of the SDUK hardly set the world of working-class readers on fire with enthusiasm (indeed, they hardly could have at the price per volume at which they were offered), a further initiative of the Society – the *Penny Magazine*, launched in March 1832 – did have a significant impact.[38] The magazine sought, in some measure, to serve as a counterweight to the unstamped press, and in an article entitled 'Progress of the people', Brougham observed (coupling the *Penny Magazine* with the *Edinburgh Journal* and the SPCK's *Saturday Magazine*) that these journals 'will surely make the people more capable of judging soundly and charitably upon matters of controversy ... and will ... purify the public taste even upon topics which too naturally excite the worser feelings of our nature'.[39] In an extended analysis of the content of the *Penny Magazine*, Patricia Anderson has noted the ideological cast that sometimes lay just beneath the surface of journal's contents:

> The interested reader of articles on natural history and geography was, on occasion, regaled with anecdotes about the 'docility' of the Newfoundland dog, the 'economical' habits of Icelandic mice, the parental 'solicitude' of storks, the 'frugality' of Swedish peasants, and the 'temperance' of Lombardy labourers. Similarly, medical and scientific articles statistically demonstrated that moral restraint prolonged life, hard work cured fatigue, and self-discipline would decrease the birth rate.

Anderson further notes that, from essays of various kinds, readers learned about the general superiority of English civilisation and 'that its continued existence required an ordered and harmonious society'.[40]

The *Penny Magazine* did not go unnoticed by the flagship of the unstamped. In the same month as Knight's publication was launched, the *Poor Man's Guardian* revelled in the fact that 'we *"levellers"* have brought these gentry to the lowly figure of a penny!'[41] In the following month, the *Guardian* mocked the anodyne and abstruse contents of the rival magazine, observing that the SDUK had 'commenced a Penny Magazine, abounding with what the false-hearted and plundering Whigs call *Useful Knowledge*, such as an account of Charing Cross, the Antiquity of Beer, the Lost Camel, &c.' The radical journal accused those behind the *Penny Magazine* of seeking 'to *withhold* really useful knowledge', arguing that the *Poor Man's Guardian* would itself provide such material. 'Which, then', the *Guardian* asks, 'will ye choose? Knowledge, calculated *to make you free* . . . or namby-pamby stuff published expressly to stultify the minds of the working people, and make them spiritless and unresisting victims of a system of plunder and oppression?'[42] To press home its political point, the journal published a special issue consisting of extracts from Colonel Macerone's *Defensive Instructions for the People* – effectively a manual detailing the essentials of street warfare; this, in the *Guardian*'s view, really was *useful* knowledge.[43]

Despite such broadsides from *The Poor Man's Guardian*, the *Penny Magazine*, at its peak, achieved a circulation which dwarfed that of any individual unstamped title. By December 1832, sales figures had reached 200,000. While not all purchasers of the SDUK journal belonged to the poorest sector of society, it is clear that the magazine did achieve significant sales among working-class literates. J. Passmore Edwards' father, a carpenter by trade, subscribed to the magazine and Edwards himself recalled that working through the paper was a positive aid to his own advancing literacy. Reading an article on John Hunter, the renowned surgeon, he tells us, he asked his mother 'the meaning of the word "anatomist," and she told me to consult the dictionary. I did so, and got a little wiser. I had to go to the same source to know the meaning of the word "modern." I read on and on, with the dictionary as tutor'.[44] John Plummer (b. 1831), the partially deaf factory worker and occasional poet, who received little more education than that provided by 'an old lady, whose chief care was to keep me quiet, rather than teach me anything', also found the *Penny Magazine* (together with stray copies of *Lloyd's Penny Sunday Times*) to be a wonderful resource: 'No miser ever hugged his gold with a more jealous care, than I did the few old torn and soiled numbers which came into my possession. For hours I would gaze on the woodcuts, and strive to decipher the letter press descriptions, in which I at last succeeded'.[45] For the radical George Jacob

Holyoake, the *Penny Magazine* served on one occasion as a form of currency. Travelling around England on foot in 1838, he found himself sharing a bed with a young musician at an Inn in Matlock, Derbyshire (the musician, a fiddler, had been given free board at the inn in exchange for entertaining the other guests). With little money to spare, Holyoake tried out an alternative way of paying for his half of the bed: 'In the morning, finding my friend had a reading disposition, I gave him some numbers of the *Penny Magazine*, which I had with me, the illustrations of which were new to him ... He declared them a sufficient reward for his accommodation, as he had incurred no expense on my account'.[46]

The back and forth movement between politically inflected rival popular publishing ventures continued into the middle years of the century. As Ian Haywood has noted, the 'struggle for control of the common reader' reached a high pitch of intensity in the late 1840s, as Chartism hit its final peak. G. M. W. Reynolds launched a series of publications in this period and Haywood sees *Reynolds's Miscellany* (established in 1846), in particular, as offering a new 'radical answer to the *Penny Magazine*'. The journal quickly established a circulation of 50,000 copies and a further title, *Reynolds's Weekly Newspaper* (1850–1924), was an even more notable success, achieving estimated sales of 350,000 by 1872.[47] Chester Armstrong (b. 1868), a weighman at a coalmine in Nenthead in Cumbria, came to Reynolds' newspaper in its later years and observes that 'it was quite inevitable that I should take to [it] as a duck to water'. The paper provided him 'with all the material required to feed the growing bias against royalty, the aristocracy, and the class arrangement of society, all of which appeared to me then as a conglomerate absurdity'.[48] It should be noted, however, that Reynolds' success was not founded solely on the political thrust of his journals. He was also a prodigious writer of popular – and often sensationalist – fiction. His serialised *Mysteries of London* and *Mysteries of the Court of London*, for example, ran to a total of 100,000 pages and were credited with sales of a million copies in the space of ten years. Patricia Anderson has justly observed of Reynolds that 'his career combined a popular political outlook with an unerring ability to pinpoint what was saleable entertainment, and ... this combination was the source of his continuing popularity'.[49]

In Reynolds' career we find, in a sense, the apotheosis of the politically driven popular publishing programmes which are the signature characteristic of the first half of the nineteenth century. These programmes were, as we have seen, partly prompted by the gradual widening of the educational franchise, as both radicals (broadly defined) and conservatives (equally broadly defined) sought to influence the political thinking of an increasingly literate working class. At the same time, the availability of cheap publications served, in its turn, to nurture the reading habit among those who received an elementary education within the gradually expanding school network. Robert Lowery observed of the wild blossoming of the unstamped that 'a taste for reading was created, and while afterwards it sought a change in some of its fare, the appetite still continued'.[50] This comment might be extended to include political publishing more generally during the course of the first long stretch of the nineteenth century, and Reynolds' career in particular might be said to resonate with Lowery's greater sense that the appetite of the common reader ultimately moved beyond the political literature which nurtured it. The key to Reynolds' great success as a writer and publisher was his ability to understand that cheap political publishing helped to foster an audience who might well prove a ready market for cut-price publications of a rather different stripe.

Working-class readers could readily enough afford the cheap political publications that were available to them in the first half of the nineteenth century. Moving on from these journals and making the transition to acquiring books was rather more difficult. The cost of books remained relatively high throughout the first several decades of the century. The *Donaldson* v. *Beckett* House of Lords decision of 1774 had confirmed that copyright was time-limited rather than perpetual (as the elite London publishing houses had repeatedly sought to claim, in the wake of the copyright legislation of 1709).[51] The ruling certainly had a significant effect on the industry, as great swathes of older canonical texts entered the public domain. Book prices fell as a result and the publishing trade expanded.[52] But the established trade dragged its feet over the new order as much as it possibly could. William St Clair notes that 'Well into the nineteenth century, many titles continued to be published by consortia of ... "pretender" copyright holders in much the same way as they had been before 1774'.[53] Beyond such retrogressive attempts to keep the old order in place, it can be said that the cost of books remained high in large measure quite simply because the cost of *producing* books remained high. As Richard Altick has noted, 'compositors were the best-paid skilled workers in London; in 1801 they made 33*s.* a week; and in 1811 the rate went to 36*s.*'. In addition, the expense of paper – a scarce commodity during the Napoleonic wars – was compounded by a heavy tax of 3d. a pound.[54] Altick further notes that 'Technologically, the book trade was far behind most other British industries' and those developments which helped to make the industry more efficient – most notably, the wide-spread use of stereotyping, the iron press, the steam press, machine-manufactured paper and machine-based typecasting – did not emerge until the century was well underway.[55]

In addition to all of these practical issues, the commercial models deployed by the publishing industry were fundamentally conservative. The enormous success of cheap political publications in the opening decades of the century ought to have drawn the trade's attention to the fact that, with a progressively expanding reading public, there was money to be made from stacking books high and selling them cheap. But the publishing industry was very slow to engage with this reality. Charles Knight offered a nice analogy for the shortsightedness of the trade as it concentrated on serving, for the most part, a single high-priced market. Publishers were, he argued, like Billingsgate fishmongers, who destroyed their surplus wares rather than sell them at a discounted price. 'The dealers in fish', he writes, 'had not recognised the existence of a class who would buy for their suppers what the rich had not taken for their dinners'. He continues:

The fishmongers had not discovered that the price charged to the evening customers had no effect of lowering that of the morning. Nor had the booksellers discovered that there were essentially two, if not more, classes of customers for books – those who would have the dearest and the newest, and those who were content to wait till the gloss of novelty had passed off, and good works became accessible to them, either in cheaper reprints, or 'remainders' reduced in price.[56]

The industry survived quite comfortably on the sales of high-priced books and the fate of at least one publisher who planned to offer cheaper wares served as something of a cautionary tale. Archibald Constable projected a reprint series, priced at 3s. or 2s. 6d., which he envisaged 'must and shall sell, not by thousands, and tens of thousands, but by hundreds of thousands, and, ay, by millions!' The 'halfpenny of profit on every copy' would, he insisted, make him 'richer than all the copyrights of all the quartos that ever were, or ever will be, hot-pressed!' He envisaged an initial 'Twelve volumes so good that millions must wish to possess them, and so cheap that every butcher's callant may have them'.[57] Constable's dream, as John Sutherland has observed, 'was forestalled by bankruptcy', and the collapse of the 'firm which had held the copyrights of Scott, the *Encyclopaedia Britannica* and the *Edinburgh Review*, all three of them goldmines ... was a terrible precedent' at which 'the whole publishing industry quaked' and it 'stifled publishing ambitions and inventiveness for years afterwards.'[58] It would not be until the mid-century that the cheap reprint became central to the way in which the publishing trade conducted its business.

Simon Eliot's extraordinarily thorough analysis of book price patterns in the period 1800–1919 nicely confirms all of this general evidence. Pricing information for the early decades of the century, he observes, reveals

> a conservative form in which the highest price group took the largest percentage, the mid-price group accounted for the second largest, and the low-price group the smallest percentage share. 1835 marked a change in which high-price books diminished and mid-price books became the largest single group. The 1840s represented a transitional period during which the low-price book began to emerge as a dominant form. By 1855 the price structure typical of the early nineteenth century had been reversed: low-price books now accounted for the largest percentage share, mid-price books came second, and high price books dropped to their lowest percentage so far recorded.[59]

For the early decades of the century, then, we can say that, while the literate public expanded, and while that expansion was nurtured by the ready availability of politically inspired cheap publications, purchasing most books remained largely outside the realms of possibility for the new generations of working-class readers.

The difficulties involved in buying books are nicely illustrated by the mill worker (and later Unitarian minister) Adam Rushton (b. 1820), who writes in his autobiography of encountering a copy of Bloomfield's *Farmer's Boy* (something of a totemic text for working-class readers) at a bookstall at Barnaby fair. Fascinated by a quick reading of some of the poems, he asks the stall-holder how much the book costs: ' "One shilling and sixpence," said the man, and I walked sorrowfully away'. Rushton manages to persuade a friend to lend him 5d., talks the stall-holder down to 10d., and thereby secures the book, but, since his companion is not as enthusiastic for the new purchase, he has to buy out his partner's share at the rate of a penny a week for five weeks. 'The book', he writes, 'served to brighten my hard factory life, and awakened hopes of deliverance from my drudgery in time to come'.[60] Others among the autobiographers were more fortunate in their choice of book-buying companions. Ben Brierley (1825–96) banded together with a group of other young men and formed a Mutual Improvement Society. They pooled their resources to buy books, taking advice from Brierley's uncle, Richard Taylor, on what they should purchase. Brierley accompanied Taylor to Manchester to spend the accumulated funds, taking with them 'a weavers' wallet in which to carry the books'. The haul was returned triumphantly to the room where the Society met and, Brierley writes, 'It afterwards became a labour of love to cover the bindings, which we did with stout nankeen, so as to make them last forever'.[61]

An even more noteworthy example of a small-scale co-operative library is provided by Robert Skeen (b. 1797) of Tweedmouth, North Durham. He writes in his autobiography of a shepherd friend and he tells of how this friend and a group of other shepherds circulated a small collection of books among themselves in a strikingly original manner:

The sheep-walks were very extensive, and in some places there were boundaries of loose stone walls. In certain crannies in these walls they agreed to deposit whatever books they might acquire – having first read them. The next who passed that way took the volume so deposited, leaving another in its place. The first, after being read, was carried miles farther on, and left in another similar depository; and so on, for a *circuit* of thirty or forty miles.[62]

On some occasions, working-class readers managed to gain access to more formal libraries. Thomas Cooper discovered that a certain 'Nathaniel Robinson, mercer' had left his collection of books for the use of the inhabitants of his native Leicester. The library had been 'thrust aside into a corner, and almost forgotten'. Gaining access to the books, Cooper was 'in ecstasies to find the dusty, cobwebbed shelves loaded with Hooker, and Bacon, and Cudworth, and Stillingfleet, and Locke' and many other writers, mostly philosophers and divines.[63] Cooper had a further stroke of luck thanks to the owner of a local store, Mrs Trevor. She kept a circulating library, from which Cooper borrowed 'the enchanting "Arabian Nights," and odd plays of Shakspeare, Dryden and Otway, and Cook's Voyages, and the Old English Baron'.[64] But Mrs Trevor also ran a 'Book Society' on behalf of the local gentry, at a subscription of two guineas per annum. One day, she whispered to Cooper that she thought she could accommodate him with the loan of the Society's books. 'Suppose I gave her ten shillings for the books of each season, and took care to fetch them in the evening about the time that shops closed, when it would be certain that none of the genteel subscribers would be in the way?' Cooper readily agreed to the proposal and walked home that night with two numbers of the *London Magazine* and the first volume of *Kenilworth*.[65]

Books could also be acquired secondhand in various ways. Mary Smith (1822–89) was delighted when her father arrived home one day 'saying he had been at a sale and had bought a lot of old books'. The miscellaneous collection of tattered volumes included 'novels, poems, plays (including some of Shakespeare's)', and the books were stored away in the attic.[66] Smith recalls that she would quietly creep up there to read when her household chores were done. Beyond small-scale local auctions, street bookstalls also served as a source for secondhand and discounted volumes, at least in the bigger cities (Fig. 4). Henry Mayhew provides an account of these enterprises in his *London Labour and the London Poor*, describing them as 'one of the oldest, and certainly not least important of the street traffics'. The volumes offered by the stalls were, of course, highly miscellaneous. Mayhew notes, for example, that the publications on sale at 1d. each at one bookstall included *Letters to the Right Honourable Lord John Russell, on State Education*; *A Pastoral Letter to the Clergy and Members of the Protestant Episcopal Church in the United States of America*; *Friendly Advice to Conservatives*; and *Elementary Thoughts on the Principles of Currency and Wealth*.[67] But a good selection of canonical works was also to be had. One stallholder told Mayhew that nothing in the trade 'sells better, or indeed so well, as English classics' and he comments that he 'learned from street book-sellers, that their *readiest* sale was of volumes of Shakespeare, Pope, Thomson, Goldsmith, Cowper, Burns, Byron, and Scott'. Another stallholder noted that every kind of book found its way to the street vendors eventually:

Why, last night I heard a song about all the stateliest buildings coming to the ivy, and I thought, as I listened, it was the same with authors. The best that the best can do is the book-stall's food at last. And no harm, for he's in the best company, with Shakespeare, and all the great people.[68]

In the years immediately running up to the publication of Mayhew's work, new books had, in fact, finally started to become more generally affordable. An editorial published in the trade journal *Bent's Literary Advertiser* in October 1851 linked the emergence of cheap publishing ventures with developments in technology and noted that the benefits of this process extended even to the poorest sectors of society:

So long as the Steam Engine exists, [the] thirst for cheap books will increase, and never be satiated. The Stationary and Locomotive engines actually feed each other. The former, at home, industriously heaps together thousands of books. The latter, on its daily journey, distributes them in its onward progress, literally over the world.

The writer notes that, in addition to serving as a distribution network, the railway also helps to sell books, as passengers buy literature to pass the time on their journeys. But the 'blessings of Cheap literature are not alone for the traveller':

The poorer classes now are reaping the fruits of the two Steam Engines. How many a long winter's evening is shortened – how many minds are expanded – how much less is spent in taverns by the mechanics 'clubbing' together to buy these cheap books, which before they never saw nor heard of.[69]

Figure 4. A London street stationer, from Henry Mayhew, *London Labour and the London Poor*, vol. 1 (reproduced by courtesy of the University of St Andrews Library, from r HC255.L6 [SR]).

Just two years later John Parker would write, in an essay entitled 'On the Literature of the Working Classes' that 'At the present time, books are plentiful, and books are cheap. Formerly books were written for the privileged few; now they are printed for the million'.[70]

The downward trend in book prices continued throughout the second half of the century (and beyond). Alexis Weedon notes that, between 1846 and 1916, there was 'a fourfold increase in production and a halving of book prices.'[71] In 1906, C. W. Bowerman, the Labour M. P for Deptford, who had worked for most of his life in the print trade, noted that 'One of the great changes I have seen as a compositor has been the cheapening of good and useful literature. Nowadays cheap editions place the best books within the reach of all except the very poor'.[72] The change that had occurred between the early decades of the nineteenth century and the opening years of the twentieth century is nicely indicated by a story which Howard Spring, the novelist and journalist, tells in his autobiography *Heaven Lies About Us*. Spring (1889–1965) grew up in Cardiff, the son of a father who had run away from his home in County Cork as a young boy and who 'did such jobs as he could get in gardens'.[73] Spring himself attended evening classes at Cardiff University, where he was frequently the recipient of prizes for his work. On one occasion, he was awarded £3 worth of books of his own choosing. Most of his fellow prize winners chose 'one, two or three' books of high value. Spring, however, 'staked out [his] claim on Everyman'. Called to the stage the first time he 'bore away a toppling pile of thirty volumes' and a second call yielded the same number of books again. Spring writes that, as he 'walked back to [his] seat, chin firmly pressed into the topmost volume, there were roars of laughter. It was a business getting home those sixty volumes. I had taken the precaution to provide myself with plenty of string'.[74] 'Everyman, I will go with thee . . .' indeed.

We have seen that editions of Shakespeare were to be had from various sources in the first half of the nineteenth century. Thomas Cooper borrowed 'odd plays of Shakspeare' from a local small-scale circulating library; Mary Smith's father acquired some individual play volumes in the job lot of books he bought at auction; Henry Mayhew found that Shakespeare's works turned up with some frequency in the cheap stock of the London streetsellers. In the final section of this chapter, I look more closely at trends in Shakespeare publishing and pricing over the course of the first long stretch of the nineteenth century, in order to establish just how expensive editions of the playwright's works were in the period, and to chart the history of how, by the second half of the century, Shakespeare had become readily affordable even to those on the most modest of incomes.

From the very first, Shakespeare's text was an expensive commodity.[75] A copy of the First Folio, bound in plain calf, probably cost about £1 in 1623, at a time when a clergyman's salary might have been between £10 and £20 per annum.[76] A century later, a correspondent in *Mist's Journal* complained about the price of Alexander Pope's edition of Shakespeare, noting that, including the expense of binding, the total cost of the set would likely run to seven guineas. In this writer's view, such a price-tag was entirely unjustified, but there was nothing that could be done about it because 'where a Bookseller has the Property of a Copy vested in him, such a Book cannot be had from any person but himself or from those that sell it under him; and therefore the Publick is obliged to come up to his Price'.[77] The rights to Shakespeare were, in this period, claimed by a London cartel headed by the Tonson publishing firm. Various challenges to the cartel's monopoly were mounted over the course of the eighteenth century – most notably by Robert Walker who, between 1734 and 1735, engaged in a publishing battle with the cartel, which ultimately led to individual play editions coming on the market at just 1d. each. But Walker was essentially driven to the wall in the process and normal pricing structures were quickly re-established. Scottish and Irish publishers also sought to provide cut-price editions, at least some copies of which were exported into the much larger English market. But even these editions were far from cheap. Alexander Donaldson, for example, was selling an Edinburgh-published complete works in 1753 for £1 2s. – much cheaper than the Pope edition, certainly, but still far beyond the means of anyone who did not have a reasonably substantial income.[78]

It was this same Alexander Donaldson who, in 1774, won the House of Lords appeal case which confirmed that copyright was time-limited and not perpetual, thus effectively breaking the strangle-hold of the London cartel's claim to exclusive rights in the Shakespeare text.[79] As we have already noted, this decision did lead to something of a shake-up in the industry, with the price of 'public domain' texts declining, as competition increased. Thus, as William St Clair has observed: 'From about 1780, the minimum price of access to certain much demanded out-of-copyright texts fell to about a half, and then to a quarter of previous levels. Editions grew three or four times as long, and there were also many more editions, often on sale at the same time'.[80] St Clair's comments certainly apply very accurately to the specific instance of Shakespeare, but the timescale of these changes was actually surprisingly long, and it was some while before a complete edition of Shakespeare could be had for a price that those in the poorest sector of society could easily afford.

We have seen St Clair note that, in the wake of the 1774 decision, many of the leading London houses continued following traditional publishing practices, including banding together into consortia, exercising what he very usefully characterises as 'pretender' copyrights. St Clair specifically observes that 'the pretender rights in Shakespeare . . . initially held up well' after 1774 and that there appears 'to have been a deliberate policy of subdividing the ownership of the pretender rights. The 1790 edition of Shakespeare, for example, was published by a consortium of no less than thirty-two London firms'.[81] This practice continued into the nineteenth century. Thus, for example, when James Boswell's revision of Edmond Malone's text appeared in 1821, the list of publishers included almost forty different firms, headed by F. C. and J. Rivington. The edition ran to twenty-one volumes and sold at twelve guineas. To put this into perspective: Joseph Gutteridge (1816–99) notes in his autobiography that he was paid £1 a week when working as a journeyman weaver in a factory.[82] At this rate of pay, the cost of purchasing the Boswell–Malone edition at its original full price would have been somewhere in the region of three months' salary for a relatively skilled worker.

The Boswell–Malone was, of course, a flagship edition, and so it is not surprising that it commanded such a high price. Sixteen years after it first appeared, it was being offered for sale secondhand at £14.[83] Cheaper alternatives were certainly available. An 1806 advert placed by Rivingtons in the then newly launched *Bent's Literary Advertiser* listed seven different editions, ranging in price from £1 7s. (for a Steevens text, in nine small volumes) to £11 (for the Johnson–Steevens–Reed edition in twenty-one volumes).[84] Even £1 7s. was, of course, an unimaginable price for any working-class reader who had been honing his or her literacy skills on 6d. editions of Paine or ½d. tracts by Hannah More and her sisters. It is noteworthy, however, that what might be called a rhetoric of affordability does enter into Shakespeare advertising from very early in the century. Thus, for instance, an advert for a two volume edition in the 10 February 1806 issue of *Bent's* boasts that it is on sale 'at the most reasonable Price hitherto offered to the Public': £1 10s.[85] The claim, like many such subsequent claims, is, of course, false (as we have seen, Rivingtons were offering a Steevens edition for 3s. less than this in the very same year) and, in any case, £1 10s. was very far from reasonable, from the perspective of the working-class reader. But the advert does at least indicate that the issue of competitive pricing was starting to find a place in the thinking of publishers, even if they were very far indeed from beginning to plan for a broad market which might include newly literate members of the poorest sector of society.

Shakespeare edition prices did decline over the opening decades of the century, but very slowly. In November 1823, Whittingham had produced a single volume pocket edition which sold at a guinea and which was characterised as 'the smallest, neatest, and cheapest edition of Shakspeare's dramas ever printed'.[86] By the following month, Rivingtons were offering an alternative one volume text – significantly styled the 'Stereotype' edition – for 15s.[87] Hurst, Robinson and Co. matched this price in 1826, with 'The cheapest diamond edition of Shakspeare' and, within a few months, Rivingtons' Stereotype edition was being advertised at 14s.[88] Twelve years later, in 1838, Longman were offering a single-volume edition advertised at '12s. only' and, in the same year, *Bent's* logged an unidentified edition – probably Rivingtons' Chalmers text – at 10s. 6d.[89] In 1841, I. J. Chidley produced an edition at 8s. and, seven years after this, Bohn offered a Chalmers edition at just 5s.[90] By 1856, Bohn was publishing this text at 3s. 6d. a price which would appear not to have been beaten until the Shakespeare tercentenary year of 1864.[91]

The tercentenary had a significant impact on Shakespeare publishing but, before coming on to this, it is worth turning back to consider the effect of an alternative form of edition publishing. Most of the texts logged here so far have been multivolume sets published as complete editions or, more commonly, single volume complete texts. But, there was also a number of editions issued in this period published in parts, and the individual elements of these editions were often cheap enough that they could have been purchased by working-class readers. Indeed, in some cases, publishers specifically attempted to sell their editions on the premise that the individual parts were readily affordable to a wide audience. Robert Tyas launched just such an edition in 1839, styling the project specifically as a 'SHAKSPERE FOR THE PEOPLE' and issuing weekly numbers at just 2d. each, with each play running to 4–6 numbers, 'but in no instance [to] exceed six'.[92] The publisher indicated that he was specifically targeting the common reader with his edition: 'Books are no longer the exclusive luxuries of the rich – they are become the necessary food of the poor'. Tyas seems to have had a certain amount in common with those involved in the SDUK publishing projects, in that he envisaged the reading of Shakespeare as an essentially improving experience, especially in times of crisis. The advert for the edition refers to 'the present great moral struggle'.[93] It is a little difficult to say quite what is meant by this, but it is worth noting that the People's Charter had been published just a few months before the edition was advertised and the Chartist struggle was reaching a high point of intensity as the first numbers of the edition appeared, with Feargus

O'Connor publicly advocating the use of physical force in support of the Chartists' demands.[94] Viewed in this light, it is tempting to see Tyas as advocating that the working-class should read Shakespeare because they will learn from him the value of social cohesion and, indeed, of political quiescence:

In the room of the artisan, in the cottage of the labourer, the PEOPLE'S SHAKSPERE (such is the proud hope of the Projectors) shall be as a household oracle; a teacher of the best human wisdom, the sacredness of human rights; the innocent and ready happiness to be found in this life, even for the lowliest; and the crowning lesson of all life's teaching – the necessity and joyfulness of wise content.[95]

Tyas was followed into the Shakespeare-by-numbers market by J. C. Moore, who began issuing a 'Penny Shakespeare' in 1845. This was projected to be published in sixty numbers, at 1d. each and in monthly parts at 4 ½d. in a wrapper.[96] Reviewing the edition, the Chartist journal, the *Northern Star*, commented that 'an edition, which should be within the reach of the poorest of the people', had, up to this point, been 'a desideratum unaccomplished. Half-crown and shilling parts, or numbers, of any work is, no doubt, cheap enough for many thousands; but such prices are above the means of a still more numerous class'. The journal welcomed the new edition, commenting that 'No man need now be without a copy of *Shakespeare*'.[97] It was probably this edition that provided W. E. Adams (1832–1906), the radical activist and journalist, with his first contact with Shakespeare's work:

a firm of printers in London, sometime about 1844 or 1845, brought out a penny Shakspeare – a play of Shakespeare's for a penny! Well do I remember this cheap treasure. It was my first introduction to the great bard. Gracious! how I devoured play after play as they came out! I was a poor errand boy at the time. When on my errands I used to steal odd moments to read my penny Shakespeare.

The series occasioned a 'painful incident' for Adams, which he remembered with an extraordinary sense of loss more than half a century later:

One day another lad – a bit of a rogue I knew – asked to look at the play I was reading. Out of pure devilment (for he couldn't read himself) he refused to return it. I followed him through many streets, thinking he was playing a joke, and imploring him to give me back my precious property. But I never saw the little book again. To this day the remembrance of grief and mortification is as vivid as ever. The scene, the book, the thief – all are clearer now than greater events of yesterday.[98]

Reading Shakespeare does not seem to have led Adams to embrace 'the necessity and joyfulness of wise content.' He became the editor of the

Newcastle Weekly Chronicle and gained for it the reputation of being the 'Pit-men's bible', on the basis of the paper's support for advanced radicalism, trade unionism and internationalism.[99]

In 1858, Willoughby and Co. advertised another edition to be published in numbers, under the banner 'Shakespeare for the million'. The individual numbers sold at 2d. each, with each one containing a complete play. The publishers claimed that it was 'The best and cheapest edition of Shakespeare extant'.[100] A more ambitious and elaborate part-published text was that announced in December 1863 by Cassell's – a firm which was very active in the field of cheap, improving literature (including such series as the *Working Man's Friend, and Family Instructor*). The Cassell's edition was to be edited by the celebrated Shakespeareans Charles and Mary Cowden Clarke and it was intended that 'by its cheapness' it would be 'within the reach of the poorest scholar'. Those involved in the project wished 'to give SHAKESPEARE'S plays a place in every household of the land, from the highest to the lowest. They feel that to a large majority of Englishmen SHAKESPEARE is at present a name – or known only by a chance quotation or allusion heard at random'.[101] The ultimate aim of the project was to produce 'a profusely-illustrated Edition of Shakespeare worthy of a place in the palaces of the great, and which will, nevertheless, from its cheapness, find its way into the lowliest cottage'.[102] The edition was certainly impressive: the pages were generously sized at 320 × 245 mm and it was lavishly illustrated, with ten or more images per play, many of them full page plates. Despite Cassell's claims, however, it was not particularly cheap. The text was issued in very affordable 1d. numbers, but each number only contained a section of a play. It is difficult to establish how many numbers, on average, made up a whole play, but the edition was issued in parts as well as numbers, initially at 7d. per part, and a complete play tended to overrun a single part. The total cost of buying the edition in parts would have been £1 16s. 3½d.[103] This is at a time, as we have seen, when Bohn was offering a single volume complete works for 3s. 6d. which is to say, about 10% of Cassell's total price.

The Cassell's edition was issued to mark the tercentenary of Shakespeare's birth. The publishers specifically presented it as an alternative to the (abortive) monument planned by the National Shakespeare Committee, claiming that they had 'very great pleasure in announcing that they have commenced the erection of a monument for which the site has already been prepared in the homes of the English people'.[104] The tercentenary sparked a great wave of Shakespeare publishing and *The Publishers' Circular* commented on 'the abundance and variety of new publications directly or indirectly connected with the poet, his life and works'. The *Circular* particularly noted that 'Editions of the Poet's works are of course the chief feature in the list, and these perhaps constitute the best monument ... that we really read, or mean to read Shakespeare, and that our homage to his genius is no mere fashion of speech'.[105]

One of the other editions launched specifically to take advantage of the tercentenary market was the Macmillan-Cambridge University Press 'Globe' text, spun off from the multivolume Cambridge edition of William George Clark, William Aldis Wright and John Glover. Alexander Macmillan himself had high hopes for this edition. Writing to the Glasgow publisher, James MacLehose on 24 May 1864, he indicated that he felt he had 'a reasonable chance of selling 50,000 of [the edition] in three years', observing that 'it would be immeasurably the cheapest, most beautiful and handy book that has appeared of *any kind*, except the Bible'.[106] Macmillan intended the Globe as an edition 'which every Englishman of the tolerably educated classes, from the intelligent mechanic to the peer of the realm, might gladly possess. It is fine enough for the latter, and cheap enough for the former'.[107] *The Bookseller* welcomed the text as being 'the cheapest and best one volume Shakspeare ever produced' and Macmillan advertised it as being offered '*at a price that will place it within the reach of everybody*' (italics in original).[108] The edition sold at 3s. 6d., a price, as we have already seen, which had been achieved by Bohn in 1856. But, this price had almost certainly already been beaten before the Globe even reached the bookstores. On 1 September 1864, *The Publishers' Circular* logged a new edition of 'Shakspere's complete works. With a memoir. Post 8vo. p. 1,020, cloth, 2s.'.[109] The text was published by John Dicks of the Strand, and it was the collected volume version of an edition that he had been issuing since April of the tercentenary year, at the rate of two plays for a penny, complete in 18 numbers and styled as 'an edition of Shakspere for the millions'.[110] Interested customers were encouraged to 'Ask for the People's Edition'. The aim of the edition was to place 'the poet's works within the reach of the great masses of the population'.[111]

Dicks was a singularly appropriate figure to initiate a project aimed at bringing Shakespeare to the masses. According to his obituary, he was a 'poor boy' who 'gradually rose in the ranks', entering 'the printing profession when almost a child'.[112] He was employed for a spell at the Queen's printing office and, in time, he entered the trade on his own account, eventually setting up a London business which became 'one of the largest and busiest printing and publishing offices in England'.[113] In 1848, Dicks entered into a partnership with G. M. W. Reynolds who, as we have already seen, was an active Chartist and who made a very successful career of providing cheap radical and sensationalist reading matter to the working-class public. Dicks served as printer for many of Reynolds' publications, buying out the rights to them on Reynolds' death in 1879. Together, Dicks and Reynolds presented a formidable team, dedicated to advancing the cause of a working-class reading public. At a 'Festival of the Establishment of Messrs. Reynolds and Dicks' held at the Crown Inn in Broxbourne in 1868, one of the contributors to *Reynolds's Newspaper* celebrated the 'immense boon' which Dicks was conferring on society by issuing his cheap editions, thereby putting 'the most brilliant intellects within the reach of the humblest and poorest persons in the land'. He continued:

The delight of perusing the works of Shakspere, Byron, Scott, Longfellow, Burns, Goldsmith, Bunyan, and others, would no longer be confined to the well-to-do classes of society; but that literary food which had hitherto been chiefly partaken of in the mansions of the rich, would now be offered for the enjoyment of the dwellers in the humblest home and poorest cottages in the land.[114]

Two years before the celebration at Broxbourne, Dicks notched up a quite stunning coup as a publisher of Shakespeare. In October 1866, John Camden Hotten proclaimed 'AN EVENT IN LITERATURE!' in an advertisement taken out in the *Publishers' Circular*.[115] Hotten was to bring before the reading public a complete works of Shakespeare for the unprecedented price of just 1s.[116] Preparation of the text was placed in the hands of the noted Shakespearean J. O. Halliwell-Phillipps, who wrote to the *Athenæum* to assert that the undertaking was not 'a refinement on the idea of any recent cheap edition. The fact is, that "The Shilling Shakespeare" was projected as long since as 1863, and after the size, type, and general appearance had been settled, the work was placed in the printer's hands early in 1864'.[117] Halliwell-Phillipps was using a little creative elision here, since the 1863 project was unconnected with Hotten's enterprise and was, in fact, an intended collaboration between the editor and the publishers C. and J. Adlard, who were responsible for his lavish 1853–65 edition. In a letter to Hotten, Halliwell-Phillipps noted that his original project had been 'abandoned on account of the difficulty I had in arranging the trade'.[118] Hotten had arrived at the 'Shilling Shakespeare' notion independently, as he wrote to Halliwell-Phillipps in August 1866: 'The idea ... occurred to me one morning in bed some months ago'.[119] Both the publisher and the editor had high hopes for the projected new edition. Hotten thought it might 'sell 100,000 copies. The Americans will take a large number. I hope to give more legible type than the "Globe" edition'.[120] Halliwell-Phillipps saw the text as potentially performing a particular class function:

One of the chief objects in the original design was the distribution of copies by employers amongst the working classes, + if you felt disposed to let copies in batches of not less than 100 be bought for distribution at 9d or 10d a piece I have very little doubt that some thousands would go in that way.[121]

A specimen page for the edition was made available to the *Publishers' Circular* at the time when Hotten placed his advert and the editor of the journal testified that it was 'perfectly legible.... The type is what is known to printers as "minion." It is round and clear, with sufficient space between the lines to make it comfortable reading for ordinary eyes'.[122] The edition never seems, however, to have advanced much beyond the specimen stage. John Dicks had been planning his own shilling edition 'in a wrapper, printed on thin paper' at just this time and, on seeing Hotten's announcement, he says: 'I immediately issued my 2s. edition for 1s, sewed in a wrapper', thus stealing the march on his fellow publisher (Fig. 5).[123] Hotten seems to have kept his Shakespearean ambitions alive at least into the early months of 1868, but Halliwell-Phillipps was increasingly gloomy of its prospects: 'I fear I could not now, with other engagements + an inability to work long hours, undertake the great labour of correcting the texts.'[124]

Responding to a query from the editor of the *Bookseller* in this same year, Dicks noted of his own shilling edition that he had sold 'about 700,000 copies in all, up to this time'. Taking the 1s. and 2s. edition together, he reckoned he had 'sold as nearly as possible 1,000,000 copies'.[125] This is a quite staggering figure, and it indicates that the edition must have circulated very widely indeed.[126] That the edition *did* circulate widely and that it made its way specifically into the hands of working-class readers is confirmed by autobiographical texts from the period. An anonymous contributor to *The Pioneer* in 1908, looking back on the tercentenary of 1864, recalled being taken to see Charles Kean in *Henry V* and noted that

It set me on to buy Dick's [sic] Penny Plays of Shakespeare, which were then the only cheap form in which the drama could be got out of a lad's scanty pocket money. And while waiting for cricket to begin, I used to delight to lie on the Old Pasture . . . and read the scenes of one or another play, the copy of which was very much worn at the creases and very tender all over, as a result of having been my pocket companion.[127]

Thomas Burt (1837–1922), a miner, trade unionist and politician who served as Liberal MP for Morpeth for forty-four years (and who ultimately

Figure 5. Cover of John Dicks' shilling Shakespeare (reproduced by kind permission of the Folger Shakespeare Library).

became a privy councillor), recalled that Shakespeare was one of two authors whose work was 'indelibly stamped on my memory' (the other was Ruskin). He too was a purchaser of the plays as they were issued individually by Dicks:

> From no *edition de luxe* did I read. The plays published by Dicks cost me one penny each, a sum well suited to my means. No matter that the print was small and the paper poor; no matter that there were neither theatre nor stage, neither actor nor orchestra. All the more scope was given to fancy and imagination.[128]

For others, it was the cheap collected edition that introduced them to Shakespeare's works. Thomas Okey, the basketmaker who became professor of Italian at Cambridge, writes in his autobiography that, when he was a child, literature in his home 'was limited to the *Daily Telegraph*' and he recalled escaping to the washhouse to read in secret. On one particular occasion, his grandfather 'catching sight of me reading there a copy of Dicks's shilling edition of *Shakespeare* – the whole, a marvellous feast of cheap publishing – sternly reproachful, exclaimed: "Ah, Tom, *that*'ll never bring you bread and cheese!" ' (in a footnote, Okey observes: 'As a fact it led in later years to a much more varied diet').[129]

It was not just those who found success in life, moving from working-class backgrounds to middle-class respectability, who discovered intellectual sustenance in Dicks' edition of Shakespeare. Tom Barclay (1852–1933), the son of Irish parents, 'worked at quite twenty factories in Leicester' during the last fifty years of his working life and styled his memoir *The Autobiography of a Bottle Washer*. He writes of the joyful experience of joining the local lending library, and he notes:

> I had read some Shakespeare before the Library opened. Dick's [sic] shilling edition in paper covers was owned by another Irish chap, one Jem Dillon, next door, a little better off than myself; he lent it me as a great favour, but I could never get far until he wanted it back again: now I could borrow Shakespeare for a whole fortnight, aye, and then renew it. But Dick [sic] the publisher deserves a word of praise: he did many a youth a grand service no doubt in bringing out that cheap edition of Sha[k]espeare.[130]

Dicks did not just flood the market with cheap Shakespeare editions; he also prompted other publishers to match his price. By 1868, both Routledge and Warne were selling shilling editions. At the Broxbourne celebration, G. M. W. Reynolds himself promised 'that all the wonders relative to this edition of Shakspere had not yet ceased, for it was intended very shortly to issue it at 8d., and if possible at 6d.'.[131] The price reduction would appear not to have been achieved in the short term, but, by 1890, Ward and Lock had certainly managed to publish a 6d. Shakespeare.[132] This was just under 2% of the price of the cheapest edition we saw advertised in 1806.[133]

Taking the nineteenth century as a whole, then, we can say that the working-class reading habit was nurtured by competing attempts to gain the allegiance of the common reader through the ready distribution of cheap political literature. An expanding reading public moved on from such polemical literature to more general forms of reading, but the publishing trade was slow to recognise the potential of this growing market. Books remained expensive for most of the first half of the century, but working-class readers proved resourceful in securing access to a wide range of texts. The tardiness of the trade's response to the new market is confirmed specifically in the case of Shakespeare, with new editions remaining prohibitively expensive well into the nineteenth century. Part publication certainly helped to make Shakespeare more affordable, but the real breakthrough came with the efforts of John Dicks who, together with Reynolds, made a real commitment to providing reading material to the poorest members of society at an easily affordable price (and, of course, Dicks and Reynolds did very well financially from their efforts as a result). Shakespeare was read by working-class readers throughout the century; Dicks made it possible for such readers to purchase their very own new copy of the complete works.

NOTES

1 William St Clair, *The Reading Nation in the Romantic Period* (Cambridge: Cambridge University Press, 2004), p. 25.
2 John Keane, *Tom Paine: A Political Life* (London: Bloomsbury, 1995), p. 307.
3 St Clair, *Reading Nation*, p. 256.
4 Keane, *Tom Paine*, p. 310.
5 Thomas Erskine, *The Speeches of the Hon. Thomas Erskine (now Lord Erskine), when at the bar, on subjects connected with the liberty of the press, and against constructive treasons* (London: printed for James Ridgway, 1813; 2nd edn), vol. 2. Erskine defended Paine, but his book records the speeches of the prosecution.
6 Quoted in Alan Richardson, *Literature, Education, and Romanticism: Reading as Social Practice, 1780–1832* (Cambridge: Cambridge University Press, 1994), p. 120.
7 Charles Manby Smith, *The Working Man's Way in the World* (London: Printing Historical Society, 1967; originally published serially in *Tait's Edinburgh Magazine*, March 1851–May 1852; published in book form London: William and Frederick G. Cash, 1853), p. 8.
8 Louis James, *Print and the People, 1819–1851* (London: Penguin, 1976), p. 29.
9 It is worth noting that at least one autobiographer turned strongly against Paine's work. John Vine Hall (1774–1860), the religious activist and compiler

of the highly successful *The Sinner's Friend*, read the *Age of Reason*, but, once his religious convictions became fully confirmed, he 'took that infamous book from off the shelf and stamped upon it, denouncing the author as a liar. I then threw it into the fire, saying "Go to the flames with you, Tom Paine; you've deceived me long enough; you shall do so no longer"' – *Hope for the Hopeless: An Autobiography of John Vine Hall*, ed. Newman Hall (New York: American Tract Society, nd), p. 27.

10 Thomas Hardy, *Memoir of Thomas Hardy, Founder of, and Secretary to, the London Corresponding Society* . . ., extract included in David Vincent (ed.), *Testaments of Radicalism. Memoirs of Working Class Politicians 1790–1885* (London: Europa, 1977), p. 49. I have included Hardy in the general bibliography since, having been born in 1751, he falls outside the chronological scope of the present study.

11 Francis Place, *The Autobiography of Francis Place*, ed. Mary Thale (Cambridge: Cambridge University Press, 1972), pp. 126–7.

12 Samuel Bamford, 'Early Days', in W. H. Chaloner, ed., *The Autobiography of Samuel Bamford*, 2 vols. (London: Frank Cass, 1967), vol. I, pp. 43–4.

13 Quoted in Keane, *Tom Paine*, p. 342.

14 Francis Oldys [pseud. of George Chalmers], *The Life of Thomas Pain, the Author of Rights of Man. With a Defence of his Writings* (London: John Stockdale, 1791; 2nd edn), verso of title page. The pamphlet, in its second edition at least, carries an advert on its final page for Samuel Ayscough's edition of Shakespeare (p. 35).

15 See R. K. Webb, *The British Working-Class Reader, 1790–1848: Literacy and Social Tension* (London: Allen & Unwin, 1955), pp. 41–2.

16 [Hannah More], *Village Politics. Addressed to All the Mechanics, Journeymen, and Day Labourers, in Great Britain* (Facsimile reprint, Oxford: Woodstock, 1995; originally published London: F. and C. Rivington, 1793), pp. 17–18.

17 For these general details, see S. J. Skedd's *DNB* entry on Hannah More: www.oxforddnb.com/view/article/19179 (accessed 11 November 2004).

18 Louis James, *Fiction for the Working Man, 1830–1850* (Harmondsworth: Penguin, 1974), p. 138.

19 Ian Haywood, *The Revolution in Popular Literature: Print, Politics and the People, 1790–1860* (Cambridge: Cambridge University Press, 2004), p. 75.

20 In fact, Cobbett's plans were frustrated and Paine's bones were ultimately lost. See George Spater, *William Cobbett: The Poor Man's Friend*, 2 vols. (Cambridge: Cambridge University Press, 1982), vol. 2, pp. 384–9, 378–9. Spater includes various contemporary satiric representations of Cobbett with Paine's skeleton, including (p. 385) *The Political Champion turned Resurrection Man*.

21 E. P. Thompson commented of the initial 2d. issue that 'No writing had obtained such popular influence since the *Rights of Man*: *The Making of the English Working Class* (Harmondsworth: Penguin, 1980; first published 1963), p. 680.

22 William Cobbett, 'To the Editor of the Agricultural Magazine. On the Subject of Potatoes', *Cobbett's Weekly Political Register*, 29:7 (18 November 1815), col. 193, 196.

23 William Cobbett, 'Apologies of Milton and Shakspear', *Cobbett's Weekly Political Register*, 29:8 (25 November 1815), col. 253.
24 Bamford, *Early Days*, p. 281.
25 [Thomas Carter], *Memoirs of a Working Man* (London: Charles Knight & Co., 1845), p. 187. Carter goes on to observe of Cobbett: 'Although I did not much respect the *man*, yet I felt a good deal of interest in reading his political disquisitions, because he seemed to me to have a happy talent for making a difficult question plain to an ordinary capacity'.
26 Christopher Thomson, *The Autobiography of an Artisan* (London: J. Chapman; Nottingham: J. Shaw and Sons, 1847), pp. 79–80.
27 George Jacob Holyoake, *Sixty Years of an Agitator's Life*, 2 vols. (London: T. Fisher Unwin, 1892), vol. 1, pp. 273, 273–4.
28 Quoted specifically from no. 112, 27 July 1833, but this range of slogans is typical of most issues of the journal.
29 Thomas Cooper, 'Éloge', in George J. Holyoake, ed., *The Life and Character of Henry Hetherington, from the Éloge, by T. Cooper, Author of the 'Purgatory of Suicides:' The Oration at Kensal Green Cemetery, by G. J. Holyoake, Editor of the 'Reasoner:' The Speech of James Watson: A Tribute, by W. J. Linton: With Hetherington's 'Last Will and Testament'* (London: J. Watson, 1849), p. 6.
30 Henry Vizetelly, *Glances Back Through Seventy Years: Autobiographical and Other Reminiscences* (London: Kegan Paul, Trench, Trübner & Co., 1893), vol. 1, p. 91. Vizetelly came from a prosperous line of printers, and so, I have not included him among the autobiographers in the appendix or bibliography to this book.
31 Thomas Frost observes that 'Henry Hetherington, with whom I was acquainted more than thirty years ago and who was the proprietor and editor of the *Poor Man's Guardian*, estimated the number of persons sentenced to imprisonment for selling unstamped newspapers at five hundred; but Mr. Heywood, a Manchester bookseller, in a paper read before the Literary Club of that town, stated that the number was seven hundred and fifty': *Forty Years' Recollections: Literary and Political* (London: Sampson Low, Marston, Searle, and Rivington, 1880), p. 8, footnote.
32 Cooper, 'Éloge', p. 7.
33 See James, *Print and the People*, p. 36.
34 Robert Lowery, *Robert Lowery: Radical and Chartist*, Brian Harrison and Patricia Hollis (eds) (London: Europa, 1979) (originally published anonymously as a series of 33 articles in the *Weekly Record of the Temperance Movement*. Publication at irregular intervals between 15 April 1856 and 23 May 1857), p. 94.
35 Henry Brougham, *Practical Observations upon the Education of the People, Addressed to the Working Classes and their Employers* (London: Longman, Hurst, Rees, Orme, Brown and Green, 1825), p. 2.
36 Charles Knight, *Passages of a Working Life*, 3 vols. (London: Bradbury and Evans, 1864–5), vol. 2, p. 56.
37 Richard Altick, *The English Common Reader: A Social History of the Mass Reading Public 1800–1900* (Chicago: University of Chicago Press, 1957), p. 270.

38 Patricia Anderson notes, in *The Printed Image and the Transformation of Popular Culture 1790–1860* (Oxford: Clarendon, 1991) that the initial circulation figures for the Useful Knowledge series ranged from 22,000 to 33,000 per month, but that these figures had declined to 6,000–10,000 within about three years (p. 46).
39 [Henry Brougham], 'Progress of the People – The Periodical Press', *Edinburgh Review*, 57 (1833), p. 241.
40 Anderson, *Printed Image*, p. 54.
41 *PMG*, 42, 31 March 1832, p. 334.
42 *PMG*, 44, 14 April 1832, p. 353.
43 In the following month, the journal carried an advertisement for a penny edition of Macerone's work, published by Hetherington himself, and the advert included the quotation ' "Get thee a sword though made of lath" – *Henry VI*. On the same page was an advertisement for Hetherington's edition of *The Beauties of the Works of Thomas Paine*, priced 3d. – *PMG*, 48, 12 May 1832, p. 392.
44 J. Passmore Edwards, *A Few Footprints* (London: np, 1905), pp. 5–6.
45 John Plummer, *Songs of Labour, Northamptonshire Rambles, and Other Poems* (London: W. Tweedie; Kettering: Thomas Waddington, 1860), pp. xv–xvi.
46 Holyoake, *Sixty Years*, vol. 1, p. 70.
47 Haywood, *Revolution*, pp. 190, 218 and see, more generally, pp. 170, 189–90. See also, for general details of Reynolds' career, Louis James' *DNB* entry on Reynolds, www.oxforddnb.com/view/article/23414 (accessed 27 October 2004).
48 Chester Armstrong, *Pilgrimage from Nenthead: An Autobiography* (London: Methuen, 1938), p. 71.
49 Anderson, *Printed Image*, p. 92.
50 Lowery, *Robert Lowery*, p. 94.
51 On copyright developments in the eighteenth century, see Mark Rose, *Authors and Owners: The Invention of Copyright* (Cambridge, MA: Harvard University Press, 1993).
52 Louis James has noted that while there were 124 letterpress printers in London in 1785, the number had risen to 316 by 1824 and to 500 by the mid-century – *Print and the People*, p. 17.
53 St. Clair, *Reading Nation*, p. 113.
54 The paper duty was reduced by half in 1836 and was fully repealed in 1861.
55 Altick, *Common Reader*, p. 262. On technological developments in the industry, see Marjorie Plant, *The English Book Trade: An Economic History of the Making and Sale of Books* (London: George Allen & Unwin, 1939).
56 Charles Knight, *The Old Printer and the Modern Press* (London: John Murray, 1854), pp. 225–6.
57 Quoted in Henry Curwen, *A History of Booksellers, the Old and the New* (London: Chatto & Windus, 1873), p. 132.
58 John Sutherland, *Victorian Novelists and Publishers* (Chicago: University of Chicago Press, 1976), p. 10. It was not, of course, the projected cheap series which broke the company, but, rather, cashflow problems and a recessionary

economic environment. The series was finally launched in 1827, after the company had re-established itself. As Thomas Frost pointed out, however, the books were never likely to achieve the sales that Constable dreamed of, because, from a working-class perspective, they were still too expensive. Frost concludes that 'though some of them had a large sale, they were bought by readers whose education and means were far above those of the masses': *Recollections*, p. 80.

59 Simon Eliot, *Some Patterns and Trends in British Publishing 1800–1919* (London: Bibliographical Society, 1994), p. 76.
60 Adam Rushton, *My Life as Farmer's Boy, Factory Lad, Teacher and Preacher* (Manchester: S. Clarke, 1909), pp. 34–5.
61 Ben Brierley, *Home Memories, and Recollections of a Life* (Manchester: Abel Heywood & Son; London: Simpkin, Marshall, & Co., [1886]), pp. 35–6.
62 Robert Skeen, *Autobiography of Mr. Robert Skeen, Printer* (London: Wyman & Sons, 1876, for private circulation), p. 5.
63 Thomas Cooper, *The Life of Thomas Cooper* (Leicester: Leicester University Press, 1971; originally published London: Hodder and Stoughton, 1872), p. 51.
64 *Ibid.*, p. 34.
65 *Ibid.*, p. 52.
66 Mary Smith, *The Autobiography of Mary Smith, Schoolmistress and Nonconformist. A Fragment of a Life* (London: Bemrose & Sons, 1892), p. 39.
67 Henry Mayhew, *London Labour and the London Poor; a Cyclopædia of the Condition and Earnings of Those that Will Work, Those that Cannot Work, and Those that Will Not Work*, 4 vols. (London: Griffin, Bohn, and Company, 1861–2), vol. 1, p. 292.
68 *Ibid.*, vol. 1, pp. 293, 296. Street sales of secondhand and heavily-discounted books also occurred outside the metropolitan areas. Thomas Wright provides an extended account of the activities of an itinerant bookseller, operating in working-class districts, in *The Great Unwashed* (New York: Augustus M. Kelley, 1970; originally published London: Tinsley Brother, 1868). Wright notes that 'One of these men will generally sell from fifty to sixty works in the course of a night, and on Saturday nights I have often known them to dispose of from 150–200' (p. 231).
69 *BLA*, 570 (11 October 1851), p. 178.
70 John Parker, 'On the Literature of the Working Classes', in Viscount Ingestre, ed., *Meliora: or, Better Times to Come. Being the Contributions of Many Men Touching the Present State and Prospects of Society*, 2nd series (London: John W. Parker and Son, 1853), p. 182.
71 Alexis Weedon, *Victorian Publishing: The Economics of Book Production for a Mass Market, 1836–1916* (Aldershot: Ashgate, 2003), p. 57.
72 C. W. Bowerman, 'How I got on', *Pearson's Weekly*, 812 (8 February 1906), p. 563. This piece is one of a series of 'Life stories by the Labour M. P.'s' published in *Pearson's Weekly* over the course of several issues of the magazine.
73 Howard Spring, *Heaven Lies About Us* (London: Collins, 1956; originally published London: Constable & Co., 1939), p. 27.
74 *Ibid.*, p. 87.

75 For further material on the editions discussed in this paragraph, see Andrew Murphy, *Shakespeare in Print: A History and Chronology of Shakespeare Publishing* (Cambridge: Cambridge University Press, 2003).
76 For the likely range of prices of the First Folio, see Peter Blayney, *The First Folio of Shakespeare* (Washington, DC: Folger Shakespeare Library, 1991), p. 32. Salary figures taken from Altick, *Common Reader*, p. 22.
77 Review of Pope's edition, *The Weekly Journal or Saturday's Post* (*Mist's Journal*), 20 March 1725, pp. 2075–6 and further comments in the issue of 27 March, p. 2081.
78 See Alexander Donaldson, *A catalogue of curious and valuable books, to be disposed of by way of sale (the lowest price being marked at each book), at the shop of Alexander Donaldson, the first fore-stair above the entry to the Royal Bank, Edinburgh* (Edinburgh: Donaldson, 1753), item 1113.
79 By this point the Tonson firm had ceased to exist, Jacob Tonson III – the last active publisher in the family – having died in 1767, and the firm's rights having been disposed of after his death. See Terry Belanger, 'Tonson, Wellington and the Shakespeare Copyrights', in *Studies in the Book Trade in Honour of Graham Pollard* (Oxford: Bibliographical Society, 1975): 195–209.
80 St Clair, *Reading Nation*, p. 116.
81 *Ibid.*, p. 113.
82 See Joseph Gutteridge, 'The Autobiography of Joseph Gutteridge', in Valerie E. Chancellor, ed. & intro., *Master and Artisan in Victorian England: The Diary of William Andrews and the Autobiography of Joseph Gutteridge* (London: Evelyn, Adams & Mackay, 1969; Originally published as *Lights and Shadows in the Life of an Artisan* Coventry: Curtis Beamish, 1893), p. 118.
83 *BLA*, 389, 10 June 1837, p. 66.
84 *BLA*, 3, 10 July 1806, p. 21.
85 *BLA*, 10, 10 February 1806, p. 13.
86 *BLA*, 223, 10 November 1823, p. 83.
87 *BLA*, 224, 10 December 1823, p. 92.
88 *BLA*, 249, 10 January 1826, p. 3; no. 254, 10 June 1826, p. 46.
89 *BLA*, 402, 11 June 1838, p. 64; no. 403, 10 July 1838, p. 84 – for the likely identity of the text, see *PC*, 27:638, 15 April 1864, list of 'Editions of and works relating to Shakspere', p. 202.
90 *PC*, 4:85, 1 April 1841, p. 98; *PC*, 27:638, 15 April 1864, p. 202.
91 *PC*, 19:461, 1 December 1856, p. 515, advert 1138. The volume is listed under 'Christmas presents published by Henry G. Bohn.'
92 *PC*, 2:33, 1 February 1839, pp. 72–3.
93 *Ibid.*, p. 72.
94 For an 'insider' account of these developments, see William Lovett, *Life and Struggles of William Lovett in his Pursuit of Bread, Knowledge and Freedom* (London: Macgibbon & Kee, 1967; originally published London: np, 1876), esp. pp. 141–50.
95 *PC*, 2:33, 1 February 1839, p. 73.

96 *PC*, 8:186, 16 June 1845, p. 181, advert 670. The full edition may not have been published. The British Library copy (shelfmark 11762g4) includes the comedies, the histories *King John, Richard II, 1 Henry IV, 2 Henry IV* and the poems, but no other plays.
97 'Pictorial Penny Shakespeare', *Northern Star*, 9:420 (29 November 1845), p. 3.
98 W. E. Adams, *Memoirs of a Social Atom*, 2 vols. (London: Hutchinson, 1903), vol. 1, p. 102.
99 For these general details, see Owen R. Ashton's *DNB* entry on Adams, www.oxforddnb.com/view/article/42327 (accessed 27 October 2004).
100 *PC*, 21:500, 16 July 1858, p. 310, advert 670.
101 *PC*, 26:630, 15 December 1863, p. 798, advert 941.
102 *PC*, 26:631, 31 December 1863, p. 826, advert 991.
103 Details of the edition are established from my own copy of the text, which has survived in its original loose parts, with coloured wrappers. Parts 1–52 are priced at 7d., parts 53–59 at 8½d. and the final part, no. 60, at 1s.
104 *PC*, 26:631, 31 December 1863, p. 826, advert 991.
105 *PC*, 27:638, 15 April 1864, pp. 199–200.
106 George Macmillan, ed., *Letters of Alexander Macmillan* (London: Macmillan, 1908), 171–2.
107 Alexander Macmillan, printed letter to booksellers, dated 15 October 1864, unpaged.
108 *BS*, 30 September 1864, p. 587; *PC*, 27:649, 1 October 1864, p. 532, advert 708.
109 *PC*, 27:647, 1 September 1864, p. 477.
110 At least, the initial advertised price in the context of this edition was two for a penny. When individual plays appear under the rubric 'Dicks' Standard Plays', they are priced (as are the other Standard Plays titles) at a penny each. The Folger Shakespeare Library holds eight plays from the series.
111 All quotations taken from an advertisement included in the *Penny Illustrated Weekly News*, 1:46 (new series), 30 April 1864, p. 726.
112 'Death of Mr. John Thomas Dicks', *Reynolds's Newspaper*, 13 February 1881, p. 1.
113 Montague Summers, 'John Dicks, Publisher', *Times Literary Supplement*, 7 November 1942, p. 552.
114 'Festival of the Establishment of Messrs. Reynolds and Dicks', *Reynolds's Newspaper*, 12 July 1868, p. 1. Victor E. Neuburg, in *Popular Literature: A History and Guide from the Beginning of Printing to the Year 1897* (London: Woburn Press, 1977), notes the extent of Dicks' activities as a cheap reprint publisher: 'his list of publications is extremely impressive in terms of quality, and he published a great deal outside the realms of fiction. There were the "Standard Plays": in 1892 1,200 items in this series were advertised, each "admirably illustrated … and issued in a coloured wrapper for the small sum of one penny each"'. Neuburg also notes that the 'series Dicks' English Novels ran to over 240 separate items' (174). In 1882, Dicks was taken to court by Chapman and Hall for issuing *Barnaby Rudge* at a price of 6d., 'whereas the lowest price of any edition published by the plaintiffs was 2s': 'Chapman and Hall v. Dicks', *The Times*, 7 August 1882, p. 4.

115 Hotten, whose career as a publisher was marked by considerable controversy, was just entering into the most productive phase of his career in the mid-1860s. Simon Eliot has estimated that, between 1865 and 1873, he published close to 500 titles, totalling 1,500,000 copies. When Hotten died in 1873, the business was bought by his general manager, Andrew Chatto, with support from his sleeping partner, W. E. Windus, the firm thenceforth becoming Chatto and Windus. See Simon Eliot, 'Hotten: Rotten: Forgotten? An Apologia for a General Publisher', *Book History*, 3 (2000), pp. 61–93, esp. pp. 62, 63.
116 *PC*, 29:697, 1 October 1866, p. 587, advert 579.
117 J. O. Halliwell, letter to the *Athenæum*, 2031, 29 September 1866, p. 404.
118 James Orchard Halliwell-Phillipps, letter to John Camden Hotten dated 18 August 1866, Edinburgh University Library Halliwell-Phillipps collection (hereafter EUL) L.O.A. 114.
119 Hotten, letter to Halliwell-Phillipps dated 14 August 1866, EUL L.O.A. 115.
120 Hotten, letter to Halliwell-Phillipps dated 1 August 1866, EUL L.O.A. 114.
121 Halliwell-Phillipps, letter to Hotten dated 26 August 1866, EUL L.O.A. 115.
122 *PC*, 29:698, 17 October 1866, pp. 608–9.
123 *BS*, 1 July 1868, p. 451.
124 Halliwell-Phillipps, letter to Hotten dated 21 February 1868, EUL L.O.A. 132. Simon Eliot writes in 'Hotten: Rotten: Forgotten' that Hotten 'issued a "Shilling Shakespeare"', citing a letter of Hotten's, dated 4 February 1867 (and preserved with the Chatto and Windus papers), to the effect that 'W. Halliwell, W. Dyce, and other gentlemen are editing my Shilling Shakespeare' (pp. 80, 92, n. 28; it is not clear whether the mistaken initials for the two editors are in the original), but I am not convinced that this is sufficient evidence that the edition did actually appear. A search of the online catalogues of the British Library, National Library of Scotland, COPAC (a consortium of UK and Irish academic libraries, including Cambridge University and Trinity College Dublin) and the Folger Shakespeare Library has not identified any Shakespeare title published by Hotten. A search on ABEbooks (conducted on 1 January 2007) provided just over 900 hits for Hotten as a publisher but, again, no Shakespeare editions were included in the results. There is certainly more to be said about Hotten's planned edition, and I would hope to publish a brief study of the topic at a later point.
125 *BS*, 1 July 1868, p. 451.
126 Stuart Sillars has indicated to me (in a private communication) that there are a couple of caveats that must be entered here. Folger Shakespeare Library PR2754 1f2 copy 4 has a label tipped in sideways before the title page, reading 'W. W. Swayne, Bookseller, Stationer, and Importer'; PR2754 1f2 copy 5 also has a Swayne identification and includes additional adverts, for US companies (following the usual British adverts); PR2754 1 f2 copies 2 and 10 have a new title page, with the imprint 'W. W. Swayne London, New York, and Boston'. Sillars concludes that this evidence points to the possibility that Dicks' edition was sold 'first as an import and then as some sort of co-publication, in the States'. This raises the possibility that some, at least, of

Dicks' 1,000,000 copies may never have circulated in Britain. He also raises a further point, noting that Folger's copy 2 includes an advert for Phillips and Company, tea merchants, advertising teas ranging from 1s. 6d. to 3s. 6d. per pound, and offering particular terms for orders over £1 and £2. It is clear that no working-class reader of the edition would be able to buy tea in these kinds of quantities, and this may indicate that the expected audience for the edition was much broader than my analysis here may suggest. I am deeply grateful to Prof. Sillars for discussing the Dicks edition with me on several occasions and for very generously sharing his findings with me. For more on Dick's edition, see Sillars, *Reading Shakespeare, Seeing Shakespeare: The Illustrated Edition, 1709–1860* (Cambridge: Cambridge University Press, 2008).

127 'T.A.', 'The Lounger', *The Pioneer*, no. 364 (30 May 1908), p. 2.
128 Thomas Burt, *Thomas Burt M. P., D. C. L., Pitman & Privy Councillor: An Autobiography* (London: T. Fisher Unwin, 1924), pp. 143–4.
129 Thomas Okey, *A Basketful of Memories: An Autobiographical Sketch* (London: Dent, 1930), p. 18.
130 Tom Barclay, *Memoirs and Medleys: The Autobiography of a Bottle Washer* (Coalville, Leicestershire: Coalville Publishing, 1995; originally published Leicester: Edgar Backus, 1934), pp. 15–16, 57.
131 'Festival', p. 1.
132 A copy of *John Dicks' Catalogue* held in the British Library, with a suggested date of 1874 still lists the hardcover and paper-covered editions as selling at 2s. and 1s. respectively. However, in a letter to *T. P.'s Weekly* in June 1911, a writer signing himself 'Not Adonis' notes: 'My first Shakespeare was issued by Dicks – something over 1,000 pages, in paper wrapper, for sixpence – and I read it all from cover to cover' (vol. 21, p. 44).
133 Francis Hughes, who was probably born in 1873, notes that when he was a teenager, the local shop in Maesteg in Wales carried journals and popular books 'you could get – Shakespeare, Milton and most of the Great poets' works in paper covers also novels and educational works by the best authors priced from 3d. to 6d.': 'I Remember', typescript, Brunel University Library, 1:359, p. 4.

CHAPTER 3

Reading

Gaining access to books was not the only problem that faced working-class readers in the early decades of the nineteenth century. The business of reading was itself often frustrated by difficulties of one sort or another. Simply finding space and time to study and think could be a serious problem. Christopher Thomson (b. 1799) notes how hard it was for him to work on his autobiography with a family of seven children 'the constant companions of his pen' and 'often four voices, and a German flute ... employed around the same three-legged deal table at which the Author was writing'.[1] Thomas Burt lived in a colliery cottage consisting of a single room, which served as 'kitchen, bedroom, wash-house, sitting-room'. To get any serious reading done, he had to retire to 'an unceiled garret, without a fireplace, and with a window which seemed to have been devised before the window-tax was abolished'.[2] Charles Shaw, the potter (born in Tunstall, Staffordshire, in 1832) derived enormous pleasure from the fact that, in his later years, he was able to set up a small study for himself in a space in his home measuring just three feet by four. He fixed this up with an iron stove, a small desk and two small bookshelves. 'I don't know what a university atmosphere is', he writes, 'I have dreamt of it, but I know when I entered this little room at night I was in another world.' Reading in his room, he observes, he 'was as a giant refreshed with new wine'.[3]

Shaw notes that it was often after nine o'clock at night before he was able to get to his room, and finding time to study was the other great problem for working-class readers. The experience of Mary Ann Hearn graphically illustrates the problems faced by those who had no alternative but to read late into the night, following a full day's work. Hearn's attendance at the local BFSS school was 'perfunctory and intermittent' and she longed to improve herself. 'In my desperate pursuit after knowledge', she writes, 'I tried hard to burn the midnight tallow (we had no oil in those days), and many a "long eight" have I wasted in the attempt'.[4] The light in her window attracted the attention of a neighbour, who commented on it to her father, and he took her to task for her late-night activities: 'He said it was not honourable of me to say "Good Night" to him at the door and pretend I was going to bed, and then wait up to read. It was setting the others a bad example, and I was never to do it again'. Hearn agreed to obey her father's command, but, before long, she returned to her studies, with near-disastrous results:

One night I awoke in terror, for the room was full of smoke. The candle was broken in the middle, and had bent over, and set the fringe on the dressing-table alight. The flames spread quickly, and already the hangings of the bed were on fire. I saw that it was hopeless for me to cope with it. On the impulse of the moment I opened the window, and in a second the whole room seemed to be in flames. In an agony of fear I called my father instantly. He was always a good friend in trouble, and he succeeded in extinguishing the fire.

As she climbed back into bed, Hearn's father observed to her 'I should think that now you have had enough of this, and that in the future you will see it is wisest to obey your father'.[5]

In fact, Hearn's midnight fire prompted her father to realise just how desperate his daughter was to gain more knowledge and, as a result, he arranged for her to have some additional schooling (this laid the foundation for her subsequently becoming a teacher). Not all working-class readers were quite so lucky. Many of them were first-generation literates (or, more accurately, first-generation *readers*), and some encountered real resistance from parents (particularly mothers) who failed to see the value of books. Mary Smith's mother 'looked upon reading, even when I was a little child, as a species of idleness; very well for Sundays or evenings, when baby was asleep and I was not wanted for anything else', though she did receive some quiet encouragement from her father.[6] John Plummer's mother was warned by friends that her son's devotion to books would 'render me crazy, a statement which had the effect of occasioning her to forbid my reading any'. Like Mary Ann Hearn, he disobeyed his parent and he notes that 'Books! books! books! was my continual cry'.[7] Where Plummer's mother thought books would drive him insane, Tom Barclay's mother – an Irish catholic who had emigrated to Leicester with her husband during the Famine – blamed his loss of religion on his reading:

'What talk you have. But sure your head is being turned with the books. I wish I never saw a sight of them same books; 'tis they that have ye ruined I'm afeared.'
  'You said last week it was the Devil.'
  'It's the same thing; he's the one that inspires the books.'[8]

Joseph Wright (1855–1930), an apprentice wool-sorter who went on to become Professor of Comparative Philology at Oxford (and compiler of the *English Dialect Dictionary*), had a mother who took direct action against books of which she disapproved. When Wright brought home a volume of Shakespeare's plays, she 'threw the book out into the street, declaring she would not have such bad stuff in the house'.[9]

Shakespeare caused problems for more than one working-class reader. To return to Mary Ann Hearn, she tells us in her autobiography that she received her 'first and only copy of "Shakespeare"' from her local minister, who inscribed the book: 'From her affectionate pastor.' A sense of outrage quickly spread through the older members of the congregation that a minister 'should give a young member of his church "a volume of plays"'. One of her fellow parishioners begged Hearn 'to let her burn it, as she was sure it was an offence in the sight of God, and several who heard of it advised me not to read it'. Hearn ignored the advice and she writes that the book 'filled me with wonder and admiration'.[10] Adam Rushton (b. 1820) was also a great reader of Shakespeare. At the age of sixteen he was put in charge of his Sunday school library and he discovered a copy of the *Iliad* among the 'nearly two hundred volumes on the book shelves'. Reading Homer, he found that for 'some time Shakespeare's characters faded from the view'. He passed the volume on to like-minded friends within the church school. However, the authorities got to hear that the book was causing a stir among some of the students and they 'looked into it, disapproved of it, and condemned it. "How did such an objectionable book get into the Library?" inquired the censors. I simply replied that I found it there.' Rushton notes that 'The book disappeared from the Library, but not its contents from our minds, nor the determination to read it again when the opportunity came'.[11] Rushton was not the only one to be subjected to interrogation about his reading habits by his religious elders. Christopher Thomson dedicated himself to Methodism for a spell when an adolescent, 'usually rising at five o'clock on the Sunday mornings, and continuing until ten at night, scarcely allowing the proper time for refreshment'. At the same time, he began to develop a great taste for books. Eventually, his reading habits started to take precedence over his attendance at chapel meetings and he was called to account for his absences. By way of defence, he says, 'I pleaded my desire for, and indulgence in reading. This appeared rather to aggravate than serve my cause'. He was told that if he 'did not at once, and unconditionally, renounce all books, except such as they should approve of' he was forever lost.[12] With a heavy heart, Thomson chose books over religion. He left the church, but continued his membership of a local circulating library and, over the course of three years, 'read various works, including Milton's, Shakspere's, Sterne's, Dr. Johnson's, and many others'.[13]

If working-class readers faced opposition in their families and their churches, they also, in many cases, had to contend with discouragement and even ridicule in the workplace. We have seen in Chapter 2 that W. E. Adams (1832–1906) had a copy of a Shakespeare play taken from him by an illiterate and unsympathetic fellow errand boy, who refused to return the book, despite Adams 'imploring him to give me back my precious property.'[14] Even late on in the century, J. R. Clynes (1869–1949), the son of an illiterate gravedigger, found himself in trouble with his foreman, when he was caught reading *Paradise Lost* while working in a mill. 'What's tha-at?' the foreman asked him. He handed the book over, but his supervisor 'stared at it uncomprehendingly'. ' "Books!" he exclaimed contemptuously. "What the 'ell dost tha want wi' books? Books'll never buy thee britches!" '[15] The reading habit often tended to lead to alienation from workmates more generally as well. As a young waterman, Joseph Terry felt keenly the difference between himself and his fellow crew members. They 'spent their time either huddled together in some forecastle, telling and listening to tales a hundred times told, and most of which I knew off by heart . . . sleeping in all sorts of places like so many pigs or else at the Ale House.' Terry himself, by contrast, occupied his spare time with 'reading, writing, composing &c'. In the summertime, he writes, 'I took some interesting book in my pocket and went forth into some quiet nook'.[16] The snobbishness of the autodidact who regards his work companions as 'like so many pigs' is evident in a number of autobiographers. Henry Jones (1852–1922), born in Llangernyw, Denbighshire, followed the trade of his father and became a shoemaker. One day he made a trip to Llanrwst to see Wombwell's Menagerie, in the company of a friend who was training as a pupil teacher. The young teacher pointed out a group of Jones' apprentice friends, 'hanging around the door of a tavern'. Jones immediately experienced an acute sense of shame and despair and he broke down 'in an agony of weeping': 'My whole life seemed to me to have been a mistake. It lay in ruins around my feet: and it was all from beginning to end my own fault. Only one thing remained. I would become "something better than a shoemaker" or I would die in the attempt.'[17] In fact, he succeeded, ultimately becoming a professor at various institutions, including the University of St Andrews, where he taught logic and English literature.

A love of reading could cause problems even for those who were master tradesmen, running their own businesses. Francis Place rose from inauspicious beginnings and built up a highly successful tailoring firm. He also established a personal library of about 1,000 volumes. He was very wary of letting too many of his customers know about his collection of books, noting that he well remembered a time 'when to be able to read and to indulge in reading, would if known to a master tradesman, have been so serious an objection to a journeyman, that he would scarcely have expected to obtain employment'.[18] When one of his customers discovered that Place had an extensive personal library, he began pickily to find fault with the tailor's workmanship, then took his business elsewhere, drawing other customers away with him. Place writes sardonically that it appeared that, to be a reader was 'an abominable offence in a tailor, if not a crime, which deserved punishment'.[19] Place's sense of conflict and oppression is nicely caught in a dream which he relates in his autobiographical writings:

A few months since I dreamed that I went along the passage to my library and into it, every thing was disarranged and there was no carpet on the floor, stooping to pick up a book, I could not rise again, something pressed me down and kept my face near the floor. I soon ascertained that it was an immense hand which covered the back of my head and shoulders, the fingers spread over me and I endeavoured to grasp the thumb but could not move.[20]

The dream offers a wonderfully ambiguous narrative: is the hand the weight of middle-class opprobrium pressing down on an upstart autodidact, or is it the burden of hard-won learning itself – those thousand volumes pushing him to the floor?

A general sense of isolation is characteristic of many working-class readers. Henry Jones became friend and mentor to a younger Welshman, Thomas Jones (1870–1955), who went from working in the local ironworks to becoming a high-ranking civil servant. Looking back on the village community from which he had sprung, the younger Jones comments that, during his years of college education, he had been 'travelling to where the home folk could not follow, into a world of books which they would never read, countries of the mind which they would never visit'.[21] Likewise, the printer and political activist W. E. Adams felt compelled, while still a teenager, to make a positive choice between reading and spending time in the company of his local childhood friends:

One Sunday afternoon the usual call was made for a ramble in the fields. Word was sent to the callers that their old companion was not going to join them. I heard from an upper room, not without a certain amount of tremor, their exclamations of surprise. They wandered off into the fields in one direction; I, with a new companion, wandered off into the fields in another. My new companion was Young's 'Night Thoughts.' The old companions were never joined again.[22]

For some readers, however, it was less a case of their love of books leading them into isolation and solitude, than it was of isolation of one sort or another drawing them on to the consolations of reading. John Wood (b. 1802), the cotton weaver and schoolmaster, born at Allerton, near Bradford, was shortsighted, and therefore 'was unable to play with other boys at games common with youths, such for instance as knur and spell, &c'. Instead, he turned his leisure hours to books and learning and came to think of his 'natural infirmity as a blessing'.[23] Emmanuel Lovekin (1820–1905), who began work in a coalmine when he was just seven, became interested in books at the age of thirteen, because a broken thigh meant that he 'had to lie in bed 13 weeks, and began to feel very strongly the desire to learn to read'.[24] The 'errand boy, account bookbinder, commercial traveller, foreman, agitator and journalist, . . . prominent labour leader and social reformer',[25] Frederick Rogers recalled that, in his youth, he was a 'dull, slow, sickly boy, with no hope or prospect in life, and careless alike whether it continued or ended'. After his day's work, he writes, 'I could forget my pain if I could creep into a quiet corner with a book and rest my tired body'. Books, he concludes, 'were my only companion, and I was entirely happy in their company'.[26]

Reading, then, served both to isolate and to lend consolation to the isolated. But, for the reader hungry for knowledge, reading in isolation was often an ineffective way of gaining real enlightenment. Rogers himself recognises this:

Mere chance and desultory reading, however assiduously pursued, never educated any man yet, and I, without training or guidance, and reading because it was the best pleasure I had found, was, after all, not much more than a human box that was full enough of information, but it was there in strange confusion, and I had no knowledge whether it was valuable or no, or how to use it if it was valuable.[27]

The frustrations of engaging in undirected reading are registered by a number of autobiographers. J. Passmore Edwards recalls that 'Having read of Locke and Newton as great names linked in fame, I resolved to buy and read their works'. He managed to pick up a copy of Newton's *Optics* and was 'just as wise at the end as I was at the beginning'; he also read *An Essay Concerning Human Understanding*, but found it equally opaque. 'This double disenchantment', he says, 'assisted to chasten my zeal in the pursuit of knowledge, and to limit my reading to humbler themes.'[28] Charles Shaw reflects ruefully that it 'was my misfortune to lack guidance at a critical period in my history, but I had to seek what came by groping'. He concluded that, while this was better than standing still, 'pathetic tragedies and failures strew the lives of individuals and nations, which might have been avoided if the light of guidance had shone in place of the shadows of groping'.[29]

The perils of untutored reading are nicely indicated in the responses of many of the autobiographers to the books that they read. Almost all of these readers found their way very quickly to a fairly predictable set of texts, with *Pilgrim's Progress* and *Robinson Crusoe* proving to be especially popular (*Paradise Lost* and Shakespeare generally followed in fairly close order). Bunyan's text, in particular, held an extraordinary appeal for working-class readers all the way through the century. John James Bezer (b. 1851) celebrates 'My own dear Bunyan' and asserts that 'if it hadn't been for you, I should have gone mad, I think, before I was ten years old!'[30] Even close to the end of the century, Harry Alfred West (b. 1880) received a copy of *Pilgrim's Progress* for his tenth birthday and, writing near the end of his life, he remarks on the 'enduring interest, moral and spiritual effect' of the book.[31] With an amazing regularity, however, the autobiographers report that they failed to grasp the fact that Bunyan's text was a work of fiction. J. A. Leatherland, born in Kettering in 1812, notes that *Pilgrim's Progress* was '*The* book of my boyhood' and he reports that he 'used to read it from morning to night, and could not but believe the pilgrimage to be a real one, and often wished my mother to set out, with me and my sister, upon the journey'.[32] Thomas Burt read Bunyan's text at his grandmother's house (the only book she possessed, apart from the Bible), and he observes: 'Not as a dream or allegory but as solid literal history did it present itself to my boyish mind. I believed every word of it. Perhaps it was the only book I ever read with entire, unquestioning acceptation.'[33] Joseph Barker (1806–75) also believed in the literal existence of such places as the City of Destruction, but his inability to distinguish between fiction and fact extended beyond Bunyan: 'I had no idea at that time that people could write and print anything in the form of a history, that was not real matter of fact.'[34] Textual confusions extended even to the Bible. Thomas Carter writes of his reading experience:

How much I needed the aid of a competent teacher will be manifest when I state that, for a long time, I believed the books of 'the Kings' and of 'the Chronicles' to be unconnected narratives of two distinct series of events; and also, that the four Gospels were consecutive portions of the history of Jesus Christ, so that I supposed there had been four crucifixions, four resurrections, and the like. I was, indeed, sometimes perplexed by the apparently repeated occurrence of events so nearly resembling each other; nor could I perceive the exact design or bearing of these events; but I knew no one of whom I could ask for the needed explanations.[35]

Carter also worked his way through a stray volume of the *Spectator* and believed that the entire contents were written by a single person. He was, he says, 'somewhat disconcerted on afterwards discovering that the work was the joint production of several persons', since he had 'drawn an amusing imaginary picture of both the author and the places he frequented'.[36]

The journey of the autodidact was, therefore, not unlike that of the Christian who so many working-class readers celebrated as a living adventurer. There were obstacles and blind alleys along the way and the passage towards knowledge was often a solitary and isolating one. This was not, however, the whole story. While some working-class readers met discouragement at almost every turn, others found support at home, at work, in their local communities, and beyond. Thus, while Christopher Thomson's mother was adamantly opposed to his love of plays – 'she condemned play reading, and regarded theatres as sinks of vice' – his father was 'very fond of reading' and entered him as a subscriber in a local circulating library.[37] In fact, not all mothers were opposed to reading or to the theatre. Joseph Arch (1826–1919), the agricultural labour leader who was born just a few miles from Stratford-on-Avon, was actually introduced to Shakespeare's plays by his mother: 'She was a great admirer of Shakespeare. She used to talk about him very often, and she was well versed in his works. She would read bits aloud to me of an evening, and tell me tales from the plays.'[38] Arch eventually married a woman who 'was no scholar, and ... did not think over questions and have a firm opinion about them as my mother did.' In one of the saddest sentences in the working-class autobiographical canon, he writes: 'She was a good, clean wife, and a good mother; she looked after my father well; she was always attending to her home and to her family; but she was no companion to me in my aspirations.'[39] But many others among the autobiographers did have spouses who served as real intellectual companions. Robert Lowery (1809–63) married a woman who 'had the same desire for reading' as he did himself. Oftentimes, they would be faced with a choice between buying something for their Sunday dinner or paying the library subscription of 8d. per week. 'What do you think', he would ask his wife, 'shall we get something for dinner, or get a book and have an early tea?' They were always, he writes, of the same mind: 'that the dinner would soon be over and gone – but if we did without it, we would not miss it much, and we would have the advantage of the library all the week.'[40] George Edwards (b. 1850), a farm worker who became General Secretary of the Agricultural Labourers' Union and MP for South Norfolk, was actually taught to read by his wife: 'She would sit on one side of the fireplace and I on the other. I would spell out the words and she would tell me their pronunciation.'[41] One of the more striking stories of spousal harmony is, perhaps, that of Fred Kitchen, born at the very end of the period covered by this survey (1890). He writes of his second wife, Elizabeth, that she had 'a taste for literature greater than my own' and was 'a rare hand at making pastries. She can quote Shakespeare, chapter and verse, and turns out excellent crumpets, which is all I now ask of life.'[42] What more, indeed, could one ask?

If the home could be a congenial place for the working-class reader, so too, in spite of Shakespeare-pilfering errand boys, could the workplace. Those who went into service, for example, often gained access to books through their employers. John Jones, born in Newland, Gloucestershire in 1774, served in a household where he found an open book-case in the dining room. 'By this means', he writes, 'I was enabled to spend many a delightful hour [reading]; and as plays were what most engaged my attention at that time, and Shakespeare's being in the collection, I read the whole of them, and some of them twice over.'[43] Reading Shakespeare prompted Jones to have a go at writing a play himself and he sent his manuscript off to London, directed to the manager of the Haymarket Theatre. After a long time waiting for a reply, he received a letter 'giving me the information that it would not do for representation, and advising me not to spend my time in such difficult undertakings'. Amused by his own youthful self, Jones notes that, for a long spell, 'I could hardly bring myself to believe that they had not copied it off, or stole the plot, or played me some dirty trick in it'.[44]

Opportunities to read while in service were particularly important for working-class women, whose access to literature was generally much more limited than that of their male counterparts. A Mrs Layton, born in Bethnal Green in 1855, borrowed 'trashy books' from a servant at a neighbouring house. She eventually gave up this reading, fearful lest, being distracted from her duties, she would lose her job (her brother had been dismissed from another household for just this reason). However, on moving to a new position, she discovered that 'reading was not considered a waste of time, and books were supplied to me to read which were suitable to a young impressionable girl, far different to the trash I had read in secret before'.[45] Later in the century, the suffragette Hannah Mitchell (1872–1956) had a similar experience. Mitchell received little more than a week's formal schooling as a child and had a mother who, she writes, 'honestly thought me lazy because I didn't like housework, and held that reading was only a recreation, meant for Sundays'.[46] She felt very keenly the fact that, while living at home, she was forced to darn her brothers' stockings while the boys were allowed to spend their time reading.[47] In due course, however, she became a maid in a schoolmaster's house and she considered herself very fortunate, even though she was badly paid: 'The work did not seem particularly hard after my strenuous upbringing, and I was not unhappy, especially as my mistress made me free of a well-filled book case.' Mitchell sometimes fell behind with her work, as she became absorbed in her reading, but, she writes: 'I could work quickly when I chose, and always had the meals ready when they came in.'[48]

For many working-class readers, masters and workmates were an important source of intellectual encouragement. Adam Rushton had an experience at work which, at first, appeared similar to that of J. R. Clynes, with his *what the 'ell dost tha want wi' books* foreman. Working in a mill, Rushton kept a collection of magazines and miscellaneous volumes under a large revolving drum. 'Great was my consternation', he writes, 'on one occasion to see the Steward (Mr. B.) rummaging amongst these books'. Mr B. asks him, sternly, 'What is this lot?' and Rushton answers 'I read a little during breakfast and tea'. Mr B. tells him 'It is against the rule' and walks away. A day or two later, however, the steward engages Rushton in a conversation concerning Charles Rollin's *Ancient History* – one of the volumes in Rushton's collection.[49] Further conversations include a discussion of the merits of the work of Thomas Paine. The rebuke had been an empty formality, and Rushton gained a new intellectual companion in his supervisor. Those who served apprenticeships with a master tradesman were also often fortunate to find in their master someone who was willing to encourage their reading. Thomas Carter trained as a tailor and served under a young master who allowed him access to a small library of books, including 'Enfield's "Speaker", Goldsmith's "Geography", an abridged "History of Rome", a "History of England", Thomson's "Seasons", "The Citizen of the World", "The Vicar of Wakefield",' and other books whose titles he had forgotten when he came to write his autobiography.[50]

Oftentimes, it was also workmates and masters who provided working-class readers with their first real introduction to Shakespeare. John Brown, a shoemaker born in 1796 at Barnwell, near Cambridge, moved to London as a very young man and found lodgings sharing a room with another member of his trade. He gave his new companion a brief account of his 'trials and travels', and they then fell into a conversation about the shoemaker-poet Robert Bloomfield. Brown quickly discovered that his roommate had a volume of Bloomfield's poems, and that it sat on 'a long shelf containing the works of our best poets, though the books were old and the binding here and there dilapidated'. The collection included an edition of Shakespeare. The two shoemakers went for a walk together and, when they returned to their room, they each selected a book to read. Brown chose the

Shakespeare, noting that it was the first time he had ever had the opportunity of reading the playwright:

> The book opened at that beautiful speech on Mercy, put into the mouth of 'Portia' in the *Merchant of Venice*. Never before had my senses been so completely captivated. I could have read all night; but observing that my friend had closed his book and looked as if inclined for rest, I put up mine also, and we both retired to bed. Yet even here, what I had been reading haunted me in my sleep. The whole *dramatis personæ* were before me palpable as life; I watched the proceedings with intense anxiety, till the Jew approached to cut the pound of flesh from the Merchant's breast, – when struggling to arrest the knife, I awoke, – and thanked God it was a dream![51]

On another occasion, Brown's companion encouraged him to read out loud from the text of *Hamlet* and he was so impressed with the 'To be or not to be' soliloquy that, he says, he read it 'over and over again ... until I had committed it to memory. I felt at that moment truly thankful for the little education I had received'.[52] His love of the playwright continued to develop and he writes that he was frequently 'up till after midnight reading Shakspeare, – when all around me was hushed in silence, save the distant rattle of some vehicle over the stones.' In due course, he began attending the theatre and he saw Kemble, Young and other celebrated actors of the day performing Shakespeare. This appeared to him 'to be the perfection of human enjoyment'.[53] Eventually, Brown moved away from London and he had a get-together with some friends, including his brother, before he left the city. Called upon to sing a song, he declined, but offered instead to recite the 'tent scene' from *Richard III*. He did this 'to the entire satisfaction of the company; and to the utter astonishment of my brother, who knew nothing of my theatrical predilections'.[54]

Tom Mann, the militant trade unionist, was also brought to a real understanding of Shakespeare by a workmate. Mann was born in 1856 in Coventry and was described by fellow-autobiographer Ben Tillett as combining 'the qualities of whirlwind and volcano', 'a genius of sheer energy'.[55] He worked for several years operating a lathe at a tool-making firm in Birmingham and, on the machine next to him, was a Scot named Jeffries, whom he describes as 'a tall, dignified person, never indulging in frivol, but absolutely obsessed by the continuous study of Shakespeare'. This workmate's 'only recreation was to read Shakespeare, and books that dealt with Shakespeare, plus seeing every Shakespearian piece performed'. This enthusiasm rubbed off on Mann, who, as a Warwickshire native himself, already had a basic familiarity with the playwright's work. 'But', he writes, 'the devotion of my fellow-workman impelled me to carefully read, mark, and learn. I derived benefit accordingly, and from that time I was never lonely so long as a volume of Shakespeare was available'. On one occasion, Mann played a Shakespearean trick on Jeffries, and the Scot was not amused by this particular instance of 'indulging in frivol'. Mann puzzled his workmate by asking him where in Shakespeare the sentence 'Oh, what a numskull to turn over the page and not to see that he's had' occurred. 'Next morning', he writes, Jeffries 'expressed regret and astonishment at his "inability to trace it; he had spent several hours trying to do so."' Mann pointed out to him that the previous day's date had been 1 April and the Scot gave him 'an unfriendly glare'.[56] Mann and Jeffries were not the only colleagues who engaged in Shakespearean exchanges at work. Will Crooks (1852–1921) – like Mann, a radical trade unionist – learned by heart many passages from Shakespeare and he had a particular fondness for *Hamlet*. He worked for a spell at a blacksmith's and his biographer, George Haw, notes that 'Often in the little forge the men would say, "Give us a bit of Shakespeare, Will." The lad, nothing loath, would declaim before them, more often than not in a mock heroic strain that greatly delighted his grimy workmates.'[57]

While some readers found time in their working day to discuss, or even perform, literary texts, others indicate that they tried to make their days doubly productive by attempting to combine work with reading. Weavers, in particular, tended to be singularly adept at this. Joseph Livesey (1794–1884), born near Preston, Lancashire, routinely laid a book on the breast-beam of his loom 'with a cord slipped on to keep the leaves from rising. Head, hands, and feet, all busy at the same time! I had a restless mind, panting for knowledge, and incapable of inaction.' He also turned his greater workspace into a kind of mnemonic zone: 'That part of the loom and the wall nearest my seat were covered with marks, which I had made to assist me to remember certain facts'.[58] Another textile worker, Joseph Barker, gives a nice sense of the complexities of combining reading with spinning warp:

Warp had to be twisted or twined twice or thrice as much as the *weft*. When the thread had been drawn out to its proper length, I had to stand till I gave it from a dozen to twenty rounds more. While I was standing and giving it those extra rounds, I contrived to get a look at my book, which I had fixed up on the jenny gallows, and read a sentence or two each draw. I thought over what I read till I had drawn out the threads a second time, and while twisting them, I got another glance at my book, and read another sentence or two, and so went on.

Barker also contrived to teach himself the rudiments of Latin while at work. He committed the grammatical rules to memory while spinning, 'then stole a little time to write a single exercise' and, in this way, he 'went through a great part of Valpy's exercises, and of Turner's'.[59] Over the course of the century, however, as industrialisation took hold and the workplace became ever more tightly controlled and regimented, the opportunities for combining work with reading declined significantly. One nice exception to this rule is provided at the very end of the century by Frank Hodges (1887–1947), born in Woolaston, Gloucestershire. Hodges writes that he was taken out of school 'the very day after attaining my twelfth birthday in order to work to supplement the family income'.[60] He was employed by the local coal mine and given the job of opening and closing a ventilation door in one of the mineshafts. To relieve the boredom of sitting idle underground for long spells, he decided to bring the family's old copy of Shakespeare down into the pit with him. He hid the book in his coat as he entered the mine and then read it, sitting in a small cabin near the door he had charge of: 'It was a difficult task, but with the aid of an oil safety lamp I managed it. I read every play and every poem until the book became so dirty that the print became scarcely visible in that dim, sputtering light.'[61] On one occasion, he was caught reading his book by an old man who worked repairing the roadways in the mine. Hodges feared he would be reported, but in fact it turned out that the roadman was illiterate and was anxious to know something of Shakespeare, so he asked Hodges to read to him from the book:

He was interested immediately, and later was fascinated. I found it wholly pleasurable work to read aloud. It has the double effect of being pleasant to hear and of impressing itself more clearly upon the mind; for I remember how much easier it is to memorise passages aloud than after reading to myself.

The visits increased in number. The roadman would make three or four visits a day just to listen for ten minutes or a quarter of an hour at a time.[62]

On one occasion, Hodges left his book in the mine overnight and the following morning he was 'horrified to find that the mice had eaten up the whole of "Venus and Adonis."' Eventually, after such extended use, the book 'literally faded away'.[63]

Hodges notes that reading Shakespeare in this way prompted him to develop a passion for books more generally, and this, in turn, spurred him on to attend evening classes. We have seen in Chapter 1 that, over the course of the nineteenth century, general educational provision for working-class children was often unsatisfactory and that, at best, it tended to offer such children little more than the basic rudiments of learning. For this reason, evening classes were a particular boon to many ambitious working-class readers over the course of the century. W. E. Adams speaks especially fondly of his experience as a student at the Working Men's College in

London, which he joined in 1855, just a year after it opened. David J. Palmer notes that the idea for the college had grown from a series of events provided by staff from King's College in 1852, including lectures on 'The Historical Plays of Shakespeare' delivered by F. D. Maurice.[64] The college had a stellar roster of voluntary staff, including John Ruskin, Dante Gabriel Rossetti, Ford Madox Brown and Edward Burne-Jones.[65] Adams considered himself particularly fortunate in being able to study with F. J. Furnivall, the energetic 'founder of more literary societies than any man living', including the New Shakspere Society.[66] For Adams, the evening classes 'were exquisite':

Part of the time Mr. Furnivall took the words as they followed in the dictionary – dissecting them, showing their origin, and tracing their transformation in sound, meaning, and spelling. Afterwards we read Chaucer and Shakspeare, getting to the root and pursuing the history of every word the poets used.[67]

Furnivall offered his students a nurturing environment in his chambers in Ely Place, Holborn, where every 'nook and corner was filled with books – all treasures of literature'. Adams remembers fondly sitting over 'biscuits and coffee till an advanced hour of the morning, talking or listening to talk about poets and poetry, and languages and literature, and having such a feast of reason and flow of soul as almost never was since Shakspeare had his bout with Ben Jonson at the Mermaid'.[68]

The London Working Men's College can be seen as something of a parallel development to a more ambitious initiative which aimed to provide workers with Mechanics' Institutes in centres of population throughout the country (Fig. 6). The first formal Mechanics' Institute was established in London in 1823, with strong support from Henry Brougham and his utilitarian colleagues. The movement quickly spread, with 20 institutions being set up in the first year and more than 500 having been established by the middle of the century.[69] The success of the initiative was, however, compromised by the extent to which the institutions were dominated by local middle class interests and political programmes. Robert Lowery, for instance, writes that 'In almost every place where I have been, in every district the mechanics' institutes are failures. For the members and committee are almost all of the middle classes – shopkeepers, clerks, and such like'.[70] 'The working classes', he observes, 'do not feel at home in institutions where the middle classes are the chief members, contributors, and managers'.[71] Thomas Frost, born in Croydon around 1821, joined a Literary and Scientific Institution, but found it unsatisfactory for the same reasons. Working-class members of the

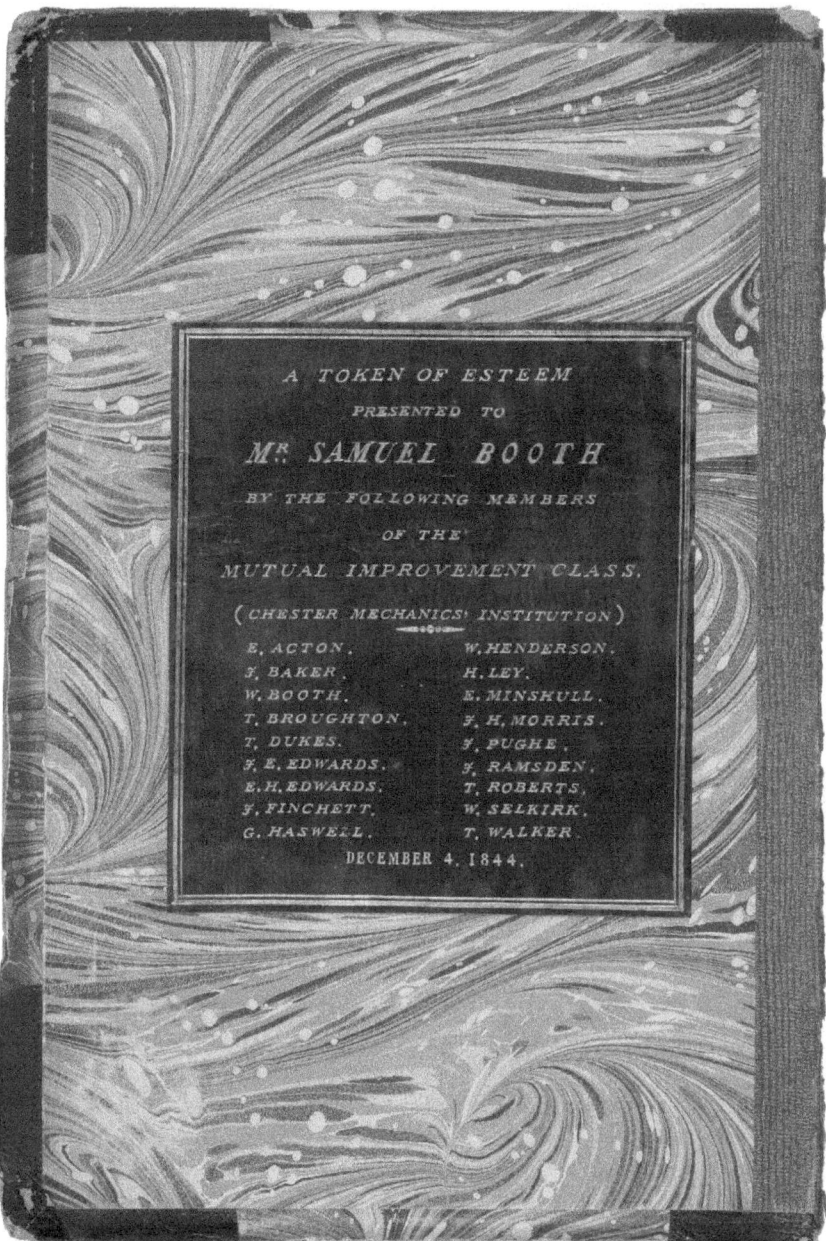

Figure 6. Embossed presentation plate of the Chester Mechanics' Institute, included in a Shakespeare collected works edition (reproduced by kind permission of the Folger Shakespeare Library).

organisation put forward a petition, suggesting the formation of a discussion class, but the committee – 'composed of the local gentry and clergy' – opposed the idea, expressing 'their fear that the young men who had signed it wished "to talk politics."' As a result, working-class membership declined, but the 'middle-class members did not regret this effect, as they objected to the presence of their assistants and workmen in the reading-room'. Shortly afterwards, the fees structure for the Institution was reconfigured, to put membership of the library out of reach for most working-class readers. 'The effect', Frost writes, 'was to drive them from the institution altogether'.[72]

Alan Richardson has observed of the Mechanics' Institutes that, by 1840s, they 'had become moribund, dominated by middle-class "sponsors," barred from addressing political issues, and catering mainly to clerks and small shopkeepers bent on acquiring a semblance of "culture."'[73] Thomas Cooper, the Chartist activist, confirms this view, in summarising the complaints of many among the working-class, noting that 'the subscription was beyond the means of the poverty-stricken artisan; in all, the rules restricting political and theological enquiry and discussion, and forbidding Sunday reading in the book-room, were irksome; and the undue influence of patrons and annual subscribers was felt as a tyranny'.[74] Smaller-scale grassroots initiatives would appear to have been more valuable to many working-class readers. Charles Manby Smith (1804–80), who served an apprenticeship as a printer in Bristol, met a chance acquaintance while 'strolling among Clifton's rocky scenery'. This friend suggested to Smith that he 'join a club of seven, which he was then endeavouring to organise with a view to mutual improvement'. Smith at once agreed and he writes '[I] have congratulated myself that I did so to this day'. The group hired a room and 'met nearly three hundred nights in the year, and talked, read, disputed, and wrote *de omnibus rebus et quibusdam aliis*, until the clock struck eleven'.[75] We have already seen in Chapter 2 that Ben Brierley (1825–96) also joined an informal local mutual improvement society, travelling to Manchester with his uncle to help carry home the stock of books purchased with the group's pooled resources. Some members of the society met on Sunday mornings at Brierley's uncle's to read 'passages from Shakespeare, Shelley, Burns and Byron'.[76] As a result of this reading, they developed an 'ambition to see Shakespeare in real gold and silk and feathers'. Eventually their desire was fulfilled, when they collectively managed to raise the price of admittance to the gallery of the Theatre Royal in Manchester, to see a production of *Macbeth*. The performance had a profound effect on Brierley, making him feel 'as though I had only had the experience of a baby', and the group as a whole took to staging their own performances, including a production of *Othello*, in which Brierley played the role of Iago.[77] Tom Mann was also involved in an informal improvement society. After his stint with his Shakespeare-loving Scots colleague in Birmingham, he moved to London, where he worked in a factory producing torpedo boat engines. Here, he established a group among his workmates, to which he gave the name the 'Shakespeare Mutual Improvement Society'. Mann served as president of the society and he notes that the subjects covered in meetings included 'Electricity', 'The Chemistry of the Sun' and 'Are other Worlds Habitable?' and that a 'good portion of the programme' was given over specifically to Shakespearean subjects.[78]

Working-class readers, then, had many obstacles to contend with, but the luckiest of them often found support either in the home or in their greater immediate circle – whether at work, or in casual or more formal local improvement societies. As we have seen throughout this chapter, a great number of working-class readers shared a strong sense of enthusiasm for Shakespeare, having arrived at the playwright's work by a variety of different pathways. Joseph Arch was introduced to Shakespeare by his mother; Mary Ann Hearn received a copy of the complete works from an admiring pastor; John Jones read his employers' edition of Shakespeare while in service; John Brown and Tom Mann were brought to a better understanding of the plays by bookish workmates; and W. E. Adams was lucky enough to study with one of the leading (if highly eccentric) scholars of late nineteenth century. For all of these readers, Shakespeare was an important part of their mental and intellectual world and for some in the period the playwright's work assumed an importance that even shaded out other reading. Joseph Blacket (1786–1810), for instance, worked his way through the writings of Josephus, together with Eusebius' *Ecclesiastical History* and Foxe's *Book of Martyrs* before he was yet fifteen years old. However, a trip to Drury Lane to see Kemble in *Richard III* led him on to read Shakespeare and he soon 'forgot the cruelties exercised in queen Mary's reign, and left the celebrated Jewish historians and others to be cherished by more permanent admirers'. 'Thus', he writes, 'did the muse of Shakespeare, with a single glance, banish the ideas of Jerusalem's wars'.[79] There were many working-class readers for whom, like Blacket, Shakespeare was the supreme writer, dominating their intellectual world for much of their lives. For the remainder of this chapter, I wish to focus specifically on a select number of individuals whose autobiographies identify them as particular Shakespeare enthusiasts, looking at the nature of their Shakespearean experience and the impact which the playwright's work had on them. The sample is quite diverse, consisting of a farm worker turned baker, turned quack doctor; a serving woman turned sailor, turned nurse; a miner and sometime poet; a mill worker turned poet, writer and lecturer; a miner turned caretaker; a book-binder turned trade unionist; and a house painter who was a confirmed eccentric. Their responses to Shakespeare are equally diverse, but in this they serve to provide a useful snapshot of the range of nineteenth-century working-class attitudes to the playwright.

To begin with the farm worker turned baker, turned quack doctor: Samuel Westcott Tilke was born in 1794 in Newton-Poppleford, Devonshire, the son of a baker whose business collapsed and who 'sunk into a state of reckless indifference, from which he never fully rallied'. Tilke first encountered Shakespeare when he came across a quotation from *Julius Caesar*, reproducing Brutus' speech 'There is a tide in the affairs of men / Which, taken at the flood, leads on to fortune ... '. The quote seemed so appropriate to his father's situation that he 'determined to read more of the same author'.[80] Virtually every single page of Tilke's *Autobiographical Memoir* contains at least one quotation from Shakespeare and, in a footnote, he alerts his readers to the fact that 'every quotation ... not having the writer's name affixed to it is taken from the works of Shakspeare, and in many instances from my memory' (p. xiii, footnote). Tilke's book is addressed specifically to his 'Young Countrymen', and it might be said to anticipate somewhat Samuel Smiles' *Self-help*, in that Tilke offers the story of his own life as an exemplary instance of 'what industry and perseverance, rightly directed may accomplish' (p. vii). Tilke advises his readers to 'Make the *most* of your time; and make the *best* use of it. In any situation of life, you can command *some* leisure; let that be occupied in self-improvement' (p. x). The reading habit should be cultivated; the 'first and best of all books' is the Bible and other religious texts such as Josephus' *Wars of the Jews* should also be carefully studied (pp. xi, xii). As far as poetry is concerned, Tilke urges caution and enjoins his young readers to remember Hannah More's warning that it is possible to find 'Serpents in beds of flowers'. Milton, Herbert, Cowper and Montgomery meet with Tilke's approval, but pride of place is reserved for 'the prince of English poets, Shakspeare, our British "Homer of his art"' (p. xiii). Tilke delineates at considerable length the 'no inconsiderable degree of instruction' he has gained from Shakespeare's works, 'which are written with a sound knowledge of divine truth'. He notes that

Shakspeare has pointed out the different grades of passion which are able either to comfort or torture the breast of man. He has taught us all that is good, and has advised us not to neglect, but to put forward to their proper uses, the various talents allotted to each; and that it is our duty to improve them to the utmost. (p. xiii)

Here Tilke includes a parenthetical comment: '(See also 1 Tim. iv. 14.)' – a rather extraordinary example of the Bible being called into service to amplify a Shakespearean truth. He continues:

At the same time he has shewn that it is impossible for man to invent a single form, or to produce a single idea, of which the model was not formed by Nature; that every thing necessary for man's existence is bounteously provided by his Maker; and that our Creator, by thus condescending to connect himself with us, has proved how great is his loving kindness towards us. It is my opinion that Shakspeare possessed a deep sense of the pure morality of the Gospel. (pp. xiii–iv)

From these general observations (which make Shakespeare sound like a pious but rather uninteresting country curate), Tilke advances to a more specific set of lessons to be drawn from Shakespeare's actual words. Effectively aligning himself with a tradition stretching back through William Dodd's *Beauties of Shakespeare* to, well, Polonius, Tilke raids the complete works to offer his reader a set of well-worn sententiae:

from his writings I learnt that 'to wilful men the injuries that they themselves procure must be their schoolmasters:' it was he that informed me that 'he cannot be a perfect man, not having tried and tutored in the world:' 'experience is by industry achieved, and perfected by the swift course of time.' He taught me to believe that 'there is a Divinity that shapes our ends, rough-hew them how we will;' and made me feel that 'mine honour keeps the weather of my fate.' (p. xv)

And so on, at some considerable length.

As might be expected from someone who saw Shakespeare primarily as a religiously minded moralist, Tilke believed that he was best reserved for reading and not performing. 'Shakespeare', he writes, 'can be far more appreciated and better understood in the closet, than in a public theatre'. He strongly urges his readers to avoid dramatic performances, on the grounds that 'thousands of young men may trace their introduction to sin and ruin to a constant attendance at the theatres' (p. xvi). For Tilke, as for Shakespeare, all the world is itself a stage and he imagines his readers venturing out into the 'theatre of the world', where they will meet a variety of Shakespearean characters made flesh, since in this world 'are to be found the *gay* Lothario, the *loving* Othello, the *treacherous* Iago, the *noble* and *sensitive* Hamlet, the *jack-in-office* Dogberry, the *volatile* Mercutio, the *money-loving* Shylock, and the *foppish* Osric' (p. xvii).

Surprisingly, for someone so opposed to the theatre, Tilke reveals that he had almost gone on the stage himself, prompted by an acquaintance who had been impressed by his reciting of Shakespeare. He auditioned for a theatre in Bath, trying out the parts of Othello, Iago, Romeo and Hamlet. The theatre manager complimented him on his Hamlet, saying that his 'conception of the author and [his] action were correct' and observing that 'all I required was a little attention to elocution' (p. 106). Should the rest of the company agree, the manager suggested, he would put Tilke on as Hamlet and, if successful, he would engage him for the season. It was, however, not to be. Tilke reports: 'I never saw him more. It was not according to the purpose of God, who had other work for me to do' (p. 107).[81] That other work was prepared for on the Clifton downs, where Tilke fell into the habit of sitting on a stone opposite the spot where the suspension bridge was erected. Here, he 'read Shakespeare's works, and also botanical and medical books, taking extracts and making observations as I read' (p. 90). The medical books enabled him to become the proprietor of a 'Medical and Steam-Bath Establishment' in Bristol, charging clients 3s. 6d. for a home consultation, with a rising scale of fees depending on distance (p. 227 and prelims). Reading Shakespeare enabled him, as we have seen, to turn the playwright into a kind of moral instructor for the ambitious young reader.

A very different kind of Shakespearean experience is provided by Betsy Cadwaladyr (1789–1860), whose father we witnessed (Chapter 1) picking up the alphabet by learning the letters tarred on the backs of sheep as he tended to his master's flock on a hillside in Wales. Betsy Cadwaladyr led an extraordinarily varied life, which included spells as a servant (at one point, single-handedly tackling a burglar while serving in a house in Liverpool), as a ship's steward, and as a nurse working at a field hospital at Scutari barracks during the Crimean War (where she fell out with Florence Nightingale, whom she considered to be inefficient and a touch self-serving). By contrast with Tilke, Cadwaladyr was a great attender of the theatre. She saw Sarah Siddons perform in both Edinburgh and Glasgow, during a stint of service in Scotland. In London, she worked as cook for the family of a fashionable London tailor, who lived across the street from the Irish actress Eliza O'Neill. O'Neill had made her name in the role of Juliet and she often spoke to Cadwaladyr, several times giving her tickets for performances at Drury Lane. Cadwaladyr observes of her playgoing: 'I never cared for comedies; but I liked the grave noble acting in tragedies'.[82]

Having seen Shakespeare in performance on the London stage, Cadwaladyr had a chance to study his plays when she went to sea on the merchant vessel *Denmark Hill*. Sailing from Bombay to Bengal, she was short of distraction, as the view offered 'nothing but the two banks of the river and the country here and there between the woods. We met no ships or boats. We had only Indian passengers on board, with whom I could not exchange a word'. Her only amusement, she writes, 'was reading Shakespeare's Plays in the cabin, by myself, and trying to look as I fancied the heroes and heroines must have done' (p. 124). The practice she had in trying to look like Shakespeare's characters must have come in useful at the end of a subsequent voyage, from Sydney to Calcutta, when she and her shipmates found themselves at a loose end while in port. They came together with the crew of another ship, the *Southampton*, and 'got up some scenes of plays, and had a grand theatre there, and one night a large assemblage of ladies and gentlemen came to see the acting.' Among the parts played by Cadwaladyr was that of Lady Macbeth, which she particularly enjoyed. Others in the company agreed that she 'played very well; Mr Thomson, the merchant, said it was a pity I did not become a professional actress; and that my eyes looked so vicious in Lady Macbeth, he should be afraid to meet me in the dark' (p. 128).

The opportunity to enter the acting profession did, in fact, present itself to Cadwaladyr when she gave up her sea-going career and returned for a spell to serving as a housekeeper in London. Her employer was, again, well-connected with the metropolitan acting profession, being an old school-friend of Charles Kemble. When her employer's sister got married, Kemble brought some of his acting friends to the house and they 'sang a great deal, and acted scenes from "Hamlet", "Douglas" and "Paul Pry"' (p. 140). Cadwaladyr was responsible for getting supper ready for the wedding party, which kept her too busy to watch the performances. But, once everything had been set up, she picked up a copy of Shakespeare's plays which had been left on a table in the kitchen. To amuse herself – and perhaps remembering her days on board ship – she began acting out scenes from *Hamlet* and other plays. While she was doing this, Kemble came to the kitchen and stood for a time in the doorway, silently watching her. He liked what he saw enough to offer to tutor her and to raise the possibility that he might engage her as an actor in his company. Cadwaladyr did not immediately respond but, some time later, she had occasion to go to Covent Garden to buy provisions and her employer asked her to call at the theatre and deliver some papers to Kemble. Here, she had something of an odd experience:

The porter said there was a rehearsal, and showed me the way I was to go. I found one or two hundred people, men, women, and children, assembled – being the full complement of the company belonging to that theatre.

I was obliged to pass very close to them, and I saw that many were poor, untidy-looking creatures, and that some were quite dirty ragamuffins, shoeless, and without stockings, or perhaps shirts. (pp. 140–1)

When she meets Kemble, Cadwaladyr asks him: 'If I come, must I play with the people I have just seen in the long passage?' He answers that sometimes she likely would and this is enough to decide her against pursuing a career in acting. 'The sight of those ragged wretches again, as I left the theatre, made me resolute to have nothing at all to do with them', she concludes (p. 141). It seems a somewhat odd decision for a woman who had, after all, experienced life on the high seas, but perhaps it indicates that she is not quite so far removed in her attitudes from Samuel Tilke as might at first appear.

An altogether less flamboyant figure than Cadwaladyr was the Cornish miner and poet, John Harris (1820–84).[83] Harris did not venture outside Cornwall until he was forty-four years old. His journey took him to (among other places) Stratford-on-Avon. In Shakespeare's birthplace, he 'seemed to be walking in some enchanted garden, where every tree and flower and sunny fountain gleamed with a splendour not of earth; and the music which rose from river and ravine was more than can be uttered.' All the while, however, he says, 'I stretched forth my hands to dear old Cornwall as the loveliest spot of earth' and he returned at the end of the trip, never to leave his native county again.[84] Commenting on his family background, Harris observes of his grandfather that 'It is not at all probable that he ever indulged much in poetry or the poets, or knew that such a man as William Shakespere had ever existed.' He tells a family story of a neighbour lending his grandfather a copy of *Paradise Lost*. When he returned it, he was asked how he had liked it, and his reply was 'The man that wrote that book ought to be hanged!' (p. 9). Harris' father was no more impressed with reading. Watching his son with a book, 'he appeared to dislike it, saying he did not think I should ever earn my living' (p. 28).

Like Mary Ann Hearn, Harris came to read Shakespeare for the first time thanks to a local clergyman. Shortly after the miner got married, the Rev. G. T. Bull loaned him a volume of the playwright's work. The effect was immediate and profound:

The first play I read was 'Romeo and Juliet,' which I greedily devoured travelling over a wide downs near my father's house. The delight I experienced is beyond words to describe, as the sun sank behind the western waters, and the purple clouds of evening fringed the horizon. The bitters of life changed to sweetness in my cup, and the wilderness around me was a region of fairies. Sometimes I cried, sometimes I shouted for joy; and over the genii-peopled heights a new world burst upon my view. Admitted into the palace of enchantment, I passed the gateway again and again, and heard music and saw visions of ethereal loveliness which filled me with a fuller existence. (pp. 63–4)

The borrowed volume prompted Harris to save up for his own copy of Shakespeare – the third book he bought for himself, after a Bible and a hymnal (p. 59).

Harris' particular interest in Shakespeare paid off for him in 1864, when he entered a poetry competition run in conjunction with the tercentenary celebrations in Coventry. The first prize was a gold watch, manufactured by 'one of the first English firms, Messrs. Rotheram' and valued at 20 guineas.[85] The case of the watch was inscribed – rather gloomily, one might feel – with Macbeth's 'Tomorrow, and tomorrow, and tomorrow / Creeps in this petty pace from day to day, / To the last syllable of recorded time'. Harris decided to enter the competition and he wrote his 'Tercentenary Ode' 'in two evenings by the kitchen fire when the children were sleeping in bed', having, as we have seen in the case of so many others, 'no place of study or retirement' (pp. 90, 90–1). Several months later, as he arrived home from working in the local tin mine, his wife told him excitedly 'You have won the prize – the gold watch' (p. 91), a telegram having arrived earlier that day. Harris was invited to Coventry to be presented with the watch as part of the tercentenary celebrations, but considerations of time (ironically, we might feel, given the nature of the prize) and money meant that the trip was out of the question for him. In due course, the prize itself arrived, delivered by the local postman, who 'would not leave until he had seen the case opened, and its contents spread before his eyes'. On seeing the watch, the postman 'danced around the room, clapped his hands and shouted, "We have beaten them all! Hurrah! hurrah! The *barbarians* of Cornwall are at the very top of the tree! Huzza! huzza!"' (p. 92). Harris himself notes that a copy of the poem was framed and preserved in the Shakespeare Museum in Stratford-on-Avon, 'the only working man's literary contribution in the place' (p. 93).

It may not be too fanciful, perhaps, to say that the story of the 'Tercentenary Ode' has many interesting subaltern resonances. What we witness here is a provincial appropriation of Shakespeare in his tercentenary year – and in the context, we will remember, of a singular (and very public) elite metropolitan failure to mark the tercentenary adequately.[86] The small town of Coventry, lacking both the urban weight of

Birmingham to the northwest and the originary cultural gravitas of Stratford to the southwest, nevertheless stakes its own claim on the playwright through its poetry competition and accompanying ceremonials.[87] For his neighbours, Harris' success represents the triumph (partly through appropriation) of an often-derided peninsular culture over its inland counterpart. And the workingman's poem itself finds a place in the very shrine of cultural idolatry: the Shakespeare museum in Stratford. This is, however, rather a lot of weight for a single poem to carry and it must be acknowledged that the 'Tercentenary Ode' itself indicates that, while Harris may have studied Shakespeare very carefully, poetically this particular apprenticeship would appear to have been less than entirely successful. A representative flavour of the work can be had from a set of stanzas registering that Shakespeare is 'Loved now the wide world round, / Where human hives are found', then listing the many and varied members of society by whom the playwright is appreciated:

> By prince, and peasant following the plough,
>   The sailor out at sea,
>   The yeoman on the lea,
> The miner digging in the earth below:
>   The shepherd in his plaid,
>   The rosy village maid,
> The warrior watching by the red camp fire;
>   The mother with her child,
>   The satchell'd schoolboy mild,
> The college student, daily pressing higher:
>   The dweller of the street,
>   In the great city's heat,
> The mountaineer, within his lodge of reeds;
>   The silent solitaire
>   On the wide desert bare:–
> All own his witchery where the daylight speeds.[88]

Over the course of his life, Harris published a total of seventeen volumes of poetry. Sad to say, however, very little of what he wrote was of a much higher standard than the 'Tercentenary Ode', though at least that one poem did gain him a golden reward.

If Shakespeare inspired Harris to write poetry, he prompted another autobiographer-poet to write literary criticism. Gerald Massey (1828–1907) was born in a hut on a canal near Tring, in Hertfordshire. He grew up in extreme poverty, briefly attended a National school, and was sent to work in a silk mill when he was just eight years old. An energetic autodidact, he teamed up with John Bedford Leno during a spell living in Uxbridge and formed a 'Young Men's Improvement Society'. In July 1850, Massey married Rosina Jane Knowles, a clairvoyant from Bolton, Lancashire. Massey had seen Knowles performing publicly under hypnosis before he married her and he 'was indignant at the treatment to which she was subjected in order to satisfy people's curiosity'. However, as they struggled to get by while he tried to make a living from journalism, lecturing and writing, Massey was compelled to put his wife back on public display, advertising a series of demonstrations of 'Mesmerism and Clairvoyance' and noting in the publicity material that 'The Clairvoyante, Mrs. Gerald Massey, long known as the "Somnambule Jane", has manifested the peculiar power of Clairvoyance or Second Sight, for a period of eleven years, during which time she has been satisfactorily tested by numerous persons'.[89] Rosina Massey suffered, in many respects, a rather wretched life, losing several children within a matter of months of their birth. Eventually, she took to heavy drinking, which led in its turn to an early death.

Before she died, Massey's wife performed a singular service for her husband. Some time in the 1860s, he developed a strong interest in Shakespeare's sonnets, expressed in the first instance in a lengthy review of Charles Cowden Clarke's *Shakespeare Characters; Chiefly those Subordinate*. Massey began planning to write more extensively on the subject and his wife helped him in his labours in a rather striking manner. Using her clairvoyant powers, she 'provided references to books about which they both knew nothing, but that were relevant to the development of his theories'.[90] Massey was careful to stress that it was not Shakespeare himself who was tracking down these references from beyond the grave. Rather, it seems, Rosina was simply tapping into some kind of spiritualist precursor to the *World Shakespeare Bibliography*. Massey developed his theories regarding the sonnets in a series of publications – initially an article in the *Quarterly Review* (April 1864), then a volume entitled *Shakespeare's Sonnets Never Before Imprinted*, which was later re-written and reissued as *The Secret Drama of Shakespeare's Sonnets*. Massey had sufficient confidence in his theories to offer to pay £100 to anyone who could refute the conclusions of his *Quarterly Review* article. His biographer, David Shaw, has noted that it was fortunate for Massey that 'no serious attempt at a refutation of his developing theories was made in order to claim his £100, which he certainly did not possess'.[91]

In *The Secret Drama* (1872), Massey observed that no one had yet investigated the sonnets with sufficient diligence to seek out the 'scattered and embedded bones of fact, and put them together again and again, until they should fit with such nicety that the departed spirit ... in these remains, should stir with the breath of life, and clothe itself in flesh once more, and take its original shape'.[92] Massey's own reassembling of the skeleton of the collection was a profoundly complex affair. Essentially, he believed that there were two sequences of sonnets: one written for the Earl of Southampton, the other for William Herbert. He also believed that the poems were never intended to be revealing of Shakespeare's own autobiography and that many of them were written as if from a particular speaker, such as Southampton himself, or Lady Penelope Rich. Massey adds his own special twist to the narrative by suggesting that, in addition to commissioning some of the sonnets from Shakespeare, William Herbert also wrote a number of the poems himself. Thus, Massey concludes, Herbert was the W. H. who was the 'only begetter' of the sonnets, in the sense that he was the one who obtained for Thomas Thorpe 'the Southampton Sonnets together with such other odds and ends of Shakspeare's poetry as the Poet had given to him; that he added to these the sonnets which had been written for himself at his own suggestion; he giving the subject and having a hand in their composition' and that he also included poems (at least four in total) written wholly by himself.[93] In Massey's view, Shakespeare himself never intended that the poems should be published, certainly not, at any rate, under his own name.

What Massey's theorising ultimately allows him to do is to retrieve Shakespeare from the kinds of speculation about his life that was already beginning to take hold in response to then current interpretations of the sonnets – even in advance of Wilde's *Portrait of Mr. W. H.* (and his comments at his 1895 trial). Thus, Massey observes that

> it is assuredly the most just to conclude that a want of discretion was far more in keeping with the character of Herbert than with that of a man who was so full of self-respect, domestic prudence, practical sagacity, wise reserve, and *canny* discreteness as was our Shakspeare; he who passed his London-life without blemish of his honour, stain on his reputation, or suspicion of his morality, and who when the sonnets were printed, had more incentives than ever for observing the decencies of life, and the respectabilities of personal character.[94]

Massey's theory is, perhaps, neither more nor less fanciful than most of the other interpretations of the sonnets that were written in the same period (or, indeed, than many of those that have been published since). What is most striking about his view of Shakespeare here is, we might say, its curiously middle-class cosiness. His picture of the playwright strangely anticipates that offered in the very next year by Henry Morley, in his *First Sketch of English Literature*. Morley had been a lecturer in English at King's

College London and was appointed Professor of English at University College London in 1866, holding the post jointly with a professorship at Queen's College from 1878. In his *First Sketch*, he writes of Shakespeare and his family:

His wife and babies he would not take with him into the unwholesome atmosphere of the great town, or bring into contact with the wild life of the playhouse wits. The children would be drawing health from the fresh breezes of Stratford; the wife would be living a wholesome life among her old friends, neighbours, and relations; while he worked hard for them where money could be earned, took holiday rests with them when theatres were closed, and hoped that he might earn enough to enable him to come home for good before he was very old.[95]

In some respects, however, the resonances between the writings of the working-class speculator and the middle-class professor are not particularly surprising, since what many autodidacts longed for was, essentially, middle-class respectability and acceptance. This may, indeed, be what links Cadwaladyr with Massey and with Tilke, since her rejection of scruffy bit-part actors and supernumeraries might also in itself be interpreted as a desire to maintain a hard-won respectability. We might also note here, specifically in relation to the filiations between Massey and Morley that, as we have seen throughout this book, the highest achievement of many of the most successful working-class self-improvers was to become, precisely, university professors.

Try as they might, however, many working-class autodidacts never did manage to find a comfortable place for themselves in the world of middle-class culture. Joseph Skipsey (1832–1903) was one such. He was born at Percy Main, near North Shields, the son of a miner who was shot dead during an industrial dispute when Skipsey was just four months old. Because his mother received no compensation for the killing, the Skipsey children were all sent to work in the pits from the earliest age possible. Skipsey himself entered the mine when he was just seven, having received no formal schooling. Like Frank Hodges much later in the century, his first job in the mine was as a trapper, opening and closing ventilation doors. This left him with enough time on his hands during the working day that he was able to teach himself how to read:

he managed to possess himself of printed bills, either obtaining them from small shops or from places where they were stuck up, and he got good-natured pitmen to give him the ends of their farthing dips, and, with a piece of chalk, he copied the letters on the sill, getting the names of the letters (which he had some chance knowledge of before he entered the pit) and explanations of meanings from those pitmen who were kindly disposed and who were able and willing to help him.[96]

By the time Skipsey was fifteen years old, he had begun to read seriously and an uncle who owned a few books lent him a copy of *Paradise Lost*, which 'was a revelation to him' and he 'thought of nothing else day or night' (p. 18). Some time after this he heard of Shakespeare for the first time and he saved up his scant pocket money to purchase a 5s. edition of the plays.[97] Skipsey subsequently observed of the volume: 'The book altered the aspect of the world to me' (p. 19).

Skipsey published his own first volume of poetry in 1859, with further collections following over the years. His poems gained him some middle-class sponsorship and attempts were made to secure suitable employment for him outside the mining industry. In 1888, he served for a time as porter at Armstrong College, where he 'fulfilled his duties admirably'. But the disjunction between his menial role as porter and his local literary fame proved to be too disruptive. Robert Spence Watson, one of Skipsey's sponsors, notes in his biography of the poet that he (that is, Watson) came to see that 'it was quite impossible to have a College where the scientific men came to see the Principal and the artistic and literary men came to see the porter' (p. 71). As a result, Skipsey left the college, but another opportunity arose for him in the following year. At that time, the (perhaps appropriately named) Misses Chataway, who had been serving as custodians of the Shakespeare birthplace property in Stratford-on-Avon, decided to retire and a new custodian was wanted. Skipsey was urged by his friends to apply for the job and he received support from a wide array of prominent figures in the arts, including Edward Burne-Jones, Dante Gabriel Rossetti, F. R. Benson, Andrew Lang, Bram Stoker, William Morris and Edward Dowden. Skipsey was called to interview and was appointed to the custodianship, despite some reservations about his strong Northumbrian accent. He and his wife moved into the birthplace and began the business of showing visitors over the house, giving the history of the property and its contents and providing details of Shakespeare's life. The move to Stratford was, however, not a success. Skipsey was particularly troubled by large parties of Americans who 'were especially difficult to satisfy'. They were, Watson writes, 'very sceptical. How did he know which room Shakespeare was really born in? Was the history he gave of a table, a chair, or a desk really true?' Even more fundamentally, they asked how he could 'know there ever was such a man as Shakespeare?' Armed with some knowledge of the work of their compatriot Delia Bacon, visitors from the

U.S. proudly declared that, in America, it had been 'shown satisfactorily that lord Bacon of Verulam had written the plays'. The relentless questioning of his basic assumptions eventually broke Skipsey, as Watson indicates:

And so the talk went on, and poor Skipsey's temper ran short, and his mind was often bewildered, and at the end of a busy day he was quite exhausted and unfit for anything. I found that he had begun to doubt that the story which he had been taught was really in any sense true. The constant suspicion and doubts freely and often cleverly expressed had worked upon his mind. He felt that if he were to make this his life's labour he would end by doubting the very existence of Shakespeare, and so he resigned his place and came home to the North. (p. 74)

Skipsey ultimately returned to working in the pits. For a time, later in life, he began to believe that he was, like Rosina Massey, clairvoyant, though, unlike Mrs Massey, he made no money from his imagined gift.[98]

Frederick Rogers (1846–1915) had a rather more robust attitude to those who denied that Shakespeare had written the plays attributed to him, observing in his autobiography that he 'snorted scornfully at the Baconians and their theories of authorship when they came my way'.[99] Rogers, who was born at Whitechapel in London, had brief stints at a dame school and a BFSS school before becoming an errand boy at an ironmongers at 2s. per week. Subsequently, he trained as a bookbinder and he remained associated with the trade for almost four decades, while also becoming involved in trade unionism and social activism, including agitating for adult education. As with so many of the other autodidacts, Shakespeare was a profoundly important figure for Rogers and he observes that 'I cannot recollect the time when I did not know something of Shakespeare. He has been part of my intellectual life ever since I had an intellectual life' (p. 157). We have already seen that, as a sickly youngster, Rogers often sought refuge in books, and his extensive reading in his teenage years included the 'odd play of Shakespeare' (p. 15). Like Cadwaladyr, Rogers was also an enthusiastic theatre-goer, though, unlike Cadwaladyr, his experience was, initially at least, of the cheap London theatres, rather than of Drury Lane. Most of the cheap theatres specialised in domestic drama, but the Standard offered plays of the 'legitimate' canon and Rogers recalls passing 'happy Saturday nights, watching Miss Marriott as Hamlet or James Anderson's Ingomar, for the small sum of fourpence – threepence for admission, and a penny for apples by way of refreshments' (pp. 7–8).

Rogers involved himself in the Working Men's Club movement and, through this work he came in contact with the Dean of Westminster, who served as president of the association. Making regular visits to the Abbey,

Rogers found himself discussing such issues as 'the beauties of Shakespeare's pastoral plays' with Dean Stanley, who he credits as being one of those among the cultured classes who sought 'to break down the partition walls which divided them from those whom it was foolish custom to regard as beneath them' (p. 74). Rogers himself carried out considerable work in the clubs, lecturing on a variety of subjects. Ultimately, he became disillusioned with the educational programme, as he felt disappointed by the response of those who frequented the clubs. Writing of the 1880s, he observes:

> I was losing my illusions as to the possibilities of the club movement. Its social value I saw, but I was seeking other values, and when one morning, in the midst of a lecture on Shakespeare, I was asked to make a break to let the man come round with the beer, I knew my work at the clubs was drawing to an end. (p. 96)

Rogers moved on from the clubs to Toynbee Hall, where he enjoyed the benefit of university extension lectures and classes. Just as W. E. Adams had studied Shakespeare under F. J. Furnivall, so Rogers was able to join a Shakespeare class being run by Sidney Lee, one of the foremost Shakespeareans of his generation. Rogers developed a much less moralistic interpretation of Shakespeare's work than many of the other autobiographers, seeing the playwright as bringing with him 'the sense of an exhaustless capacity, a limitless freedom' and as offering 'the complete expression of the idealism and the life of a great England' (pp. 157, 157–8). For Rogers, the life in question was 'full-blooded and impetuous ... daring and dreaming noble, but in fierce revolt against all that would tame or curb the hot passions of the flesh, or check the dancing, bubbling fountains of human joy' (p. 158). Where Samuel Tilke saw Shakespeare as possessed of 'a deep sense of the pure morality of the Gospel', Rogers celebrates what he regards as a 'shout of defiance' in Shakespeare against the puritan 'preachers of self-restraint', who 'so interpreted their gospel as to make it suppress every warm and generous impulse, and in the name of virtue turn to sourness all that was sweet in life' (p. 158). Rogers relishes the spirit of the times of the Renaissance, seeing a kind of near-anarchic *jouissance* as forming the context for Shakespeare's writing:

> Authority had fallen, and men held themselves free, alike from the restraints of morals and of faith. Intoxicated with the new wine of national liberty, they hated fiercely, revelled gloriously, and loved and died in heroic fashion, and if there was no pity in their hate neither was there any stinting of their love.

If other working-class commentators on Shakespeare sound strikingly similar to their contemporary middle-class counterparts, Rogers might almost be said here to be sketching out a very early rough draft of the Introduction to *Radical Tragedy*.

Again, by contrast with Tilke, Rogers retained a strong interest in theatrical performances of Shakespeare throughout his life, eventually moving on beyond the delights of the thruppeny East London playhouses. In addition to Miss Marriott, he saw many other performers play Hamlet, including Barry Sullivan, T. C. King, Forbes Robertson and Henry Irving. This last actor he considered his favourite and he observes: 'no Hamlet I ever saw left in my mind such a sense of intellectual greatness, and of artistic completeness as did the Hamlet of Henry Irving' (p. 133). Rogers eventually got to meet Irving, when the actor attended an event to honour the memory of Christopher Marlowe, at which Rogers gave a speech. Irving was sufficiently impressed by what he heard that he invited Rogers to be a guest at his production of Tennyson's *Becket* at the Lyceum and to attend the onstage supper which followed the performance: 'Becket lay dead on the stage, amid the flashing lightning and the rolls of thunder, the curtain fell', then the invited guests filed out on to the stage and 'By the time they got there it was transformed into a great supper room, in which was a great table built into a half-circle ... and a magnificent stand-up supper was laid for those who cared to partake' (pp. 171, 171–2). Rogers was also an enthusiastic supporter of the work of William Poel and the Elizabethan Stage Society, which was dedicated to mounting productions in a style as close as possible to that of the Renaissance stage. Rogers strongly approved of the venture and observed of Poel's production of *Measure for Measure* in 1893 that 'It was Shakespeare in his own clothing and it had a strange and beautiful witchery about it' (p. 169).

Among Rogers' publications in addition to his autobiography was a book entitled *The Seven Deadly Sins*, which appeared from A. H. Bullen's 'Shakespeare Head Press' in Stratford-on-Avon, in 1907. Rogers observes of his connection with Bullen that it 'is an episode in my life to which I look back with unalloyed and exalted pleasure, and must ever be counted among the happiest of my literary memories (p. 255). His opinion of the publisher is extremely high, not least because of the edition of Shakespeare which Bullen produced at the Stratford press. The 'Stratford Town' edition was published in ten volumes, at a price of 10 guineas, with a further limited edition being issued on vellum at a higher price. We have travelled a long way here from the realm of Dicks' Shilling Shakespeare.

The final Shakespeare enthusiast I discuss in this chapter is William Margrie, who has the noted distinction of being identified by the *Dictionary of National Biography* as a 'philosopher and eccentric'; more prosaically, he earned his living primarily as a house painter.[100] Margrie was born in Camberwell, south London, in 1877, and he was educated at Gloucester Road board school. In *A Cockney's Pilgrimage in Search of Truth* (1927), he observes: 'I find that my principal interests are London, Shakespeare, Evolution, and Self-Culture. In other words, I am a worshipper of life, for London, Shakespeare, and Evolution are large slices of life.'[101] Margrie became known as the 'Sage of Peckham', and his love of London led him to found the 'London Explorers' Club', dedicated to enjoying all aspects of the capital's architecture and culture.[102] His enthusiasm for south London was such that he asserted that, 'when Shakespeare wrote the line – "The uncertain glory of an April day" – he ... was obviously thinking of glorious Camberwell'.[103] Margrie's investment in evolution caused him, controversially, to become a staunch supporter of eugenics and his eccentricity is given full reign in *The Mighty Heart: A Survey of England as It Is and a Vision of What It Might Be* (1925), where he advances proposals for an 'Isle of Eugenics'. This was to be established on 'the Isle of Wight, the Isle of Man, or Jersey. Its present population should be persuaded to go elsewhere'. Once the island had been cleared 'superior young couples should be induced to settle there. Once on the island, they could do as they liked, always provided they became parents'. Candidates for transfer to the island would be 'university men and women who had done well, young workmen who had invented something, athletes who had broken records, witty comedians of both sexes, and so on' – an interestingly eclectic mix, at least. Margrie also envisaged that, on the mainland, local communities should run their own 'annual eugenic festival. This would be a good thing in itself. Young men who have passed a mental test should run races for the prettiest girl of the district as first prize'.[104] The Sage of Peckham does not seem to concern himself overmuch with the question of how the prettiest girl of the district might be likely to respond to this.

Looking back on his childhood, Margrie notes that 'Soon after I learnt to read I purchased a copy of "Comic Cuts" (½d)'. This, he claims, introduced him to Plato, Shakespeare and Bernard Shaw – a singular feat for a ha'penny comic.[105] In his *Diary of a London Explorer*, he writes that 'In my early twenties I went in for a course of intensive self-culture. I waded through many masterpieces, including *The Origin of Species, The Descent of Man*, Plato's *Republic, Paradise Lost*, the majority of Shakespeare's plays, and three encyclopædias'. His enthusiasm for Shakespeare led him to join the London Shakespeare League. At a general meeting of the League, he 'made a sort of workingman's Shakespeare speech and was promptly elected to the council', thereby meeting 'many interesting men and women', including Ben Greet, the actor and theatre manager, and William Poel.[106] In keeping with Poel's own theatrical programme, Margrie notes that 'The principal object of the Shakespeare League was to produce Shakespeare's plays as they were written'.[107]

Margrie retained a strong sense of enthusiasm for Shakespeare throughout his life, observing in one publication that 'Shakespeare still remains the world's brightest intellect. Plato taught us to think; Cæsar taught us to act; Shakespeare taught us to express ourselves, though nobody has been able to imitate the master'.[108] His sense of pleasure in Shakespeare was tied-in with a nationalistically minded sense of English identity, as he observes: 'We have sadly neglected Shakespeare. We don't make half as much fuss of him as Scotland makes of Burns. Yet Burns to Shakespeare is like a candle to the sun. Well, Shakespeare is the greatest master of language' and 'Good old Shakespeare! You can't praise him too much. If England had done nothing but produce Shakespeare she would have justified her existence.'[109] His interest in Shakespeare also intersected with his investment in eugenics, as he characterised Shakespeare as 'the nearest approach to a real Superman' and it also intersected, rather humorously, with an interest in phrenology, as he observes elsewhere that 'there is some connection between the size and shape of the head and ability. It would be impossible for a man with a head like a gorilla to be a Shakespeare'.[110]

Much as Margrie admired Shakespeare, he was not above having some fun at the playwright's expense and, in *A Camberwell Man*, he provides a humorous fictional account of a visit of some working-class children to the Old Vic to see *Hamlet*. The piece is written from the perspective of one of the children (given the name 'Tom Edwards') who provides a summary of the action of the play, noting that, while it was 'very long', he had 'managed to keep awake most of the time'.[111] Edwards expresses some surprise at Claudius' marriage to Gertrude, observing that 'When a king dies it's his son who takes on the job, not his brother. I'm surprised Shakespeare didn't know that. But we mustn't be too hard on Shakespeare, because in his time there were no Council schools'.[112] On the whole, he likes that play, but ultimately he concludes: 'if that's Denmark, I'd sooner live in Peckham!'[113]

Margrie was, without a doubt, the most unusual of Shakespeare's nineteenth-century-born working-class admirers. What is striking, however, looking back over the writings of Tilke, Cadwaladyr, Harris, Massey, Skipsey, Rogers and Margrie is the fact that, beyond their backgrounds and a general (and often bardolatrous) enthusiasm for Shakespeare, there is little enough that can be said to unite them in their attitudes to the playwright. There is nothing here that could be styled a distinctive or coherent working-class approach to or interpretation of the playwright. Some of them, as we have noted, do see Shakespeare as a token of a kind of middle-class respectability to which they themselves aspire. But, generally speaking, however, what these autobiographers offer is a set of discontinuous personal experiences of reading the plays. There was, however, one group of working-class readers for whom Shakespeare's work did resonate with a particular working-class programme in the nineteenth century – the movement for political reform. It is to these readers that I turn my attention in Chapter 4 of this study.

NOTES

1 Christopher Thomson, *The Autobiography of an Artisan* (London: J. Chapman; Nottingham: J. Shaw and Sons, 1847), p. vii.
2 Thomas Burt, *Thomas Burt M. P., D.C.L., Pitman & Privy Councillor: An Autobiography* (London: T. Fisher Unwin, 1924), p. 122.
3 Charles Shaw, *When I Was a Child* (Firle, Sussex: Caliban, 1877; originally published serially in *The Staffordshire Sentinel*, December 1892–May 1893, author identified as 'An Old Potter'), p. 224.
4 Marianne Farningham (pseud. of Mary Anne Hearn), *A Working Woman's Life: An Autobiography* (London: James Clarke, [1907]), pp. 46, 48.
5 *Ibid.*, pp. 49, 49–50.
6 Mary Smith, *The Autobiography of Mary Smith, Schoolmistress and Nonconformist. A Fragment of a Life* (London: Bemrose & Sons, 1892), p. 26.
7 John Plummer, *Songs of Labour, Northamptonshire Rambles, and Other Poems* (London: W. Tweedie; Kettering: Thomas Waddington, 1860), p. xvii.
8 Tom Barclay, *Memoirs and Medleys: The Autobiography of a Bottle Washer* (Coalville, Leicestershire: Coalville Publishing, 1995; originally published Leicester: Edgar Backus, 1934), p. 49.
9 Elizabeth Mary Wright, *The Life of Joseph Wright* (London: Oxford University Press, 1932), 2 vols., vol. I, p. 21.
10 Farningham, *Working Woman's*, p. 71. The same pastor had also given her a copy of *Jane Eyre*.
11 Adam Rushton, *My Life as Farmer's Boy, Factory Lad, Teacher and Preacher* (Manchester: S. Clarke, 1909), p. 50.
12 Thomson, *Autobiography*, pp. 64–5, 66.
13 *Ibid.*, p. 67.
14 W. E. Adams, *Memoirs of a Social Atom*, 2 vols. (London: Hutchinson, 1903), vol. I, p. 102.
15 J. R. Clynes, *Memoirs, 1869–1924* (London: Hutchinson, 1937), p. 45.
16 Joseph Terry, 'Recollections of My Life', typescript, Brunel University Library, 1:693, pp. 32–3, 33.
17 Sir Henry Jones, *Old Memories*, ed. Thomas Jones (London: Hodder and Stoughton, [1922]), pp. 72–3.

18 Francis Place, *The Autobiography of Francis Place*, ed. Mary Thale (Cambridge: Cambridge University Press, 1972), p. 16.
19 *Ibid.*, p. 223.
20 *Ibid.*, p. 276.
21 Thomas Jones, *Leeks and Daffodils* (Newtown: Welsh Outlook Press, 1942), p. 10.
22 Adams, *Memoirs*, vol. 1, pp. 108–9.
23 John Wood, *Autobiography of John Wood, an Old and Well Known Bradfordian, Written in the 75th Year of his Age* (Bradford: *Chronicle and Mail* Office, 1877), p. 5.
24 Emmanuel Lovekin, 'Some Notes on My Life', manuscript, Brunel University Library, 1:452, p. 2.
25 David Rubenstein, ' "Introduction" to Frederick Rogers', *Labour, Life and Literature: Some Memories of Sixty Years* (Brighton: Harvester, 1973; first published London: Smith, Elder, 1913), p. xi.
26 Rogers, *Labour, Life*, pp. 15, 40. William Heaton, born near Halifax in 1805, also found that books provided him with company: 'Having no brothers, and only one sister, who was married prior to my mother's death, I found my companions in books': *The Old Soldier; The Wandering Lover; and Other Poems; Together with A Sketch of the Author's Life* (London: Simpkin, Marshall & Co.; Halifax: T. & W. Birtwhistle, 1857), p. xviii.
27 Rogers, *Labour, Life*, p. 19.
28 J. Passmore Edwards, *A Few Footprints* (London: np, 1905), p. 6.
29 Shaw, *When I Was*, p. 227.
30 John James Bezer, 'Autobiography of one of the Chartist Rebels of 1848', in David Vincent, ed., *Testaments of Radicalism: Memoirs of Working Class Politicians, 1790–1885* (London: Europa, 1977), p. 167. Originally published serially in *The Christian Socialist*, 6 September–13 December 1851.
31 Harry Alfred West, 'The Autobiography of Harry Alfred West: Facts and Comments', typescript, Brunel University Library, 1:745, p. 11.
32 J.A. Leatherland, *Essays and Poems, with a Brief Autobiographical Memoir* (London: W. Tweedie, 1862), p. 4.
33 Burt, *Thomas Burt*, p. 115.
34 Joseph Barker, *The Life of Joseph Barker. Written by Himself*, ed. John Thomas Barker (London: Hodder & Stoughton, 1880; originally published London: Chapman Brothers, 1846), p. 54.
35 [Thomas Carter], *Memoirs of a Working Man* (London: Charles Knight & Co., 1845), pp. 28–9.
36 *Ibid.*, p. 80.
37 Thomson, *Autobiography*, pp. 65, 94.
38 Joseph Arch, *The Autobiography of Joseph Arch*, ed. John Gerald O'Leary (London: MacGibbon & Kee, 1966; originally published London: Hutchinson, 1898), p. 22.
39 *Ibid.*, pp. 35–6, 36.
40 Robert Lowery, *Robert Lowery: Radical and Chartist*, Brian Harrison and Patricia Hollis (eds) (London: Europa, 1979; originally published

anonymously as a series of 33 articles in the *Weekly Record of the Temperance Movement*. Publication at irregular intervals between 15 April 1856 and 23 May 1857), p. 63.
41 George Edwards, *From Crow-Scaring to Westminster: An Autobiography* (London: National Union of Agricultural Workers, 1957; originally published London: Labour Publishing Company, 1922), p. 3.
42 Fred Kitchen, *Brother to the Ox. The Autobiography of a Farm Labourer* (London: Caliban, 1981; originally published London: J. M. Dent, 1940), p. 200.
43 John Jones, 'John Jones, an Old Servant: An Account of his Life, Written by Himself', in Robert Southey, *The Lives and Works of the Uneducated Poets*, J. S. Childers (ed.) (London: Humphrey Milford, 1925), p. 173.
44 *Ibid.*, p. 175.
45 Mrs. Layton, 'Memories of Seventy Years', in Margaret Llewelyn Davies, ed., *Life as We Have Known It*, Anna Davin (intro.) (London: Virago, 1977; first published London: Hogarth Press, 1931), p. 29.
46 Hannah Mitchell, *The Hard Way Up: The Autobiography of Hannah Mitchell, Suffragette and Rebel*, ed. Geoffrey Mitchell, preface by George Ewart Evans (London: Faber & Faber, 1968), p. 54.
47 *Ibid.*, p. 43.
48 *Ibid.*, pp. 67–8.
49 Rushton, *My Life*, p. 52.
50 Carter, *Memoirs*, pp. 74–5.
51 John Brown, *Sixty Years' Gleanings from Life's Harvest. A Genuine Autobiography* (New York: Appleton & Co., 1859; originally published Cambridge: printed for the author, 1858), p. 35.
52 *Ibid.*, p. 41.
53 *Ibid.*, p. 45.
54 *Ibid.*, p. 169.
55 Ben Tillett, *Memories and Reflections* (London: John Long, 1931), p. 114.
56 Tom Mann, *Tom Mann's Memoirs* (London: Macgibbon & Kee, 1967; first published London: The Labour Publishing Company, 1923), pp. 17–18.
57 George Haw, *From Workhouse to Westminster: The Life Story of Will Crooks, M. P.* (London: Cassell & Co., 1907), p. 22. In 1905, Crooks, as the local MP, presided over a meeting at Poplar town hall, at which Beerbohm Tree gave a lecture on 'The Humanity of Shakespeare'. Towards the end of the meeting, a young man posed the question: 'Did Shakespeare or did he not ridicule the working classes?' Crooks, by way of an answer, 'recommended the young man to the Free Library, and broke up the meeting': *Newspaper Cuttings Relating to Shakespeare*, collected by Lemuel Matthews Griffiths, Birmingham Central Library, vol. 6, p. 55, Article 'Shakespeare and the "Common People." A Voice from Poplar' (identified as having been published in 'P.O.' and dated 29 December 1905).
58 Joseph Livesey, *The Life and Teachings of Joseph Livesey*, ed. John Pearce (London: National Temperance Publication Depot; Preston: Livesey's

Temperance Tract Depot, 1887; originally published serially in *The Staunch Teetotaller* in 1867 and 1868), p. 6.
59 Barker, *Life*, pp. 68–9, 69.
60 Frank Hodges, *My Adventures as a Labour Leader* (London: George Newnes, [1925]), p. 7.
61 *Ibid.*, pp. 12–13.
62 *Ibid.*, p. 13.
63 *Ibid.*, pp. 13–14.
64 See David J. Palmer, *The Rise of English Studies: An Account of the Study of English Language and Literature from its Origins to the Making of the Oxford English School* (London: Oxford University Press for the University of Hull, 1965), p. 35.
65 See Adams, *Memoirs*, vol. 2, p. 375.
66 *Ibid.*, vol. 2, p. 378. For Furnivall's extraordinary career, see William Benzie, *Dr. F. J. Furnivall: Victorian Scholar Adventurer* (Norman, OK: Pilgrim, 1983).
67 Adams, *Memoirs*, vol. 2, pp. 379–80.
68 *Ibid.*, vol. 2, pp. 380, 380–81.
69 See Palmer, *Rise of English*, p. 32.
70 Lowery, *Robert Lowery*, p. 114.
71 *Ibid.*, p. 115.
72 Thomas Frost, *Forty Years' Recollections: Literary and Political* (London: Sampson Low, Marston, Searle, and Rivington, 1880), p. 199.
73 Alan Richardson, *Literature, Education, and Romanticism: Reading as Social Practice, 1780–1832* (Cambridge: Cambridge University Press, 1994), p. 220.
74 Quoted in Harold Silver, *English Education and the Radicals 1780–1850* (London: Routledge & Kegan Paul, 1975), pp. 41–2, from *Plain Speaker*, 1:19 (1848), p. 148.
75 Charles Manby Smith, *The Working Man's Way in the World* (London: Printing Historical Society, 1967; originally published serially in *Tait's Edinburgh Magazine*, March 1851–May 1852; published in book form London: William and Frederick G. Cash, 1853), pp. 14, 14–15.
76 Ben Brierley, *Home Memories, and Recollections of a Life* (Manchester: Abel Heywood & Son; London: Simpkin, Marshall, & Co., [1886]), p. 38.
77 *Ibid.*, p. 39. In the absence of proper makeup, the group resorted to the chimney for material to blacken Othello's face. At the end of the play, as Othello stooped to kiss Desdemona, Brierley heard her whisper to him: 'thou munno buss me gradely, thou'll sooty my nose' (p. 42).
78 Mann, *Tom Mann's Memoirs*, p. 19.
79 Joseph Blacket, *The Remains of Joseph Blacket; Consisting of Poems, Dramatic Sketches, 'The Times, An Ode,' and a Memoir of his Life*, 2 vols. (London: Sherwood, Neely, and Jones, 1811), vol. 1, p. 4.
80 Samuel Westcott Tilke, *An Autobiographical Memoir, with remarks on the various incidents which have occurred during forty-five years of his life, and a full description of his mode of treating diseases, with reasond explanatory of his system* (London: printed for and sold by the author, 1840), p. 31. All further references are incorporated directly into the text.

81 Tilke did, in fact, appear on stage in a production of *Othello* in Cheltenham: 'I was over-persuaded by some friends to play Iago to the Othello of a Mr. P—, for the benefit of a charitable institution, and in a week after, to reverse the characters, and play for another. These were temptations to me, and revived feelings which had long been dead. I took the parts assigned me, but look back to the fact of my having done so with deep regret' (p. 122, footnote).

82 Elizabeth Davis (pseud. of Betsy Cadwaladyr), *The Autobiography of Elizabeth Davis*, ed. Jane Williams (Cardiff: Honno, 1987; originally published London: Hurst & Blackett, 1857). Cadwaladyr adopted an anglicised name after growing frustrated with the inability of those outside Wales to pronounce her own name correctly. All further references are incorporated directly into the text.

83 By an interesting coincidence, Harris worked in the same mine as another small-scale poet, Thomas Oliver (b. 1830). Oliver eventually emigrated to Australia and, while making his voyage there, he contributed a poem to the ship's daily newspaper. A fellow passenger accused him of plagiarism, convinced that he had tried to pass off a passage from Shakespeare as his own. Oliver writes: 'I solemnly declare I had never seen any of Shakespeare's works till years after that time; he could not have paid me a greater compliment I am sure, but it was no compliment after all, it was only a display of the man's ignorance, he could not have read any of Shakespeare's works': *Autobiography of a Cornish Miner* (Camborne: Camborne Printing and Stationery Co., 1911), p. 22.

84 John Harris, *My Autobiography* (London: Hamilton, Adams & Co., 1822), pp. 93–4. All further references are incorporated directly into the text.

85 John Harris, *Shakspere's Shrine, An Indian Story, Essays, and Poems* (London: Hamilton, Adams, & Co., 1866), p. 130. Taken from a series of quotations from press coverage of the competition, included in the 'Introduction to Shakspere's Tercentenary Ode'.

86 A further nice example of cultural appropriation is provided by the poet's son, John Howard Harris, who writes that, after the poet's death, he discovered the dust-covered volumes of his father's edition of Shakespeare, which 'bore evidence of good usage'. 'Before coming into his possession', he writes, 'they must have formed a portion of a collegian's equipment, from the occurrence of the words "Coll. Exon.," written on the first leaf of each': *John Harris, the Cornish Poet. The Story of His Life* (London: Partridge, [1884]), p. 67.

87 The *Birmingham Daily Gazette* reported: 'For this entertainment great preparations had been made. Flags were hung in the streets, and a handbill was issued by the Mayor, requesting the shopkeepers to close their shops at five in the evening. The Corn Exchange had assumed a very pleasing and appropriate appearance under the hands of the decorators. the back of the orchestra was ornamented with crimson drapery, in the form of which the city arms were arranged and choicest flowering shrubs' – see Harris, *Shakspere's Shrine*, p. 129.

88 Harris, *Shakspere's Shrine*, p. 134.

89 David Shaw, *Gerald Massey: Chartist, Poet, Radical and Freethinker* (London: Buckland, 1995), p. 59.

90 *Ibid.*, p. 120.
91 *Ibid.*, p. 117.
92 Gerald Massey, *The Secret Drama of Shakspeare's Sonnets Unfolded, with the Characters Identified* (Np: 'for subscribers only', 1872), p. 19.
93 *Ibid.*, p. 432.
94 *Ibid.*, p. 435.
95 Henry Morley, *A First Sketch of English Literature* (London: Cassell & Co., 1896 edition; first published 1873), p. 398.
96 Robert Spence Watson, *Joseph Skipsey: His Life and Work* (London: T. Fisher Unwin, 1909), pp. 17–18. All further references are incorporated directly into the text.
97 As we have seen in the previous chapter, Bohn was offering a 5s. edition of Chalmers' text at precisely this time.
98 Henry James based his short story 'The Birthplace', in *The Better Sort* (New York: Charles Scribner's Sons, 1903), on Skipsey's experience in Stratford. In James' story, Morris Gedge (his figure for Skipsey) comes himself to feel disillusioned with the Shakespeare myth, to the frustration of his wife, who wishes to hold on to their cosy lifestyle at the house. Gedge eventually reveals his hand to a young American couple, whose views he finds sympathetic. In an odd, Frenchly philosophical moment, Gedge speculates on the question of whether such a thing as an author really can exist:

> 'Practically' – he felt himself getting the last of his chance – 'there *is* no author; that is for us to deal with. There are all the immortal people – *in* the work; but there's nobody else.'
> 'Yes,' said the young man – 'that's what it comes to. There should really, to clear the matter up, be no such Person.' (p. 283)

99 Rogers, *Labour, Life*, p. 157. All further references are incorporated directly into the text.
100 See Peter M. Claus' entry for Margrie: www.oxforddnb.com/view/article/94697 (accessed 1 August 2006).
101 William Margrie, *A Cockney's Pilgrimage in Search of Truth* (London: Watts & Co., 1927), p. v.
102 See Margrie's obituary in *The Times*, 12 January 1960, p. 16, and Margrie's own *The Diary of a London Explorer: Forty Years of Vital London Life* (London: Watts & Co., [1934]).
103 William Margrie, *A Camberwell Man: Being a Record of the Beneficent Activities of Horatio Chucklewit, J. P., Pork Butcher, Orator, Patriot, and Children's Champion* (London: Watts & Co., 1926), p. 9. Where Margrie's texts are not in some way directly autobiographical I have included them in the general section of my bibliography.
104 William Margrie, *The Mighty Heart: A Survey of England as It Is and a Vision of What It Might Be* (London: Watts & Co., 1925), p. 43 (all quotations).
105 William Margrie, *My Eighty Years in Camberwell: Highlights – Flashes – Milestones* (London: William Margrie, [1958?]), p. 4.

106 Margrie, *Diary*, p. 10 (all quotations).
107 *Ibid.*, p. 11.
108 William Margrie, *English Grass: Signifying the Soul and Soil of England* (London: Watts & Co., 1936), p. 40.
109 *Ibid.*, pp. 62–3.
110 Margrie, *Mighty Heart*, p. 19.
111 Margrie, *Camberwell Man*, p. 40.
112 *Ibid.*, p. 41.
113 *Ibid.*, p. 43.

CHAPTER 4

Political Shakespeare

In one of the most frequently quoted passages from his *Reflections on the Revolution in France*, Edmund Burke dwells at length on what he refers to as 'the atrocious spectacle of the 6 October 1789',[1] when, as he says, history records that the king and queen of France

> lay down, under the pledged security of public faith, to indulge nature in a few hours of respite, and troubled, melancholy repose. From this sleep the queen was first startled by the voice of the sentinel at her door, who cried out to her to save herself by flight – that this was the last proof of fidelity he could give – that they were upon him, and he was dead. Instantly he was cut down. A band of cruel ruffians and assassins, reeking with his blood, rushed into the chamber of the queen, and pierced with a hundred strokes of bayonets and poniards the bed, from whence this persecuted woman had but just time to fly almost naked, and, through ways unknown to the murderers, had escaped to seek refuge at the feet of a king and husband, not secure of his own life for a moment.[2]

As Jonathan Bate has pointed out, Burke provides a literary context for his evocative description of the revolutionaries' night-time raid when, in setting up the passage, he refers to Louis XVI's rejection of an approach from the National Assembly, by observing that they had held up to his lips not 'the balm of hurt minds', but 'the cup of human misery full to the brim'.[3] The 'balm of hurt minds' is, of course, 'the innocent sleep ... sore labour's bath' and Burke is quoting from Act 2, scene 2 of *Macbeth*. What he does here, then, as Bate argues, is to create a link in the reader's mind between the near-murder of the French royal couple and their attendants, on the one hand, and the murder of Duncan and his attendants, on the other. As Bate observes, Burke forges 'an association between sleeplessness and regicide, which will be invaluable for his subsequent argument. The power of allusion is such that it is almost as if he is comparing the assassination of Duncan to the execution of Louis XVI even before the latter event has taken place.'[4]

Burke meditates directly on the relation between historical events and dramatic representation elsewhere in the *Reflections*. He argues that the treatment of the French royal family is so extreme that no morally minded writer in a properly civilised (which is to say, non-revolutionary) society could possibly consider representing it sympathetically on the stage: 'Poets who had to deal with an audience not yet graduated in the school of the rights of men, and who must apply themselves to the moral constitution of the heart, would not dare to produce such a triumph as a matter of exultation.' Conversely, in the face of the real events of 6 October, he finds himself somewhat embarrassed by the fact that he has himself in the past been deeply moved by theatrical performances, considering 'the tears that Garrick formerly, or that Siddons long since, have extorted from me' to be 'the tears of folly'.[5] Burke thus, in a sense, invokes theatricality to sharpen the focus of the particular tragedy of the French royal family, while also disavowing theatricality as a way of indicating that the tragedy is so great that it finally exceeds the boundaries of drama.

Paine picks up on the theatrical aspect of Burke's writing in replying to the *Reflections* in his *Rights of Man*. The account of the attack on the royal family is, for Paine, the work precisely of a would-be dramatist, rather than of a credible historian:

> As to the tragic paintings by which Mr Burke has outraged his own imagination, and seeks to work upon that of his readers, they are very well calculated for theatrical representation, where facts are manufactured for the sake of show, and accommodated to produce, through the weakness of sympathy, a weeping effect. But Mr Burke should recollect that he is writing History, and not *Plays*; and that his readers will expect truth, and not the spouting rant of high-toned exclamation.[6]

He further argues, in the same vein, that he 'cannot consider Mr Burke's book in scarcely any other light than a dramatic performance', as he has taken 'poetical liberties [in] omitting some facts, distorting others, and making the whole machinery bend to produce a stage effect'.[7] Where Burke invokes *Macbeth* to gain sympathy for the king and queen of France, Paine replies with a Shakespearean invocation of his own: 'if the age of aristocracy, like that of chivalry, should fall, (and they had originally some connection), Mr Burke, the trumpeter of the Order, may continue his parody to the ends, and finish with exclaiming, "*Othello's occupation's gone!*"'[8]

We have seen in Chapter 2 of this study that the battle between Burke and Paine set in motion an ongoing series of initiatives and counter-initiatives aimed at drawing the common reader to one or other side of the political divide. The two writers' opposing deployments of Shakespeare also found echoes across the century. Jonathan Bate, again, has noted that, for example, anti-radical cartoonists quickly found their way to connecting Paine with *King Lear*'s 'Mad Tom', and he observes that, in James Gillray's *The Rights of Man* (May 1791), Paine is portrayed as a figure shouting 'Fathom and a half! Fathom and a half! Poor Tom!' As Bate writes, the 'identification stuck, for it was soon used by other caricaturists, who no longer needed to quote directly from *Lear*'.[9] But, as we have seen Paine himself demonstrate, Shakespeare could be mobilised by radicals just as easily as by conservatives and, in this chapter, I explore the ways in which working-class writers across the century sought to make use of Shakespeare to further a (broadly defined) radical agenda.

In an article on 'Shakespeare and Radicalism', Antony Taylor has noted that the 'lack of hard knowledge about the personal details of Shakespeare's life ... helped reformers reconstruct an imaginary Shakespeare, allowing them to project plebeian fantasies on to the sparse details of his biography'.[10] There is certainly much evidence to support Taylor's contention. To take a handful of instances: in 1834, Ebenezer Elliott, the 'corn law rhymer', asked in his volume of poems, *The Splendid Village*, 'why should we wonder, if mechanics write well in these days?', pointing out that 'a wool-comber, Shakspeare by name, hundreds of years ago, [wrote] better than any body else, rich or poor, learned or unlearned, before or since'.[11] Six years later, the *Chartist Circular* declared that 'natural genius is a very common gem among the poor, and *belong[s] almost exclusively to the working masses*' (italics in original). As proof of this assertion, the *Circular* noted that 'Burns, the poet, was a Paisley ploughman', 'Bloomfield, the poet, was an English shoemaker' and 'the father of Shakspeare was a butcher'.[12] At the middle of the century, Mary Smith went to London for the Great Exhibition and she also took in Westminster Abbey, writing of her visit: 'The immortal dead of England are there, if not in their urns, in their effigies, inciting the uplifted eyes of the youth of both sexes, and of all classes and conditions. Our noblest Shakespere was a poor man's child.'[13] Even the Cornish poet John Harris, in what we have seen is a rather anodyne 'Tercentenary Ode' to Shakespeare, characterised the playwright as 'Labour's noblest son, –/ The people's honour, leader, champion strong; / the glory of the soil'.[14] In the same year, an event held at the Theatre Royal, Drury Lane, to raise money for the People's Shakspeare Memorial Fund, James Bruton delivered a poem in which he praised Shakespeare as a 'wondrous man! . . . / Sprung from no aristocracy of birth; –/ But lowly born!'[15] Two years later, in April 1866, the *Leicester Chronicle and Mercury* reported on a Shakespeare birthday celebration where a certain A. Garland recited a poem linking his own humble origins with those of the playwright:

> Shakespere! for long years thy praises have been sung,
> In various lands by many a powerful tongue;
> E'en kings and nobles rich and great agree,
> To offer homage to thy minstrelsy;
> How then shall I an unknown working man,
> Who far from thee, absorbed, admiring scan,
> Thy beauteous verse, study thy works sublime,
> E'en in thy praises tune my tongue to rhyme?
> I have a right, a kindred right I claim,
> Though rank nor titles gild my humble name,
> 'Tis from his class, the class the proud discard,
> For Shakespere was himself the people's bard.[16]

These examples, taken together, illustrate the manner in which, in some circles in the nineteenth century, Shakespeare was granted the status of a card-carrying member of the working class. This class co-option of the playwright facilitated the deployment of his work as a form of radical text over the course of the century. A notable example of such deployment is provided by Robert Lowery (1809–63). In April 1834, the *Newcastle Chronicle* reported that, in a speech delivered at a meeting on Newcastle Town Moor on the fourteenth of the month, Lowery had observed of those activists gathered on the moor that they 'were men of the same passions and the same dimensions as their oppressors; they were fed on the same food and partook of the same air with them; if they were pricked would they not bleed, and if they were wronged should they not revenge themselves . . . ?', at which, the crowd cheered.[17] In Chapter 3, I suggested that the entire occasion of John Harris' 'Tercentenary Ode' could be seen as a kind of multi-layered subaltern moment, but I also noted that this was, perhaps, foisting quite a heavy critical burden onto a rather slight piece of poetry. Here, however, we encounter a rather more broad-shouldered cultural moment. Lowery identifies his working-class audience with the ethnically outcast Shylock of *The Merchant of Venice*. Just as Shylock asserts his right to be considered as being as fully human as his Christian oppressors, so Lowery asserts the right of his class to be regarded the equals of their rulers. And just as Shylock's assertion of equivalence rather darkly raises the spectre of vengeance in the face of wrong, so too does Lowery's.

Robert Lowery was, at least for much of his life, a confirmed Chartist, representing the Newcastle association at national meetings, and serving as a 'Chartist missionary' in Cornwall and Dublin.[18] In the 1830s and 1840s, Chartism served as the principal point of focus for radical activity in Britain. The Reform Act of 1832 was a great disappointment to working-class political activists, as it offered only a very limited extension of the franchise and it failed to effect real change within the political system. The People's Charter itself (from which the movement derived its name) was published on 8 May 1838, and it called for universal male suffrage (without a property qualification); ballots to be held in secret; annual parliaments; members of parliament to be placed on salary; and equal electoral districts. The demands were resoundingly rejected by parliament, and the government continued to refuse the Chartists' demands up to and including 1848, after which point the movement went into decline. While it failed to achieve its most tangible aims, however, the Chartist movement did, for an extended period, succeed in galvanising working-class support for a reformist politics. As Martha Vicinus has observed:

> The Chartist promise was so total that for a time it absorbed all other working-class activity; political, trade union, and cultural. From Brighton to Aberdeen, working men and women met weekly to seek the salvation of their class through their Chartist Association; Chartism became a way of life, a rich and varied experience that had a profound impact on its participants.

Vicinus notes that Chartism prompted the creation of 'a class-based literature, written by and for the people'.[19] Within the context of this greater cultural project, Shakespeare might be said to have become almost a kind of literary patron saint for the Chartist movement, invoked repeatedly in a variety of contexts. Returning to the *Chartist Circular*, we find the journal's writers frequently deploying Shakespeare to serve their political ends. The 11 July 1840 issue of the periodical strikingly anticipates the UK and US 'culture wars' of the 1980s when it notes that 'gentlemen critics complain that the union of poetry with politics is always hurtful to politics, and fatal to the poetry', before going on to assert that 'these great connoisseurs must be wrong, if Homer, Dante, Shakspeare, Milton, Cowper, and Burns were poets'. The writer continues by asking:

> What is poetry but impassioned truth – philosophy in its essence – the spirit of that bright consummate flower, whose root is in our bosoms? Are there no politics in 'Hamlet[']? Is not 'Macbeth,' – is not the drama of 'Wallenstein,' and a hundred other works of great authors, sublime political treatises[?][20]

The writer of the article emphasises the point being made by offering three quotations from the history plays: two from *1 Henry IV* and one from *3 Henry VI*. The first two quotations are concerned with sleep – or, rather, with *wakefulness*, specifically the wakefulness of kings, contrasted with their subjects' happy slumbers: King Henry's 'How many thousand of my poorest subjects / Are at this hour asleep ... Uneasy lies the head that wears a crown' and Prince Harry's 'Why doth the crown lie there upon his pillow, / Being so troublesome a bedfellow? . . . Like a rich armour worn in heat of day, / That scald'st with safety'. The final quotation again offers a contrast between the troubled world of the monarch and the simple pleasures enjoyed by the poorest of his subjects:

> Gives not the hawthorn bush a sweeter shade
> To shepherds looking on their seely sheep
> Than doth a rich embroidered canopy
> To kings that fear their subjects' treachery?
> O yes, it doth – a thousandfold it doth.
> And to conclude, the shepherd's homely curds,
> His cold thin drink out of his leather bottle,
> His wonted sleep under a fresh tree's shade,
> All which secure and sweetly he enjoys,
> Is far beyond a prince's delicates,
> His viands sparkling in a golden cup,
> His body couched in a curious bed,
> When care, mistrust, and treason waits on him.

In context, these speeches are complexly framed, and such moments as these – Henry V's disguised midnight ramble on the eve of Agincourt is, of course, another example – operate after the fashion of a kind of literary necker cube, turning sympathy now one way, now another. Prince Harry's tender meditations on the burdens of kingship are, for example, a prelude to his taking the crown from his sleeping father's side and placing it on his own head, imagining his father's sleep as an anticipation of his death – the wish, as the awoken king chides him, being father to the thought. The *Chartist Circular*'s invocation of these passages out of context has the effect of flattening Shakespeare's text, so that we lose the highly textured ambiguity of the original. At the same time, however, it is hard not to admire the roguish inversion which the *Circular* performs here. The words of kings are made to speak against kingship and for the virtues of the lives of ordinary people. The speeches, intended in context to draw sympathy – albeit tempered sympathy – to the plight of rulers, are offered fully at face value and therefore create, we might say, an inversion of the values of the original. It really *is* better, the journal suggests, to lie 'in smoky cribs, / Upon uneasy pallets', to be 'the wet sea-boy' sleeping, to 'snore out the watch of night', to gain 'sweeter shade' from the hawthorn bush, to drink from the 'leather bottle' rather than the 'golden cup', to 'sleep under a fresh tree's shade' (and equally, we might say, 'subjects' treachery' and treason are to be celebrated, rather than feared). The strategy employed here is not unlike that we have seen Paine use against Burke, where the Irishman's subtle invocation of *Macbeth* is met with the radical's transvaluing of Othello's anguished cry of lost identity, so that it becomes a trilling expression of empty affect, lamenting a crumbling, decadent order.

The *Chartist Circular* made use of Shakespeare to further its political programme in other ways as well. Just as Robert Lowery adapted Shylock's speech to a contemporary political context, so too did the *Circular* rewrite well-known Shakespearean passages to turn them to new political ends. The 16 May 1840 issue of the journal presented its readers with a meditation on 'The Seven Stages of Whiggery', lambasting the supposed reformers for their failures. In power, the Whigs were tyrannical, 'With fair round numbers, by fat places bought, / With acts coercive, Ireland still in chains, / Full of crude laws and modern quackeries'. Finally, they had lapsed into 'second childishness and mere oblivion, / Sans power, sans fame, sans friends, sans everything'.[21] The writer of the 'Seven Stages' is presumably operating from the assumption that the journal's working-class readers will be likely to have a knowledge of Shakespeare's original, since such knowledge would sharpen the power of the parody.

Like many such journals, the *Chartist Circular* had its brief day in the sun and then perished, having run for 146 issues between September 1839 and July 1842.[22] A political publication with rather more staying power was Feargus O'Connor's *Northern Star*, which ran from 1838 until 1852, achieving a peak sales figure of some 50,000 copies. On 25 April 1840 – just past Shakespeare's birth / deathday – the *Star* initiated a new series in its poetry column, headed 'Chartism, From Shakspeare'. The series continued for several issues, and it offered quotations from the playwright which resonated with the political debates of the day. In the first instalment, all of the quotations were taken from *1 Henry IV*. Some were simple truisms, of the kind that would have appealed as much to a Samuel Tilke or a William Dodd as to any card-carrying radical: 'Tell truth and shame the devil', 'Out of the nettle danger, we pluck the flower safety', 'The better part of valour is discretion.' As in the case of the *Chartist Circular*, little attention was paid to the context of the quotes reproduced, but it is noteworthy that the bulk of them were taken from speeches by Hotspur: a potent (if admonitory) role model for the aspiring rebel. Many of the quotations resonated with the *Northern Star*'s own particular programme. So Hotspur's 'I am whipp'd and scourg'd with rods, / Nettled, and stung with pismires, when I hear / Of this vile politician' omits the immediately following name 'Bolingbroke', presumably so that the reader can mentally insert in its place 'Melbourne' or the name of some other detested member of the government. Hotspur's swaggering impetuosity seems to have held a particular appeal for a journal that aligned itself solidly with the 'physical force' wing of Chartism. Thus, his rejection of the charms of Lady Percy find a place here: 'This is no world / To play with mammets, and to tilt with lips; / We must have bloody noses, and crack'd crownes, / And pass them current too.' Worcester's complaint to King Henry that 'being fed by us, you used us so / As that ungentle gull, the cuckoo's bird, / Useth the sparrow . . . '[23] also assumes a broader meaning as, cut adrift from the context of internecine aristocratic feuding, it becomes a general comment on a voracious ruling class feasting on the fruits of others' labours. As in the case of some of the quotations taken from Hotspur, Worcester's speech also serves to justify direct physical action: 'We were enforc'd, for safety sake, to fly / Out of your sight, and raise this present head'.[24]

The second instalment of 'Chartism from Shakespeare' included quotations from a wider range of plays: *Coriolanus, Julius Caesar, Antony and Cleopatra* and *King John*. The techniques of deployment remain much the same. The First Citizen's 'We are accounted *poor* citizens; the patricians, *good*. What authority surfeits on, would relieve us. . . I speak this in hunger for bread, not in thirst for revenge' is a predictable enough inclusion from *Coriolanus*, but also reproduced is Volumnia's 'Had I a dozen sons, – each in my love alike . . . I had rather had eleven died nobly for their country, than one voluptuously surfeit out of action'. Volumnia is, of course, fiercesome in her support of the Roman patrician order, but the point of attraction of the quote is that it offers an exhortation to direct action. Something similar might be said of many of the other quotations deployed here. For example, the following speech from Lepidus is reproduced from *Antony and Cleopatra*:

> Noble friends,
> That which combined us was most great, and let not
> A leaner action rend us. What's amiss
> May it be gently heard. When we debate
> Our trivial difference loud, we do commit
> Murder in healing wounds. Then, noble partners,
> Touch you the sourest points with sweetest terms,
> Nor curstness grow to the matter.[25]

Lepidus is, of course, a thoroughly ineffectual character. His efforts to reconcile his fellow triumvirs Antony and Caesar prove ultimately to be futile and he himself is deposed by Caesar, who annexes his revenue. But, again, the point of attraction of the speech is the face-value message it conveys in a Chartist rather than a Shakespearean context. Like all radical movements, Chartism was riven with disagreement, most notably between its constitutional and its physical force wings. So, Lepidus' speech offers a plea for unity, for division to be expressed within the confines of the movement itself and for it to be expressed in conciliatory tones. (We might also say, of course, that, had the Chartists read their Shakespeare a touch more closely, they would have seen that this would not be possible.)

'Chartism from Shakespeare' continued for several more issues of the *Northern Star*.[26] By 23 May 1840, some of the quotations were explicitly being framed in a specific contemporary context. An entire scene (1.3) of *2 Henry IV* was included in this issue. The scene presents a discussion between the Archbishop of York, Thomas Mowbray, Lord Hastings and Lord Bardolph. At issue is their intended uprising against the king and whether the time is right for such a bold move. Lord Bardolph is deeply cautious, worrying that, though Northumberland has promised decisive support, the rising would be futile if that support should fail to materialise. The spirit of Harry Percy haunts proceedings, as the archbishop, concurring with Bardolph, observes that 'indeed, / It was young Hotspur's case at Shrewsbury'. The argument for action finally wins the day but, of course, as Bardolph feared, Northumberland proves unreliable and the planned rising fails, with the leaders being arrested. The *Star* reproduces the scene under the heading 'Frost and Physical Force'.[27] The reference here is to events that had occurred in Newport, Wales, on 4 November in the previous year (1839). John Frost was a linen draper in Newport, who had identified himself closely with the Chartist cause. Prompted by the arrest and sentencing of the popular radical leader Henry Vincent, Frost placed himself at the head of a group of armed volunteers, who sought to take over the town. W. E. Adams notes in his memoir of the times that

> the attempt at Newport was an entire failure. A great storm in the hills delayed the march of the reputed insurgents, frustrated the intended surprise, and enabled the authorities to prepare for the defence of the town. But much blood was shed, and some dozen lives were lost, during the attack on the Westgate Hotel.[28]

One of the other factors that severely hampered Frost's campaign was that those under his command were to have been one of three groups launching a co-ordinated attack within the town. The other leaders were William Jones and Zephaniah Williams. These other two groups either arrived late or never appeared, leaving Frost's men to carry forward the action on their own, against the odds. Frost, Jones and Williams were all sentenced to be hanged, drawn and quartered, though this was subsequently commuted to transportation for life to Van Diemen's Land. The parallels between the

Shakespearean scenario and the history of Frost's misbegotten campaign are abundantly clear. Again, we find an aristocratic conflict being reconfigured in the context of the journal, so that it offers comment on a contemporary radical situation. What is particularly striking here is that the abstracted Shakespeare scene is used to rehearse a set of genuine issues for the *Star*'s activist readers: When is the right time for action? How can insurrectionary conflicts be properly co-ordinated? Can allies be trusted to deliver on their promises? The journal returned to Frost's case in a further instalment of its series, on 6 June 1840. Among the crop of quotes included in the issue is one from *2 Henry VI*, in which King Henry laments the fate of Humphrey Duke of Gloucester, beginning 'Thou never did'st them wrong, nor no man wrong' and concluding

> Even so myself bewails good Gloster's case,
> With sad unhelpful tears; and with dimm'd eyes
> Look after him, and cannot do him good;
> So mighty are his vowed enemies.[29]

The passage is given the heading 'Frost's Case', and it effectively uses the Shakespeare text to offer a simple expression of human sympathy with the condemned man's plight.

In the year following the appearance of the 'Chartism from Shakespeare' series in the *Northern Star*, a group of radicals broke away from the main Leicester Chartist organisation and set up a rival branch, to which they gave the name the 'Shakespearean Chartist Association'. Over the course of the year the membership grew, reaching a peak of about 3,000.[30] The choice of name was not entirely motivated by literary concerns. The title was effectively derived from their meeting place: the Shakespearean Room at the Leicester Amphitheatre. However, from the very first, the group did have strong connections with the playwright. They met two or three times a week to hear lectures on a variety of subjects, including the works of Shakespeare, with portions of the plays being read out. Together they compiled and published a *Shakespearean Chartist Hymnbook*, which sold for 3d.[31]

The leader of the Shakespearean Chartists was Thomas Cooper, an extraordinary figure whose life precisely encompasses a broad range of the experiences which we have identified as being characteristic of the nineteenth-century working-class reader and Shakespeare enthusiast. Born in Leicester in 1805, he was the illegitimate son of a dyer, who died when Cooper himself was still a child. He attended two local dame schools, the second of which was run by 'Old Gatty', 'an expert and laborious teacher of the art of reading and spelling'.[32] He next attended a National School, experiencing the monitorial system at firsthand and noting that 'the course of instruction was limited to reading the Scriptures, writing, and the first four rules of arithmetic, simple and compound' (p. 14). His mother moved house when he was ten years old, and he had a final spell of formal education at a school run by 'Daddy Briggs', who provided him with instruction free of charge in exchange for Cooper serving as his assistant.

Cooper borrowed books from the other boys attending Briggs' school, including 'Enfield's Speaker, and Mavor's British Plutarch, and the abridgment of Goldsmith's Histories of England, Greece, and Rome'. In addition to these volumes there was *Robinson Crusoe, Philip Quarll* and ' "Salmon's Geography," containing the Lord's Prayer in thirty languages' (p. 33). His schoolmates were not his only resource for reading matter. The woman at the local shop where he went to buy pencils and water-colours kept a circulating library and he writes:

from her shelves I drew the enchanting 'Arabian Nights,' and odd plays of Shakspeare, Dryden, and Otway, and Cook's Voyages, and the Old English Baron; and the Castle of Otranto, and Guiscard; and the Bravo of Venice; and Hardenbras and Haverill; and Valentine's Eve; and the Castles of Athlin and Dunbayne; and the Scottish Chiefs – and a heap of other romances and novels that would require pages even to name. (p. 34)

Like Christopher Thomson, Cooper developed a passion for Primitive Methodism in his teens. He found himself 'getting into secret places twenty times in a day, to pray for the pardon of my sins' (p. 38). Again like Thomson, what finally caused him to react against the church was his elders' opposition to his 'reading any book but the Bible, unless it was a "truly religious book." ' Cooper 'rebelled completely' and 'ceased to frequent the little chapel' (p. 39).

In need of a trade, Cooper became apprenticed to a shoemaker named Joseph Clark, 'a lively young fellow of four-and-twenty, who had been in London for improvement' (p. 42). Clark was 'capricious in temper' but, as we have seen with a number of other autobiographers, Cooper's workmate opened up a new world of culture for him:

Clark ... rehearsed to me what he had seen and heard of London actors, and repeated the criticisms of the Londoners on the personations of Shakspere's characters by Kemble and Young and Mrs. Siddons, and later performers. All this directed me to a more intelligent reading of Shakspeare, for myself; though I did not yet feel the due impression of his greatness. (p. 43)

At the beginning of his twenties, Cooper embarked on an extraordinary programme of self-improvement. His aim was that, by the time he was twenty-four, he would have managed to master Latin, Greek, Hebrew and French, together with a course of Algebra, 'a large and solid course of history, and of religious evidences' and that he might be 'well acquainted . . . with the current literature of the day' (p. 57). In addition to all of this, he intended to commit to memory the entirety of *Paradise Lost* and seven of Shakespeare's plays. Cooper's programme of studies required extraordinary sacrifices and self-discipline. He writes that he was 'seldom later in bed than three or four in the morning' (p. 60) and that he 'not unfrequently swooned away, and fell along the floor, when I tried to take my cup of oatmeal gruel, at the end of my day's labour' (p. 67). But the work also had its compensations. Of his study of Shakespeare, he writes that 'the sweetness, the marvellous power of expression and grandeur of his poetry seemed to transport me, at times, out of the vulgar world of circumstances in which I lived bodily' (p. 64). There were also moments of high elation, such as when he managed to read Caesar's *De Bello Gallico* in the original Latin. He finished it sitting on a local hill at five o'clock in the morning, with the sun shining on the landscape around him. He said to himself triumphantly: 'I have made a greater conquest, without the aid of a living teacher, than the proudest warrior ever made – for I have conquered and entered into the possession of a new mind' (p. 60).

The new mind that he forged – like the young body that suffered so much in its creation – was fragile, and, predictably, Cooper eventually suffered from a complete mental and physical breakdown. In the summer of 1827, he felt the slow onset of collapse: 'I had, now, "Hamlet" entirely and perfectly by heart, and thought of beginning to commit "Lear" to memory, but dare not; and I felt also compelled to halt at the end of the fourth book of "Paradise Lost."' Eventually, he was forced to abandon the whole programme, 'for anything that required thinking brought on pain and nervous torment; and I grew very sad, and often wept, when alone' (p. 68). At one point, his state of collapse was so advanced that a neighbour felt for his pulse in vain and told his mother that he was dead: 'My eyes were closed, and I could not open them, and I could not speak. The sensation I felt was as if a huge stone lay on my chest' (p. 70).

Cooper was confined to bed for nine weeks, though he did eventually make a full recovery. Some time after this, he moved back to Leicester and he considered returning to his studies as soon as he could repossess himself of a suitable collection of books. In the interim, however, he attended a Chartist lecture and he found himself asking 'What is the acquirement of languages – what is the obtaining of all knowledge . . . compared to the real honour . . . of struggling to win the social and political rights of millions?' (pp. 146–7). Cooper threw himself as wholeheartedly into the Chartist struggle as he had into his autodidactic programme. He was instrumental in setting up the Shakespearean Chartist Association, and he lectured to his fellow activists on Shakespeare, Milton and Burns, in addition to such miscellaneous topics as Geology and Phrenology (p. 169). He also took to styling himself as the 'Shaksperean General'.[33]

Cooper's political aspirations were as wide as his intellectual ambitions. In *Radical Leicester*, Alfred Temple Patterson has noted that 'Having established absolute supremacy over the main body of Leicester Chartists, his next aims were to augment his following and increase Leicester's importance within the movement'.[34] Ultimately, he planned to carve out a central role for himself in the higher reaches of the national movement. Before he could achieve this, however, Cooper found himself caught up in series of events which led to localised rioting in the Potteries. He was arrested and charged with aiding riot and arson and, though acquitted, he was immediately re-arrested on charges of conspiracy and sedition. While fighting his legal battles, Cooper returned to Leicester and attempted to raise funds for his expenses by staging dramatic performances in conjunction with his Chartist colleagues and with the help of some professional actors. The first work to be staged was John Home's *Douglas*, and the *Leicestershire Mercury* reported that Cooper 'hoped as many as possible would attend as the surplus would go to the purchase of dresses for Hamlet, which was in course of preparation'. The *Mercury* was no supporter of Cooper and the radicals and it took a great delight in reporting that the performance of *Douglas* was a comprehensive failure. The audience was unruly and Cooper was unable to impose his authority on the crowd:

The noisy occupants of the circus would not 'listen to the voice of the charmer;' nay, when he *insisted* upon silence, they had the audacity to laugh in his face; he threatened to call in the police, and was dared to do it; and when at last, as a *dernier resort*, he ordered 'the *sensible* men present – the Chartists of the Shaksperean Association – that they should by fours seize upon the collars of single obstreperous individuals, and *drag* them out,' – the very height of disobedience manifested itself, – not a foot stirred, not a hand was raised, and absolute mutiny stared the 'General' in the face.

The *Mercury* also reported, perhaps tipping its hand, that one person in the audience 'more knowing than the rest' had shouted that 'the noisy parties were bribed by the *Leicestershire Mercury*, to cause a row!'[35] Despite the disruptions to the performance of *Douglas*, the production of *Hamlet* went ahead as planned, with Cooper himself taking the lead role – after all, as he pointed out himself, he 'knew the whole play by heart' (Cooper, *Life*, p. 228). The play was given twice and drew capacity crowds of 3,000 each night, but the performances failed to meet their intended aim of raising funds for the radical's legal expenses. As Cooper himself explained: 'the people who went on the stage as actors and actresses, all demanded payment, both for the cost of their dresses and their time, and so the income hardly covered expenses' (p. 229).

Cooper's defence failed and he was sent to Stafford Gaol to serve a two-year sentence. During his initial stint in prison he was without reading matter, but he drew on the texts he had committed to memory to pass the time in his cell. In a letter to a fellow activist, written from the jail and published in the *Northern Star*, he comments 'I committed the first three books of Paradise Lost, and the whole of Hamlet to memory, when about two and twenty years of age. These, and other delightful treasures of the "immortal mind" cannot be stolen from me'. Late at night, he recited some of the poetry to himself 'in a very low under tone, of course, – for prisoners are not allowed to speak aloud'.[36] Eventually, Cooper was permitted to resume his reading and he declares that he 'could revel in Shakspeare and Milton as soon as I got possession of my books' (p. 252). During his time in prison, he also composed an extended epic poem in Spenserian stanzas, entitled *The Purgatory of Suicides*. W. J. Linton, in *Threescore and Ten Years, 1820–1890, Recollections*, described the poem as being 'remarkable if only for being produced under prison difficulties, but also as evincing much thoughtful reading, and not without passages of true poetic beauty'.[37] This may seem to be a case of damning with faint praise, but, as anyone who has tried to read much of the poem will attest, it is a rather generous assessment. Martha Vicinus' judgment on the *Purgatory* that, while a 'monument to Cooper's learning, it is virtually unreadable' is rather closer to the mark.[38]

Towards the end of his stint as a prisoner, an anonymous benefactor – probably Lord Sandon, who had been impressed, during a visit to Stafford prison, by his knowledge of Hebrew – offered to pay for Cooper to attend Cambridge, on the sole condition that he agree to give up his political activities. Cooper declined but, in fact, his connections with radical politics diminished very considerably in his later years. He had an abiding interest in religion, and George Julian Harney noted, in writing an obituary of Cooper, that his 'mental changes from Wesleyanism to – well, I had best say – Straussism, and from ultra-scepticism to evangelist Christianity, were startling'.[39] In the years after leaving prison, Cooper concentrated largely on preaching and religious activity. The Gospel was not his only text, however, and he continued, throughout his life, to lecture on 'the Genius of Shakspeare' (Cooper, *Life*, p. 322). In 1867, at the age of sixty-two, he visited Stratford-on-Avon, and commented of it that it was 'a town in which I should certainly go to reside for life, if I were a man of fortune, and had "nothing to do" ' (p. 391).

While Cooper turned away from active involvement in the Chartist movement following his stint in prison, the movement itself effectively foundered in 1848, when parliament once more rejected the principal demands of the Charter and outlawed a mass meeting planned for London on 10 April. In the wake of the Chartist failure, radical politics fractured, with many looking to Europe for their political bearings. Among the continental figures who served as a source of inspiration for British radicals was Louis Kossuth (1802–94), the Hungarian revolutionary and nationalist, who briefly served as President of the Hungarian Republic in 1849, before the Russians intervened and he was forced into exile. He lived for a spell in England, before moving on to Italy. In 1853, a presentation was made to Kossuth at the London Tavern. It consisted of 'a neatly-constructed model of Shakespeare's house at Stratford-upon-Avon, in which was placed a splendidly-bound copy of "Knight's Shakspeare" '.[40] The front cover of the Shakespeare edition included a silver plate, on which was inscribed: 'Purchased with 9215 pence, subscribed by Englishmen and women, as a tribute to Louis Kossuth, who achieved his noble mastery of the English language, to be exercised in the noblest cause, from the page of Shakspeare.' Kossuth explained in his acceptance speech that this latter claim was literally true. During an early spell in prison he was confined on his own 'without a book to read, without a pen to write'. When he asked his jailers for some books, he was told that he could have nothing political. 'Well, give me Shakspeare, with an English grammar and a dictionary', he replied and his guards agreed to his request. Initially, with no prior knowledge of English, the volume 'was a sealed book' to Kossuth. But, in time

> the light spread over me; and I drank, with never-quenched thirst, from that limpid source of delightful instruction. Thus I learnt the little English I know. But I learnt something more besides. I learnt politics. What, politics from Shakspeare? Yes, gentlemen. What else are politics than philosophy applied to the social condition of men? and what is philosophy but knowledge of nature and of the human heart? and who ever penetrated deeper into the recesses of those mysteries than Shakspeare did?

Kossuth was one of a clutch of continental leaders who achieved iconic status for British radicals in the middle decades of the nineteenth century. Others included Giuseppe Mazzini (1805–72) and Giuseppe Garibaldi

(1807–82), republican radicals who were key figures in the *Risorgimento* (the 'resurgence' which led ultimately to the unification of the disparate collection of Italian states into a single national entity).[41] Like Kossuth before him, Garibaldi also visited England, spending 'twelve hectic days in London' in April 1864, during which he was as much feted by the establishment as he was warmly welcomed by British radicals.[42] The sense of excitement generated by the visit is nicely caught by George Elson, a chimney sweep born in Northampton in 1833. Elson notes that the Italian's 'fame and marvellous successes in the liberation of Italy aroused intense popular enthusiasm, inducing many thousands of admirers to wait for hours in London streets to witness his triumphant procession'. Elson joined the crowds to watch Garibaldi's progress through London in the carriage of the Duke of Sutherland. He writes of his experience:

At the impulse of the moment I ran up to the side of the carriage on which Garibaldi was seated, with his face turned towards the Duke, and before either were aware of my presence my cap was off, and I was waving it round his glorious head. I shall never forget how quickly he turned, and perceiving at a glance the honour I meant to pay him, instantly his face beamed with smiles.[43]

Garibaldi's visit to London coincided with the Tercentenary celebration of Shakespeare's birth. The two events became intertwined in various ways.[44] John Bedford Leno notes in his autobiography, for instance, that he 'was an active member for the committee appointed to meet ... Garibaldi, and in the movement to honour Shakspeare'.[45] Likewise, George Howell, the bricklayer born in Somersetshire in 1833, registers that on 11 April 1864, he was 'in London as one of the Garibaldi Reception Committee, and met him at the Nine Elms station' and, twelve days later, he was back in London 'to attend the Shakespeare demonstration' – an event which he helped to organise.[46] The Tercentenary celebration also became interlocked with Garibaldi's visit in a very direct fashion. Both events were mired in controversy. In the case of the Tercentenary, as we have already noted in the introduction to this study, the official committee set up to honour the playwright's birth fell prey to infighting and intrigue and, as one insider put it, 'toppled over like a house of cards'.[47] And while Garibaldi's visit was broadly welcomed by the establishment, some figures in the government began to grow anxious about his continuing presence in the country. Gladstone met with Garibaldi to express the government's concern, and the Italian left the country aboard the Duke of Sutherland's yacht on 23 April. The official reason given for his leaving was ill health, but this was widely viewed with scepticism.[48]

Garibaldi's departure thus coincided exactly with the anniversary of Shakespeare's birth. The collapse of the official Tercentenary committee had, as we have already seen, prompted a much smaller-scale initiative by a Working Men's Committee, who arranged, for the afternoon of 23 April, a tree-planting ceremony on Primrose Hill, which they proposed should thenceforth be known as 'Shakespeare's Hill'.[49] The rhetoric of the Working Men's Committee was fully in keeping with what we have seen in other sources from the time. The committee's address 'to the workmen and operatives of the United Kingdom' registered that Shakespeare 'sprang from the class to which you belong' and noted that he was 'a philosopher and poet of the loftiest order, and shows in his immortal works the invincible regard of a mighty and well-ordered intellect for truth, justice, humanity, and liberty'.[50] The oak sapling (in fact a substantial young tree) was planted by Samuel Phelps, who was regarded as 'deservedly a favourite of the London working men – having taught them to understand and enjoy Shakspeare by his high-minded management of Sadler's Wells'. At the end of his brief speech, Phelps declared: 'In the name of the workmen of England I plant this tree.'[51] The gathering on Primrose Hill to mark the Tercentenary provided a ready-made crowd for a demonstration of a different kind. As Richard Foulkes has noted: 'At the end of the ceremony a splinter group of 60–70 gathered at the top of the hill and encouraged the crowds to regroup around them, of which about 4,000 did so.'[52] The purpose of the second meeting was to stage a protest 'against the manner in which General Garibaldi had been hurried away from England, and to demand further explanations from the Government as to the cause of his hurried departure'.[53] The political demonstration was declared illegal by the police, who broke the meeting up with some measure of force.

The morphing of the Primrose Hill Tercentenary celebration into a pro-Garibaldi demonstration and its subsequent suppression by the police had significant long-term consequences. The demonstration meeting was chaired by the Cambridge-born barrister, Edmond Beales who, working in conjunction with others, carried the momentum of the Primrose Hill protest forward, ultimately founding the Reform League (with Garibaldi as honorary president), to call, once again, for substantial changes to the electoral system.[54] The right to assemble for political purposes was one of the central claims of the League, and it led to a further confrontation with the police in July 1866, when a crowd of 20,000 defied a government ban and broke through the railings at Hyde Park. In 1867, the government finally acceded to the call for reform and the franchise was extended to include 'roughly two-thirds of the male working-class population [making] the working class the majority of the national electorate'.[55]

The 1867 Act was far from perfect (it still required a property qualification and, of course, it continued to restrict the franchise to male voters only), but, as W. E. Adams noted, many radicals came to the conclusion that the principle of the legislation was worth accepting, particularly as it was felt that 'the restrictions and counterpoises . . . could be modified or even swept aside afterwards'.[56] The broadening of the franchise led, two years later, to the founding of the Labour Representation League, the object of which was

> to promote throughout the kingdom the registration of working men's votes without reference to their opinions or party bias; its aim being to organise fully the strength of the operative classes as an electoral power, so that, when necessary, it may be brought to bear, with effect, on any important political, social or industrial question in the issue of which their interests are involved. Its principal duty will be to secure the return to Parliament of qualified working men: persons who, by character and ability, command the confidence of their class, and who are competent to deal satisfactorily with questions of general interest, as well as those in which they are specifically interested.[57]

J. R. Clynes noted that the League's resolution 'was received throughout the length and breadth of Britain with a shout of gargantuan laughter. Working men in Parliament, forsooth! What would the absurd fellows think of next?' Within a year, however, a candidate – George Odger – was put forward in a by-election in Southwark and he came second to the Conservative, beating the Liberal candidate into third place. Odger (1813–77) was born in Roborough, south Devon, the son of a miner.[58] He trained as a shoemaker and worked at the craft all his life, in addition to being active in trade union affairs and radical politics. He had been a member of the Working Men's Committee responsible for the Primrose Hill celebration and was also involved in the popular welcome afforded to Garibaldi. He entered parliamentary contests on five occasions, twice withdrawing rather than run against the official Liberal candidate. He never did succeed in gaining a seat in parliament. However, in the general election of 1874, the Labour Representation League fielded twelve candidates and two were successful. As Clynes puts it, with a rather dramatic flourish: 'Thomas Burt and Alexander Macdonald, the forlorn hope of the mighty army of British workers, flung open the gates of St. Stephen's; and those gates have never been quite shut against us since.'[59] These were, effectively, the first tentative steps that would ultimately lead to the emergence of Labour as a formal political party and, ultimately, to the election of a Labour government.

In the final decades of the nineteenth century, then, the focus of radical politics shifted away from large-scale populist lobbying groups such as the Chartist Association and from influential, but still essentially peripheral, figures such as Thomas Cooper, towards the actual centre of political power in Westminster, as the first generations of left-wing activists began to gain a foothold in parliament. Many of these individuals shared the Shakespearean enthusiasms of their predecessors – even if they did not carry such enthusiasm to quite the same lengths as the 'Shakespearean General' from Leicester. As we have already seen from J. R. Clynes' account, Thomas Burt was one of the very first of this group to enter parliament, being elected Liberal MP for Morpeth in 1874 and holding his seat for a total of forty-four years, becoming a privy councillor in 1906 and ending his political career as Father of the House. Burt was a miner and trade unionist and he writes in his autobiography that 'in my wildest dreams, the idea of becoming a member of Parliament had never entered my head'. When he was approached to stand in the general election, he responded with a quote from *Titus Andronicus*: 'O! brothers, speak with possibilities, / And do not break into these deep extremes.'[60] We have already seen (in Chapter 2) that Burt had read Shakespeare in Dicks' penny-a-play issue and the experience left a deep impression on him:

Though since then over sixty years have elapsed, vividly do I remember the time and the surroundings. A new world of poetry and romance was presented to my mental vision. Except in short tags, Shakespeare was then wholly unknown to me. Often had I heard him denounced from pulpits; often had I been warned not to read his plays, the preacher not infrequently, all unconsciously, quoting him, so completely had the great dramatist's words and phrases entered into the very texture of our language.

Burt regarded Shakespeare's plays as 'among the greatest creations of the human intellect'.[61] Later in life, he attended a local debate on the subject 'Burns and Shakespeare: Which was the Greater Poet?' The case for Burns was put forcefully by a Scotsman, Dr Alexander Trotter. Burt, however, cast his lot with the playwright and, he writes, there was 'an overwhelming vote in favour of Shakespeare, some of us, indeed, being so benighted as to assert that he is the world's greatest poet'.[62]

Joseph Arch joined Burt on the Liberal benches in parliament from 1885, when he was elected MP for North West Norfolk. He had first stood for election in 1880, when he was defeated in Wilton, Wiltshire. In 1884, however, the franchise was extended to include rural labourers, a move which benefited Arch, as leader of the National Agricultural Labourers' Union. Arch was born in Barford, Warwickshire, in 1826. The village is hardly more than a half-a-dozen miles away from Stratford-on-Avon and Arch imagined that Barford was a place 'which William Shakespeare may have seen, and even entered'.[63] As we have seen in Chapter 3, Arch was introduced to Shakespeare's work by his mother, and his interest in Shakespeare endured throughout his life: 'Shakespeare and the Bible were the books I was brought up on, and I don't want any better. I have heard and read a good deal since then, but I have never come across anything to beat them.'[64] Antony Taylor notes that Arch 'began many of his speeches with a quotation from Shakespeare' and that, speaking in Stratford in 1878, he cited Shakespeare 'as an enthusiast for redistribution of wealth using King Lear's speech: "Distribution should undo excess / And each man have enough."'[65]

While Burt and Arch both served as Liberal MPs, by the turn of the century the first generation of Labour MPs was beginning to enter parliament.[66] In 1906, the *Review of Reviews* ran a feature on 'The Labour Party and the Books that Helped to Make It'. The author of the article, William T. Stead, sent a standard letter to Labour MPs, indicating that he was writing on 'the books which have been most useful to those who have fought their way up from humble beginnings to the front rank' and asking if they could offer 'some notes or memoranda ... as to the books which you found by experience most useful to you in the early days when your battle was beginning?'[67] Shakespeare appears in the MPs' lists of books again and again. John Johnson (b. 1850), coalminer and MP for Gateshead, observed: 'My first poet is Shakespeare, a constant companion. I have read Dante's work, but I fear not with the same profit' (p. 576). James Rowlands (b. 1851), watchcase maker and MP for Dartford, Kent, noted that 'After Shakespeare I absorbed Byron and Shelley, while not neglecting the minor poets' (p. 579). The bargeman W. C. Steadman (1851–1911), who represented Finsbury Central, commented: 'I have gained most of my experience in the hard school of adversity from my boyhood days upwards', but he also noted that he had 'read a large number of books', including 'the Bible, Shakespeare, and ... S. Webb, H. George, R. Blatchford, Thorold Rogers, Kingsley and Ruskin' (p. 580). Stephen Walsh (1859–1929), a Liverpool-born coalminer who served as MP for Lancashire, Ince, wrote that 'from very early years Shakespeare has been a prime and constant favourite. Falstaff, Brutus, Mark Antony, Cassius, quaint old Dogberry, and the tender half petulant, yet innocent old Verges – all these have been almost living realities with me' (p. 580). Annie Kenney (who named her son Warwick 'after Shakespeare's Warwick the Kingmaker'), the Lancashire-born suffragette, had fond memories of the role Walsh played in a dispute in 1908.[68] John Burns, the trade unionist and politician, was agitating to prevent married women from working at the pit-brow in the mining industry, and Kenney was worried about the consequences that would follow from this. She contacted Walsh and he agreed to attend a public meeting at which he debated the issue with Burns. Kenney notes that the 'discussion ended by each quoting Shakespeare, both trying to prove their case about women by using verses written by one of the world's masters of philosophy and poetry'.[69]

Walsh entered parliament in 1906 – the same year as J. R. Clynes became an MP. Clynes (1869–1949) was born in Oldham, the son of an illiterate Irish farmworker who found employment as a gravedigger in Lancashire. Clynes himself worked as a 'piecer' in a mill in Oldham, while reading voraciously in his spare time. In his autobiography, he writes that he would often 'repeat appropriate passages of poetry in time with the glide and thrust of the jennies'. He worried that, if anyone caught him, they would think he was mad, but 'the everlasting noise was my safeguard, and my small voice was swept away'.[70] Early in life he happened upon the quotation 'Be not afraid of greatness; some men are born great, some achieve greatness, and some have greatness thrust upon them'. The original context of the quotation seems not to have been registered by Clynes, as he found it genuinely inspirational: ' "Be not afraid of greatness!" What a creed! How it would upset the world if men lived up to it, I thought. I often puzzled over it; little dreaming then that a certain fame would come to me, also, in my turn' (p. 31). Clynes is being a touch modest here. His 'certain fame' was that he became a privy councillor in 1918, served as Lord Privy Seal and Deputy Leader of the House in the first Labour administration and was then appointed Home Secretary in Ramsay MacDonald's second government, in 1929.

From that first encounter with *Twelfth Night*, Clynes retained a strong interest in Shakespeare. Much of his reading was done at the Oldham Equitable Co-operative Society's library, and here Shakespeare came alive for him, as much as a writer specifically of real political substance as anything else:

I sat at the table reading Shakespeare, Ruskin and Dickens, or whatever else I could get hold of. I remember my discovery of *Julius Caesar*, and how the realisation came suddenly to me that it was a mighty political drama, not just an entertainment.

The haughty Tribune who reproved the mechanics for daring to walk abroad on a labouring day 'without the sign of their profession' was typical of many who sat on the benches of the House of Commons in my boyhood; and men of like spirit sit there yet. (p. 49)

Clynes was encouraged in his reading by the Society's librarian, who would often look over the young man's shoulder to see what book he had in hand: ' "Shakespeare!" he would murmur in satisfaction. "Stick to Shakespeare and the Bible. They're the roots of civilisation." ' Clynes concludes: 'In that drab reading-room, history became real to me, and its characters changed from dusty puppets into men and women, fanatics and patriots, many of whom had died for their beliefs. Wat Tyler and Jack Cade seemed heroes' (p. 50). Again, as in the case of the *Chartist Circular* and the *Northern Star*, Clynes' interpretation serves to drain Shakespeare's text of its rich ambiguity, since it could never in any sense be said that Cade is presented straightforwardly as a hero by the playwright, even if some complex element of sympathy forms a part of his portrayal. (And Tyler does not, of course, appear directly as a character in any of the plays.)

Clynes was able, when necessary, to turn his knowledge of Shakespeare to solid practical ends. At one point in his career as a trade union official, he was asked to negotiate with a man he characterises as 'a particularly dogged employer of the old school'. Clynes takes up the story:

With considerable persistence I succeeded in obtaining an interview with him. I quoted a line from *Much Ado About Nothing*, and he stared in astonishment. Then we plunged into a discussion about Shakespeare's comedies, which lasted us till luncheon was announced.
   Hearing the butler's voice, he started and dragged out a big gold watch.
   'Tut, tut! I'd no idea the time had gone so quickly,' he said. 'You'll stay to lunch, of course!'
   Over the fish we commenced a new argument about Shakespeare's value as a historian and, later, my host queried a remark of mine that I knew certain scenes from some of the historical plays off by heart. So, when the coffee cups had been removed, I declaimed the whole of one longish scene from *Julius Caesar* to him. (pp. 80–1)

At the conclusion of this extended discussion of Shakespeare, Clynes 'tactfully led back the conversation to the subject of the strike'. The employer quickly conceded the men's demands and Clynes was able to convey to them 'the good news that the concessions for which they had decided to fight were granted' (p. 81).

Clynes' encounter with this recalcitrant employer, who is finally accommodating in the face of the trade unionist's knowledge of Shakespeare, represents, I want to suggest, something more than just another example of the strategic deployment of Shakespeare for political ends. Clynes and his host reach an agreement because Shakespeare serves as common ground on which representatives of two distinct strata within society can meet and negotiate, both culturally and in more pragmatic, quotidian terms. The story indicates the extent to which Shakespeare had, over the course of the nineteenth century, become a common cultural property. With the dawn of a new century, however, culture – very broadly defined – would begin to shift in various ways that would make such a coming together over the shared iconic figure of Shakespeare increasingly less likely.

NOTES

1 Edmund Burke, *Reflections on the Revolution in France*, ed. Frank M. Turner (New Haven: Yale University Press, 2003), pp. 68–9.
2 *Ibid.*, p. 60.
3 *Ibid.*
4 Jonathan Bate, *Shakespearean Constitutions: Politics, Theatre, Criticism 1730–1830* (Oxford: Clarendon Press, 1989), p. 89.
5 Burke, *Reflections*, p. 69.
6 Thomas Paine, *Rights of Man, Common Sense and Other Political Writings*, ed. Mark Philp (Oxford: Oxford University Press, 1995), p. 100.
7 *Ibid.*, p. 110.
8 *Ibid.*, p. 100.
9 Bate, *Shakespearean Constitutions*, p. 99. Bate also very nicely observes that 'the complexity of Shakespeare's play works against any simplistic reading of the allusion: once it is recalled that Poor Tom is in fact Edgar, a very different complexion is put on the parallel, and one begins to call into question the appeals to "nature" of *Edmund* Burke'.
10 Antony Taylor, 'Shakespeare and Radicalism: The Uses and Abuses of Shakespeare in Nineteenth-Century Popular Politics', *Historical Journal*, 45:3 (2002), p. 362.
11 Ebenezer Elliott, *The Splendid Village: Corn Law Rhymes; and Other Poems*, 2 vols. (London: Benjamin Steill, 1834), vol. 1, p. 48.
12 'The Genius of Working Men', *Chartist Circular*, 33 (9 May 1840), p. 136 (italics in original).
13 Mary Smith, *The Autobiography of Mary Smith, Schoolmistress and Nonconformist. A Fragment of a Life* (London: Bemrose & Sons, 1892), p. 176.
14 John Harris, *Shakspere's Shrine, An Indian Story, Essays, and Poems* (London: Hamilton, Adams, & Co., 1866), p. 134. I should note, perhaps, that Harris shifts, in the poem, from the register of labour to that of aristocracy: the immediately following lines characterise Shakespeare as 'The towering prince of toil, / The matchless monarch in the realm of song'.
15 James Bruton, untitled poem included in *Addresses Delivered at the Theatre Royal, Drury Lane, in Aid of the People's Shakspeare Memorial Fund. December 5th, 6th, 8th, 9th, 10th April, 1864* (London: Thomas Hailes Lacy, [1864]), np.
16 'Shakespere's Birthday', *The Leicester Chronicle and Mercury*, 56 (28 April 1866), p. 5.

17 Robert Lowery, *Robert Lowery: Radical and Chartist*, Brian Harrison and Patricia Hollis (eds) (London: Europa, 1979) (originally published anonymously as a series of 33 articles in the *Weekly Record of the Temperance Movement*. Publication at irregular intervals between 15 April 1856 and 23 May 1857), p. 207. The reformist George Jacob Holyoake specifically advocated that those who wished to become involved in public speaking should make a careful study of Shakespeare, observing that

> The prompting of Lucio to Isabel, when pleading before Angelo for the life of her brother . . . is one of the happiest practical lessons in the art of persuasion on record. As a piece of perceptive teaching, neither the rhetoric of modern or of ancient times, so far as I have knowledge, has produced anything so wise, so concise, and yet so comprehensive, as Hamlet's directions to his players. It is a manual of delivery in miniature.

– *Public Speaking and Debate* (London: T. Fisher Unwin, nd; the first edition appears to have been published in 1849), p. 31.

18 For these details, see Brian Harrison's *DNB* entry on Lowery, www.oxforddnb.com/view/article/42341 (accessed 15 March 2006).

19 Martha Vicinus, *The Industrial Muse: A Study of Nineteenth Century British Working-Class Literature* (London: Croom Helm, 1974), p. 94.

20 'The Politics of Poets', *Chartist Circular*, 42 (11 July 1840), p. 170. For a much more extended and considered discussion of the use of Shakespeare in the *Chartist Circular* see Peter Holbrook, 'Shakespeare, "The Cause of the People", and *The Chartist Circular* 1839–1842', *Textual Practice*, 20:2 (2006), pp. 203–29 and see also, for a broader consideration of working-class journals, Paul Thomas Murphy, *Towards a Working-Class Canon: Literary Criticism in British Working-Class Periodicals, 1816–1858* (Columbus: Ohio State University Press, 1994).

21 'The Seven Stages of Whiggery', *Chartist Circular*, 34 (16 May 1840), p. 138.

22 See Holbrook, 'Shakespeare', p. 208.

23 The quotation continues to 'Sworn to us in your younger enterprise'.

24 'Chartism, From Shakespeare', *Northern Star* (hereafter *NS*), 3:128 (25 April 1840), p. 7 (all quotations).

25 'Chartism from Shakespeare', *NS*, 3:129 (2 May 1840), p. 7 (all quotations).

26 Owing to pressures of space, I pass over here the quotations included in 3:130 (9 May 1840), p. 7.

27 'Chartism from Shakespeare', *NS*, 3:132 (23 May 1840), p. 7.

28 W. E. Adams, *Memoirs of a Social Atom*, 2 vols. (London: Hutchinson, 1903), vol. I, p. 197.

29 'Chartism from the Poets', subheading 'Shakspeare', *NS*, 3:134 (6 June 1840), p. 7.

30 See Jeremy Crump, 'The Popular Audience for Shakespeare in Nineteenth-Century Leicester', in Richard Foulkes, ed., *Shakespeare and the Victorian Stage* (Cambridge: Cambridge University Press, 1986), p. 273.

31 See advert placed in the *NS*, 5:251 (3 September 1842), p. 5. Despite my best efforts in feeding variations on the title to various library catalogues, I have

failed to locate a copy of the *Hymnbook*. There is, however, clear evidence that the book was indeed published. J. A. Leatherland was, in his younger days, an avowed Chartist, but he later came to repudiate radical politics and to regret his association with the group. In his autobiography, he notes with some little embarrassment: 'a Song that I penned ... inserted in the "Chartist Hymnbook," became very popular', the first line of the song being 'Base Oppressors, break your slumbers': *Essays and Poems, with a Brief Autobiographical Memoir* (London: W. Tweedie, 1862), p. 17 (footnote).

32 Thomas Cooper, *The Life of Thomas Cooper* (Leicester: Leicester University Press, 1971; originally published London: Hodder and Stoughton, 1872), p. 7. All further references are incorporated directly into the text.

33 Thomas Cooper, letter (dated 29 August 1842) to *NS*, 5:251 (3 September 1842), p. 6.

34 Alfred Temple Patterson, *Radical Leicester* (Leicester: University College Leicester, 1954), p. 324.

35 *The Leicestershire Mercury*, 7:337 (17 December 1842), p. 3.

36 Thomas Cooper, letter (dated 30 August 1842) to *NS*, 5:251 (3 September 1842), p. 6. This letter in fact refers to his first period of confinement in the jail, prior to his being sentenced.

37 W. J. Linton, *Threescore and Ten Years, 1820–1890, Recollections* (New York: Charles Scribner's Sons, 1894), p. 41.

38 Vicinus, *Industrial Muse*, p. 110. The epic (together with Cooper's Christmas poem, *The Baron's Yule*) did, however, prompt the following contemporary comment in *Douglas Jerrold's Shilling Magazine*: 'It is now fairly a race between the classes; and I fancy that the energetic sons of the people, such as can write "The Suicide's Purgatory," [*sic*] and "The Baron's Yule," with the few hours that they wring from toil, or snatch from rest, will out-run the college-taught and castle-sheltered sons of fortune' – Mrs Leman Gillies, 'The Press and the People', *Douglas Jerrolds' Shilling Magazine*, 3 (1846), p. 254.

39 George Julian Harney, obituary for Thomas Cooper, *Newcastle Weekly Chronicle*, 12 July 1892, p. 5.

40 All quotations are taken from 'Presentation of the Shakspeare Testimonial to Kossuth'. The source is probably the *Illustrated London News*, 14 May 1853, page number unknown. I have found the material in Lemuel Matthews Griffiths, *Newspaper Cuttings Relating to Shakespeare* at the Birmingham Central Library, vol. II, p. 88.

41 When W. E. Adams visited his old comrade George Julian Harney in Cambridge, Massachusetts, in 1882, he found the walls of his friend's home decorated with pictures of his heroes and fellow radicals. Included among the portraits were images of Cobbett, Frost, Marx, Kossuth, Mazzini and Shakespeare – see Adams, *Memoirs*, vol. I, p. 224.

42 Derek Beales, 'Garibaldi in England: The Politics of Italian Enthusiasm', in J. A. Davis and P. Ginsborg, eds, *Society and Politics in the Age of the Risorgimento: Essays in Honour of David Mack Smith* (Cambridge: Cambridge University Press, 1991), p. 192.

43 George Elson, *The Last of the Climbing Boys, an Autobiography* (London: John Long, 1900), pp. 214–15. The daughter of Roger Langdon, the railwayman and self-taught astronomer, also remembered the Garibaldi excitement: 'While we were at Durston we had the pleasure of seeing Garibaldi. His train was crossed on to another line. We children were playing as usual on the bank above the station, and when Garibaldi's carriage stopped right in front of us of course we all screamed with delight, and our noise brought everybody out, and the men got so excited they crawled all over the top of the carriage and shouted for all they were worth': Roger Langdon, *The Life of Roger Langdon, Told by Himself, with Additions by his Daughter Ellen* (London: Elliot Stock, [1909]), p. 69.

44 It is an indication of the extent to which the events became intertwined that the 'Editorial' of the *Comic News* for 7 May 1864 observed that 'It was unfortunate that the Garibaldi excitement and the Shakespeare sensation should have been simultaneous. The confusion which the two names have given rise to in the vulgar mind has been very unfortunate, many people having been discovered in remote localities talking wildly of the dramatic works of William Garibaldi, and the military achievements of Giuseppe Shakspeare': cutting included in Birmingham Central Library Tercentenary Shakespeare Scrapbook, vol. 1, p. 151.

45 John Bedford Leno, *The Aftermath: With Autobiography of the Author* (London: Reeves & Turner, 1892), p. 62.

46 George Howell, 'The Autobiography of a Toiler', 6 vols., manuscript, George Howell Collection, Bishopsgate Institute, London, vol. F, 6th page of section headed 'Chapter VI'. For Howell's involvement in the Primrose Hill affair, see the signatories to the prospectus of the event, included in Stratford Records Office (hereafter SRO), file ER1/107.

47 Henry Vizetelly, *Glances Back Through Seventy Years: Autobiographical and Other Reminiscences* (London: Kegan Paul, Trench, Trübner & Co., 1893), vol. 1, p. 110. Vizetelly was a member of the committee and he provides a full account of the controversy. See also Richard Foulkes' excellent account, in *The Shakespeare Tercentenary of 1864* (London: Society for Theatre Research, 1984).

48 For these details, see Foulkes, *Tercentenary*, pp. 42–3.

49 The *Morning Star* reported on an excited supporter of the name change: ' "Shakspere's 'ill!" cried the enthusiast with outstretched finger. "Lor!" replied [his] practical friend, "I thought he was dead!" ' 2 May 1864, included in SRO ER1/58 (vol. 1).

50 Prospectus for the Tercentenary event, SRO, ER1/107.

51 *Illustrated London News*, 30 April 1864, p. 422, included in SRO DR330. The sapling, incidentally, did not thrive; the Society for Theatre Research planted a replacement oak at the quarcentenary – see Richard Foulkes, 'Shakespeare and Garibaldi on Primrose Hill', *Camden History Review*, 9 (1981), p. 16.

52 Foulkes, *Tercentenary*, p. 43.

53 *The Times*, 25 April 1864, p. 7, included in SRO, DR330.

54 See also Taylor, 'Shakespeare and Radicalism', p. 378.

55 Richard W. Schoch, *Not Shakespeare: Bardolatry and Burlesque in the Nineteenth Century* (Cambridge: Cambridge University Press, 2002), p. 162, n. 23.
56 Adams, *Memoirs*, vol. 2, p. 534.
57 Quoted in J. R. Clynes, *Memoirs, 1869–1924* (London: Hutchinson, 1937), p. 21.
58 General details of Odger's career are taken from F. M. Leventhal's *DNB* entry www.oxforddnb.com/view/article/20539 (accessed 14 November 2006).
59 Clynes, *Memoirs*, p. 22.
60 Thomas Burt, *Thomas Burt M. P., D. C. L., Pitman & Privy Councillor: An Autobiography* (London: T. Fisher Unwin, 1924), p. 210.
61 *Ibid.*, p. 143.
62 *Ibid.*, p. 189.
63 Joseph Arch, *The Autobiography of Joseph Arch*, ed. John Gerald O'Leary (London: MacGibbon & Kee, 1966; originally published London: Hutchinson, 1898), p. 19.
64 *Ibid.*, p. 22.
65 Taylor, 'Shakespeare and Radicalism', p. 369.
66 Robert Smillie (1857–1940) might be added to the list of Labour MPs discussed here. He too had a life-long interest in Shakespeare and he notes in his autobiography: 'I read and re-read the great plays. It was a new and enchanting world. Those tragedies and comedies, to an ardent young mind which had hitherto been "cribb'd, cabin'd, and confin'd," caught and held in the iron clutch of the industrial machine, were a sheer revelation' and 'I can quote, if need be, freely and extensively from the best passages of his works, and a Shakespearean quotation has often stood me in good stead when I lacked words of my own': *My Life for Labour* (London: Mills & Boon, 1924), p. 50 (both quotations). I have, however, excluded Smillie from the general discussion here, as he was born in Belfast and grew up in Glasgow, and so falls outside the geographical parameters of my study. (Smillie, incidentally also anticipates BBC Radio 4's *Desert Island Discs*, as he writes in *My Life*: 'Outside the boards of the Bible I know of no greater mental stimulus than Shakespeare. If I were doomed to dwell on a desert island alone for the rest of my life, with two books, those are the two I would pack', pp. 50–2.)
67 William T. Stead, 'The Labour Party and the Books that Helped to Make It', *Review of Reviews*, 33:198 (June 1906), p. 568 (further references are incorporated directly into the text). Because these pieces are so short and are concerned exclusively with books, I have not treated them as autobiographical texts.
68 See Brian Harrison's *DNB* entry for Kenney, www.oxforddnb.com/view/article/34285 (accessed 15 March 2006).
69 Annie Kenney, *Memories of a Militant* (London: Edward Arnold, 1924), p. 131.
70 Clynes, *Memoirs*, pp. 31–2, 32 (further references are incorporated directly into the text).

CHAPTER 5

Decline and fall

In July 1901, the journalist J. E. MacManus made a trip from London to Stratford-on-Avon. In a tongue-in-cheek report on his journey, he noted that, when in Stratford, 'it is difficult to get away from Shakespeare'. 'Little boys', he wrote,

> stop you and recite Shakespeare by the yard in the hope of pennies. I conciliated one of these tender victims with a sixpence, and asked him his private opinion of the poet. 'Wot do I think of 'im?' he whispered hoarsely, 'why, we 'ates 'im worse'n the school board inspector.'

MacManus returned to London, arriving in Euston at 10:30 p.m. He concluded that a run up to Stratford 'would be an ideal trip for a fine summer's day if one could eliminate the castles and Shakespeare'.[1]

MacManus was, of course, offering a flippantly amusing account of his day trip and, reading his article, we might be prompted to wonder, among other things, why a young Warwickshire schoolboy should have been speaking to him in an accent that appears to anticipate the Dick van Dyke sub-dialect of Cockney. Nevertheless, his schoolboy's hatred of Shakespeare does have a certain ring of truth to it. We have seen (in Chapter 1) that, while working-class children were unlikely to have encountered Shakespeare in school throughout most of the 1800s, the situation began to change as the century drew to a close and such children spent more and more time in the classroom – driven there, in many cases, precisely by the dreaded school board inspector. Shakespeare, increasingly, became part of the curriculum to which these children were exposed and the nature of that exposure was often unsatisfactory. Jonathan Rose has observed that 'If Shakespeare still had a proletarian following in the nineteenth century, it melted away in the twentieth' and he touches on an argument suggesting that one reason for this may have been the fact that 'a bureaucratized system of compulsory education reduced Shakespeare to tedious classroom drill'.[2] There is some evidence to support this view. The London Shakespeare League sponsored a meeting at University College in May 1906 to discuss the topic of Shakespeare and education. The meeting was addressed by Dr C. W. Kimmins, chief inspector of the Education Department of the London County Council, and by Israel Gollancz, professor of English at King's College, London. Kimmins observed that 'It was a melancholy thing that the introduction of Shakespeare in ... schools was usually through preparation of a piece for examination purposes, with difficult and obscure passages'. 'Such a method', he noted 'often created a distaste for literature in the schools'.[3] When Gollancz addressed the meeting he offered some practical examples which confirmed that much Shakespeare teaching did, indeed, amount to 'tedious classroom drill'. The King's professor drew upon a letter he had received from a frustrated schoolmaster:

A stuffy school classroom on a hot summer's afternoon; twenty healthy schoolboys sit in order, each with his eyes fixed on one of the pages of a badly printed book dog-eared from much use and smudged with ink. Upon all their faces is a look of unutterable mourning and melancholy. There is dead silence in the room save for the buzzing of flies and the droning of a voice that would have sounded appropriate by the shores of Styx. The boys are studying 'The Winter's Tale'...

Reaching the lines 'O Proserpine! / For the flowers now that, frighted, thou let'st fall' the class stops, while the master reads out an extended series of notes on the word 'frighted'. The notes deal with 'the word from the point of view of comparative philology, etymology, historical grammar, orthography, and pronunciation'. Gollancz's correspondent notes that one boy 'in the midst of all this wasted learning, tempted by the magic of the lines, would turn back to the text, but he stays his hand, for he knows that "distinction in Shakespeare has to be obtained by sticking to the notes"'.[4] Another school teacher had written to Gollancz to say that he 'knew of a master who always set his imposition in Shakespeare ..., and the boys spent their wet evenings in writing out "Macbeth," and sold the manuscript to their comrades at 1d. per hundred lines'.[5]

While the experience of Shakespeare as mind-numbing classroom drudgery was common enough in the period, it was by no means universal. Jonathan Rose himself notes that 'it seems unfair to blame the 1870 Education Act for the decline of the people's bard. In school memoirs, some of the most rhapsodic passages harken back to Shakespeare recitals in class'.[6] Again, there is evidence to support this contrary view. In Chapter 1, we noted Daisy Cowper's happy experience of studying and acting out scenes from *The Merchant of Venice* and *As You Like It* in the classroom.[7] Likewise, when Charles Morley published *Studies in Board Schools* in 1897, he reported of a working-class London school he visited that, when the teacher called for a recitation

Many hands were held out, from which one was selected – that of a girl of thirteen, with a most intellectual headpiece. She threw out her chest, tossed back her head, and began – in tones that thrilled me by their depth and fire – Henry V.'s fine reply to Westmorland on the field of Agincourt.

Morley noted that, following the recitation, 'the master bombarded them all with questions on Henry, the Salic Law, and treaties. I was quite astonished to hear the quick replies'.[8]

Again, as with J. E. MacManus' Stratford trip, the details here do not ring entirely true; it is, for example, hard to imagine any schoolchild in any age enthusiastically answering questions on the Salic Law (Laurence Olivier's film of the play treats the Archbishop of Canterbury's disquisition on the law as a moment of comic impenetrability). Nevertheless, the contradictory evidence presented here should serve as a caution against too easily assuming that, at some readily identifiable point early in the twentieth century, popular interest in Shakespeare simply collapsed, and that the cause of that collapse can be straightforwardly assigned to a narrowly defined set of developments in the field of education. Having said this, it is clear that the high level of nineteenth century working-class investment in Shakespeare which has been charted in the previous two chapters of this study certainly did begin to fall away from the early decades of the new century. The reasons for this decline are complex, and they will be examined in some detail in this chapter. While education does not in any sense provide a full explanation for the contraction of Shakespeare's popular audience, it does, nevertheless, serve as a useful starting point for exploring the issue.

The general paradigm for the nineteenth century Shakespeare enthusiast that has been mapped out in this study is of someone who, thanks largely to the work of the church societies, gained basic reading skills during a relatively short school career and then honed those skills either through personal initiative or with the help of like-minded friends, co-workers or fellow activists. So, we might say, the experience of basic education served as a stepping stone to further either solo or communal educational endeavour. The 1870 Education Act and the legislation which followed on from it in subsequent years had the effect of fundamentally changing the nature of the working-class educational experience. Once the Board School system was fully established, with compulsory attendance up to the early teenage years being enforced, working-class children were provided with a much more substantial educational experience than their predecessors had been. Some contemporary commentators suggested that the effect of this more wide-ranging basic educational provision was, paradoxically, to make the move forward to a more ambitious self-directed programme of study less likely. As early as 1873, for example, Thomas Wright noted that while the '*means* of self-education and culture are now within the reach of almost every working man', such self-education was less often pursued than in the past, and he attributed this in part to

> the idea that education is completed within the school period; that a boy who has 'been through' an 'arithmetic,' a grammar, a geography, and who (while still fresh from school) can repeat you the list of his country's kings, and stand cross-examination in the genealogies of the patriarchs, is a scholar of mark [and] can need nothing more in the way of education.[9]

The radical activist W. E. Adams also reflected on advances in educational provision in his autobiography, published in 1903. In common with Wright, he laments the fact that later generations had 'failed to make the best use ... of the enormous advantages they enjoy over the generations that preceded them' and he goes on to argue that, at the time when he is writing:

> We have greater freedom, but less inclination to turn it to the best advantage; more knowledge, but less desire to use it for the best purposes. Nothing is more disappointing to early reformers than the comparatively little benefit that has accrued to society from the millions of money that have been spent and that are being spent on School Boards and Board Schools.[10]

Surveying the evidence from a wide range of nineteenth century working-class autobiographies, the modern historian John Burnett concludes that these writings 'demonstrate a contrast between the struggles and sacrifices of highly motivated individuals for education and self-improvement in the earlier part of the century and the more passive acceptance of the majority when schooling became compulsory after 1876'.[11] In this sense, we may say that the great tradition of autodidacticism which drove forward the likes of Thomas Cooper and so many others, bringing them to a fruitful engagement with the work of Shakespeare and other canonical writers, seems, in some measure at least, to have begun to falter as the century drew to a close.

When we move from the nineteenth century into the twentieth, the nature of educational provision changes further. As the school-leaving age was gradually raised, the need for a clear demarcation between 'primary' and 'secondary' schooling began to emerge. Alice Foley was born in Bolton in 1891, the daughter of a father who, having worked casually as a scene-shifter, 'had learned by rote most of the Shakespearean soliloquies' and who frequently, 'with unexpected dignity . . . stalked round the house declaiming magnificent passages from the plays'.[12] In her autobiography, she laments the fact that, beyond her early teen years, no formal educational pathway was open to her: 'little persuasion or encouragement was available to promising pupils to continue their studies. One entered the establishment as an infant of five, remained the requisite number of years demanded by law, then faded out at age thirteen into the adult world without fuss, farewell, regrets or good wishes.'[13] As the twentieth century progressed, however, this situation would change in various ways. As the distinction between primary and secondary schooling was gradually sharpened, a route opened up for working-class children to advance beyond the educational opportunities provided by the board schools in their earliest decades of existence. Such children – in limited numbers, admittedly – were afforded the opportunity to gain access to grammar schools and other secondary facilities through scholarship schemes. These schemes tended to act as a point of division within the working class, sorting students into opposing groups. Anita Hughes (b. 1892), the daughter of a gardener, had to leave school at the age of twelve, following her sister into the local Lancashire mill. In her autobiography (dated 1977), she recalled:

I could never forget my last day at school – I was heartbroken and just sobbed. In the meantime I had sat for an Exam at the High School in Golden Hill but failed. My Mother said that even if I passed I couldn't stay at school – Father said they could not make flesh of one [daughter] and fish of another but I wanted to try anyway.[14]

It is hard not to feel that there is something particularly poignant about the fact that the school Hughes failed to enter is located in 'Golden Hill'. Like Hughes, Robert Roberts, born in Salford in 1905, also wished to stay on at school and he competed for a bursary to attend a technical college. With no active support available to him from his school, he 'sat an incomprehensible paper and failed'. His father, hearing the result, told him to 'Get out and find work!' At the Labour Bureau, he was given a card and told to 'put what you would like to be at the bottom'. He wrote 'Journalist' on the form, but, he records, 'They did not require any journalists. A boy was needed, though, to sweep up, brew tea and abrade union nuts in a brass shop. I took that'.[15] Roberts' experience might usefully be contrasted with that of Richard Hoggart, born just over a decade later than him, in 1918. Hoggart notes of the pupils at his elementary school that 'almost all of us were being prepared as recruits for the big Hunslet works and were therefore given an education no better than was needed in that role'.¹⁶ Hoggart himself, however, was one of a small handful of boys to be picked out and successfully prepared for a scholarship examination that would take them not to the Hunslet works, but to Cockburn grammar school. Hoggart thrived at Cockburn, finding 'much help and kindness there'.¹⁷

The difference in the cultural resources made available to the scholarship boy or girl and to those who did not benefit from the advantages of the grammar school is nicely illustrated by contrasting the Shakespearean experience of Hoggart with that of V. W. Garratt, born in Birmingham in 1892. Garratt attended a church school which was taken over by the School Board and he notes that the 'classes were large and teachers few, individual tuition was scant'.¹⁸ For a time, as a child, he lived in the village of Langley in Warwickshire and, with a group of friends, he made a trip on foot to Stratford-on-Avon, the aim being 'to see Shakespeare's house'. Finding the property, Garratt and his friends were disappointed to discover that 'a charge was made to go in'.

What, pay to see Shakespeare's house! How do they expect poor children to pay for everything that happens to be interesting to them? If they wouldn't let us inside the house, they could at least have made it a little more thrilling by having a band outside or a few flags flying from the roof. To peep through the windows might lead people to think we wanted to break in . . . [O]ur best plan was to view it from a distance for a few minutes in silent admiration, and then go and find his burial place in the church.¹⁹

Hoggart's experience was entirely different. In his fifth year at Cockburn, he was stopped in the corridor by one of the masters from the English Literature group, who told him that arrangements had been made for him to attend the annual school camp at Stratford. The school recognised that Hoggart's family would not be able to pay the £6 cost of the trip, but a whip-round had been quietly organised among the teachers to enable him to attend. Hoggart 'enjoyed the week and all the plays very much', winning a prize for an essay he wrote about his experience. The 'plays themselves', he writes 'made the Stratford week a landmark and a gateway'.²⁰ Thus, where Garratt could do little more than, metaphorically, press his nose against the window-glass of Shakespeare's house, the scholarship boy Hoggart was, so to speak, allowed to take possession of the keys to the front door.

Hoggart's experience at Cockburn set him on a path that would take him farther and farther from his roots, as he observes: 'I was beginning the movement out and away, step by step, slowly but irrevocably leaving that house, that home, that culture, those unhappy people to whom I would for ever after be emotionally linked'.[21] This is, of course, a pattern that we have already witnessed among many of the nineteenth-century autobiographers: recall, for instance, W. E. Adams feeling compelled to choose the company of Young's *Night Thoughts* over that of his childhood friends, or Henry Jones being driven on to further study – and a university professorship – by his sense of shame at the behaviour of his fellow shoemaker apprentices.[22] However, I want to suggest here that what is different about the way in which the educational system begins to work from the early part of the twentieth century onwards is that it acts as a mechanism for selecting out a small (but gradually increasing) percentage of working-class children in order to groom them specifically for making the transition to membership of the middle class.[23] In the nineteenth century, the project of advanced autodidacticism might possibly, in some cases (Henry Jones, Thomas Okey and Joseph Wright are the most notable examples), lead to the middle-class respectability of a university career. But, in the majority of cases, it served simply as an end in itself; for most of the autobiographers considered here, concentrated programmes of reading led to greater knowledge but not to a change of career or of class position (the desires of, say, a Betsy Cadwaladyr for respectability notwithstanding). For those who began to benefit from an opening up of access to the grammar schools from the early decades of the twentieth century onwards, the situation was quite different. Access to advanced education for these generations of working-class children almost invariably meant alienation from their home communities and translation to a different class. As Hoggart himself writes of his own generation of working-class grammar school students, having been accepted into the system, 'their main friendships would be of the classrooms not the streets; they would dance to different drums. No parents would go with them, [their] first day [at grammar school] or any other.'[24]

A nice sense of this duality and alienation is provided by Raymond Williams (who was born in 1921, the son of a railway signalman), in his autobiographical novel *Border Country*. The figure for Williams himself in the novel is known as 'Will' at home, though his registered name is 'Matthew'. When his father goes to talk to the boy's headmaster about the possibility of school and university scholarships, he is forcibly struck by the experience of referring to his son by his 'official', rather than his home, name: 'It was the first time he had used the name, in talking about Will. He found, as he went out, that it had pleased him.' For the adult Matthew/ Will himself (translated, in the novel, from a literary critic to a historian), summoned home by his father's illness, the disjunction between his two worlds is, by contrast, unsettling: 'He was trained to detachment: the language itself, consistently abstracting and generalizing, supported him in this. And the detachment was real in another way. He felt, in this house, both a child and a stranger. He could not speak as either; could not speak really as himself at all, but only in terms that this pattern offered.'[25]

The process of sorting working-class children into those who would be expected to remain within their native communities and cultures and those who would be offered the opportunity to advance into a different world was intensified after 1944, when R. A. Butler's Education Act formalised the process whereby children were subjected to an '11 plus' examination in order to determine which secondary school they would attend.[26] Butler's Ministry of Education envisaged a tripartite system consisting of grammar schools, secondary moderns and technical schools. In practice, the technical sector failed to flourish and for most children secondary education operated, broadly speaking, through a dual structure.[27] The effects of the mature system in one working-class community were registered in a study published by the sociologists Brian Jackson and Dennis Marsden in 1962. The authors found that, though the selection point was set at eleven, streaming and preparation of students effectively began earlier:

In all but the smallest schools there were systems of pre-selection enabling the teachers to give particular attention to the needs of those likely to go to grammar school. Some, for instance, were moved up into the 'scholarship' class two or even three years in advance. For most this meant that hard work, many tests and a thorough grounding in those skills of arithmetic and language to be examined by the eleven plus, began at seven or eight years of age.[28]

The broadening of access to third level education from the late 1940s also meant that many of the children studied by Jackson and Marsden were able ultimately to progress from their grammar schools on to college or university. Taking an overview of the lives to date of their complete pool of subjects, the authors concluded: 'There had been moments of stress, but most grew through this and accepted both the way in which they had been trained, and the world for which they were being prepared. They are now middle-class citizens.'[29]

In a later study of Brian Jackson's, a young woman who was a successful product of the system (given the name 'Pauline Duce') indicates the extent to which the new values of the grammar school were quickly internalised by working-class pupils:

Grammar school taught me to read widely, yet at the expense of my parents. I thought an evening could not be spent in a pleasanter way than doing my homework and then reading – and not joining in conversation but when spoken to, to quit.

> In early adolescence when I was with my non-grammar school friends I was well satisfied with detective novels or a 'funny' film and 'pop music', but now I have learnt to appreciate finer things such as real music and more subtle entertainments. Previously I had to go to a cinema for my entertainment but walks and hikes give me more thrills.[30]

While the bulk of those studied by Jackson and Marsden made the transition from working-class roots to middle-class respectability, there were some who fell by the wayside and, in the case of many such children, lack of success at grammar school meant precisely a rejection of the cultural values that the system tried to inculcate in them. One of the students tracked by Jackson and Marsden was wholly dismissive of the experience he had had at the local grammar school (which the authors wrote about under the fictional name 'Marburton College'): 'Christ no, I didn't like Marburton College. Too fast, they just got me there and they crammed my nut from the moment I arrived.' He rejected what the school offered him, complaining about 'having all that crap about Shakespeare and Dickens rammed down my throat. I wouldn't read a word of it now.'[31] In the Jackson–Marsden study, this former student is very much the exception rather than the rule, but Ray Gosling, the writer and documentary filmmaker, born in Chester in the late 1930s, vividly details in *Sum Total* the tensions that the smart working-class child experienced in embracing what the educational system had to offer. An English teacher brought him to see the vitality and relevance in the work of Shakespeare. He taught his students

> that Shakespeare was as important and vital and wonderful as Auden and all that, because what he had to say about the human condition, about life wasn't a tale of an Italian aristocrat of the fifteenth century but the stuff beneath the costume. It was – all human life is here, the whole of life – with the *News of the World* story thrown in for the interest, to keep the story going. It wasn't that I admired him. It wasn't the person who taught that mattered but the way it came across. This was important. He made for me the whole of language come alive, and the whole of literature vital – the social scene, the human scene, the temporal conflicts, the eternal struggles.

However, as Gosling registers, there was a cost to all of this. Access to culture and to advanced thought and literary appreciation required, in return, not just adherence to the values of the system, but also the rejection of those who were unable to, or failed to, or refused to make the transition from one world to another:

> But, and there was a big But. The books were in a package deal with The School and the way up, on to the best possible University, and on to the best possible

outlet in teaching or commerce, or what have you. We were the one in 130 of our age group. We were the top of the cream. They could talk about the ones who missed the message and went in for Beatnik, or Brewery, or Drifting, or Nothing; the ones who wouldn't or couldn't keep climbing, as failures, not just of the system but failures for themselves. They hadn't done themselves justice. We were the select who could appreciate and make judgements and it was a sin unto ourselves if we abandoned being the select, the upper intelligentsia.[32]

A nice contrast, in this regard, is provided by the respective attitudes of Gosling and Hoggart. For all his uneasiness about the middle-class world that he came to move in, Hoggart indicates clearly, in his classic study *The Uses of Literacy*, the extent to which he had become simply incapable of understanding the emerging new popular culture of the late 1950s, as he dismisses the world of the milk bar and the jukebox with blank incomprehension, describing those who indulge in these forms of entertainment as mostly being 'rather less intelligent than the average, and therefore even more exposed than others to the debilitating mass-trends of the day. They have no aim, no ambition, no protection, no belief'.[33] This is, indeed, the mindset of 'The School' in its most dismissively contemptuous form. Gosling, by contrast – admittedly (and very importantly, of course) a generation younger than Hoggart – positively embraced the new popular culture in all its forms. Of a trip to Leicester, he writes:

I went out and into the Town. I tried to find a juke box caff, something I knew, some little part of my own country. I couldn't find one. Had an egg and chips somewhere, and went into a pub after. It was all old old working class with no lads, no juke box, and no old gels. Found a cinema. They were showing Presley's *Jailhouse Rock*. I went in on my own, and came out with my own bird tagging on my arm. Said good-bye, by the bus-stop, and promised to come over again.[34]

For all of Gosling's swaggering embrace of popular culture, however (and, indeed, his own Kerouacian narrative style), he was, in fact, visiting Leicester for a very particular reason: to be interviewed for a place to study English literature at Leicester University. He spoke with his interviewer 'about Larkin and Silkin, Amis and Gunn' – a selection of very contemporary writers, to be sure, but, still, rather more rarefied territory than *Jailhouse Rock*.[35] Hoggart, too, had studied English (at the University of Leeds) and he reflects very interestingly on the complexities of his experience. Recalling that it was not until he 'stood in a field in North Africa in 1942, reading *Macbeth* from a tattered edition found in some barracks' that he 'felt for the first time the impact of Shakespeare', Hoggart observes of his time at Leeds: 'It was as though, to get through to the point at university at which you sat those eight or nine papers on different periods and genres, you could not allow the force of the works to flood into you; you might have been pushed off course.' 'You did not', he concludes, 'for those three years dare to release yourself to the power of the works; you controlled your responses to them, almost unconsciously.'[36] Hoggart points here to another educational factor which might be seen as serving to contribute to the decline in Shakespeare's popularity among a mass audience. The characteristic note of much working-class reaction to Shakespeare in the nineteenth century is rapturous awe, bordering on unabashed bardolatry. We have seen this again and again in previous chapters, and Christopher Thomson might be allowed to stand here for generations of like-minded enthusiasts when he writes 'Many a time have I felt my soul light up with pure and holy fire at the altar of our Shakespeare'.[37] Adopting such an attitude would not have served Hoggart terribly well in his Leeds finals – certainly, it would not have won him the first class degree he ultimately achieved. But the requirements of the Leeds English faculty were, we might say, the product of developments in higher education that had taken shape gradually from the middle of the nineteenth century onwards.

The second half of the nineteenth century was, in general, a period of increasing professionalisation. Julia Swindells has noted that 'From 1841 to 1881, there was a massive expansion of the professions, of work describing itself and seeking to describe itself as professional'.[38] This development was most noticeable in medicine, and David Vincent has observed, for example, that

> The Medical Registration Act of 1858 was designed to create an impermeable barrier between the trained, certificated, disinterested practitioner and the self-taught amateur wise-woman or the self-promoting vendor of unproven remedies. Those not on the register of the General Medical Council who still claimed that they could cure the sick were now isolated from the professional doctor.[39]

By contrast with the changes which occurred in the field of medicine, the dedicated study of English literature was slow to emerge as a professional discipline, and certainly, Oxford and Cambridge universities were notoriously reluctant to accept that it constituted a worthwhile academic pursuit. However, the London institutions did lead the way, with University College and King's College establishing chairs in English in 1828 and 1835 respectively. David J. Palmer has observed that to Henry Morley, who taught at both institutions in the latter half of the century, 'belongs the distinction of being the first to devote an academic career in England solely to English studies' and 'with him English studies became fully professional'.[40]

The particular field of Shakespeare studies offers a clear example of an accelerating growth in professionalism over the course of the nineteenth century. The two greatest Shakespeare scholars at the end of the eighteenth century were George Steevens and Edmond Malone. Both survived on family inheritances, and they studied and edited Shakespeare as respected gentlemen amateurs. This tradition carried on into the early decades of the new century, with Alexander Dyce (an Anglican clergyman with an inherited income), John Payne Collier (a journalist), Charles Knight (a publisher) and James Orchard Halliwell-Phillipps (wealthy by virtue of having run off with his patron's daughter) all producing important editions of Shakespeare. From the 1860s, however, all of this changed. The towering edition of the nineteenth century was that issued by Macmillan in nine volumes between 1863 and 1866. It was referred to from the first as the 'Cambridge Shakespeare' because it was produced in association with the Cambridge University Press and was edited by Cambridge scholars William George Clark and William Aldis Wright (with the early assistance of H. R. Luard and John Glover), who made extensive use of a large collection of early texts held at the Wren Library at Trinity College, Cambridge. After the Cambridge edition, all serious Shakespeare editing would be undertaken by professional academics. Such scholars also captured the market for serious Shakespeare commentary, with, for example, Edward Dowden (appointed to Trinity College Dublin's first chair in English literature in 1867) publishing his enormously influential *Shakspere: A Critical Study of His Mind and Art* in 1875 (the book had, by 1909, reached its fourteenth edition) and his *Shakspere Primer* in 1877.[41]

The ever-increasing professionalisation of Shakespeare studies and their domination by university scholars did not, of course, necessarily have the effect of locking out working-class readers from encountering and appreciating Shakespeare, and we might note, for example, that the publication of the Cambridge edition coincided almost exactly with the appearance of John Dicks' enormously popular cheap editions of the playwright's works.[42] It would be true to say, however, that the absorption of Shakespeare by the universities did, over time, tend to contribute to establishing a connection between the playwright and a gradually emerging conception of an elite culture that distinguished itself from its populist counterpart. In this sense, rather than being a writer to be informally discovered, read and cherished (as was the case for most of the nineteenth century), Shakespeare became an author who needed to be studied – and studied in the company of properly professional commentators and interpreters. Thus, David Vincent has observed that, by the end of the nineteenth century, those 'who sought to exercise their imaginations after work discovered that Shakespeare and Milton were becoming more accessible but less familiar as the "classics" were divorced from mass-produced literature and from oral and literary categories of creativity practised by the mass of the population'.[43]

A similar bifurcating and hierarchising effect can be seen at work in the theatre of the time. Shakespeare was genuinely popular with working-class theatre audiences for almost the entirety of the nineteenth century. We have seen, for instance, Thomas Cooper's shoe-maker master, Joseph Clarke, recounting his experience of Shakespeare productions in London and knowledgeably discussing the performances of Siddons and Kemble. Thomas Frost saw *The Tempest*, *A Midsummer Night's Dream* and *A Winter's Tale*, among other plays, at the Princess's Theatre; he also saw Kean and Phelps act, though the former was not at his best as he had 'lost his front teeth which affected his voice detrimentally'.[44] Charles James Billson notes that, in the later nineteenth century, a chimney-sweep named Kelley, a great admirer of Shakespeare, regularly attended a Leicester theatre and he 'used to occupy a prominent seat in the gallery, from which prompter's box he would correct in a loud voice any actor who deviated from the exact words of the poet'.[45] These examples could be multiplied considerably (I have given others in my introduction), and we can further say that, in fact, attracting a working-class audience was commercially very important to nineteenth-century theatre managers. The bigger theatres in particular needed to draw in large crowds for long runs in order to pay for the extravagant costuming and sets which increasingly became a feature of the nineteenth-century stage. By the turn of the century, however, styles began to change. Richard Foulkes has identified a new 'progressivist' aesthetic, which ran counter to the populist thrust of much previous practice:

Shakespeare traditionalists, working on commercial lines, had basically served public taste, though often giving it a nudge and a jolt in the process. Since their production methods were costly they necessarily sought to attract large and socially diverse audiences for long runs. The progressives, opting for simpler staging, set their sights on the more discerning playgoers, who could appreciate the artistic merit of what they saw.[46]

Cary DiPietro has expanded Foulkes' analysis to indicate the extent of the backlash amongst the theatrical elite against populist productions of Shakespeare from the beginning of the new century. He notes, for example, that, in 1911, 'Edward Gordon Craig was criticizing the pageantry and spectacle of the degraded money-making theatre, "the coloured Christmas card culture which in the teeth of common sense and conventional good taste displays its impertinence night after night, year after year upon our English stage" '.[47] The ultimate effect of the efforts of the theatrical reformers from the beginning of the new century was, as Foulkes concludes, that Shakespeare became 'an unapproachable icon, associated with high culture and erudition rather than the fount of popular entertainment'.[48]

Foulkes' observations here concerning Shakespeare and the theatre resonate with a much larger argument advanced by John Carey in *The Intellectuals and the Masses: Pride and Prejudice Among the Literary Intelligentsia, 1880–1939*. Carey argues that, in response to the near-universal levels of literacy effected by the 1870 Education Act, the intellectual class sought to redefine culture in a way that excluded a mass audience.[49] He argues that

The intellectuals could not, of course, actually prevent the masses from attaining literacy. But they could prevent them reading literature by making it too difficult for them to understand – and this is what they did. The early twentieth century saw a determined effort, on the part of the European intelligentsia, to exclude the masses from culture. In England this movement has become known as modernism.[50]

Shakespeare was not, of course, a modernist writer, but he could be interpreted in ways that resonated with modernist thinking – as Hugh Grady, Richard Halpern and Cary DiPietro have all very ably demonstrated.[51] And certainly one of the writers Carey discusses in his book was very clear on Shakespeare's location in relation to the issue of class: 'genius like Shakespeare's is not born among labouring, uneducated, servile people. It was not born in England among the Saxons and the Britons. It is not born to-day among the working classes.'[52] Thus, where, in the nineteenth century, working-class activists comprehensively claimed Shakespeare as their own, firstly by imagining the playwright himself to be of humble origins, then by reading his work through the prism of radical political concerns, here, we see a reactionary denial of the possibility that the working class could ever produce a figure of Shakespeare's magnitude. And, we might say, within the context of the greater modernist project, what the working class could not produce they were also unlikely to be able properly to understand.

That members of the working-class were, in fact, being driven away from an appreciation of literature receives some confirmation in a government report on *The Teaching of English in England* (1921), where the authors indicate that

We were told that the working classes, especially those belonging to organised labour movements, were antagonistic to, and contemptuous of, literature, that they regarded it 'merely as an ornament, a polite accomplishment, a subject to be despised by really virile men.' Literature, in fact, seems to be classed by a large number of thinking working men with antimacassars, fish-knives and other unintelligible and futile trivialities of 'middleclass culture,' and, as a subject of instruction, is suspect as an attempt to 'side-track the working-class movement.'[53]

Carey's study indicates that, in the period running up to the beginning of the Second World War, the modernist movement sought to effect a strong distinction between high culture and populist culture, and I have suggested that Shakespeare increasingly found himself being appropriated to the elitist side of that binary. During the course of the war, the vision of culture being split between high and low began to infiltrate government thinking on the arts. The Arts Council of Great Britain had its roots in a wartime organisation known as the Council for the Encouragement of Music and Arts (CEMA). One of the driving forces behind CEMA in its earliest years was Thomas Jones – the same Thomas Jones we encountered in Chapter 3 of this study, being mentored by fellow Welshman Henry Jones.[54] Thomas began his working life in the local ironworks, before eventually going on to become an academic and then a high-ranking civil servant. He saw CEMA as having a 'social service' mission, with the twin aims of helping artists and serving audiences, but with the latter function being uppermost in his mind.[55] As the war progressed, the culture of CEMA gradually shifted. In December 1941, R. A. Butler – who would, as we have already seen, be responsible for formalising the 11-plus system – offered the chairmanship of CEMA to John Maynard Keynes. Keynes was a friend of Butler's father-in-law, the art patron Samuel Courtauld. His appointment set the arts organisation on a track very different from that favoured by Jones. As Robert Hewison has observed: 'Not only did Keynes see to it that in future subsidy would be concentrated on professional organisations, he also reversed CEMA's policy of not funding work in London. As his critics saw it, Keynes ensured that the future Arts Council would be both élitist, and metropolitan in bias.'[56] In time, Hewison notes, Jones and the other populists 'gave way to those, like Sir Kenneth Clark, who saw the arts as an essentially professional activity and CEMA's duty as the maintenance of standards'. Clark himself became, in due course, chairman of the Arts Council (which received its Royal Charter in 1946) and Hewison observes of him that he 'epitomised the tastes of the mandarin aesthete, passionate about the art and artists, less passionate about people'.[57]

Hewison indicates that the immediate post-war orientation of the Arts Council set it on a course that would see it essentially serving the needs of the few rather than the many. As he observes, the Council 'missed opportunities that had existed . . . to define the arts so as to embrace a wider range of activities and to include a broader definition of the audience for them'. The narrow focus of the body remained in place for decade after decade. The Council's failure to promote a policy of inclusivity is summed up in its repeated response to the question of whether the function of the body was to 'raise or spread'. As it repeatedly contemplated this question, the instinct of the Council was always to think of its primary mission as being to elevate standards rather than to expand access. Hewison quotes from W. E. Williams, who served as secretary-general of the council from 1951 to 1963:

'Might it not be better to accept the realistic fact that the living theatre of good quality cannot be widely accessible and to concentrate our resources upon establishing a few more shrines like Stratford and the Bristol Old Vic?' Williams's answer to his own question was: '"Few, but roses" – including, of course, regional roses.' But the regional roses became fewer as the Council's regional offices were wound up and the council withdrew from directly managing regional theatres and theatre tours.

When a financial crisis in 1952 wiped out the Council's reserves, Williams concluded: 'It seems wiser that the Arts Council should now concentrate its limited resources on the maintenance and enhancement of standards.'[58]

Taking the long stretch up through the middle decades of the twentieth century, then, we can say that working-class children coming to Shakespeare in the board schools often tended (at least early in the century) to encounter the playwright in the context of oppressive drudgery; that when, in time, older working-class schoolchildren were brought to an appreciation of the true worth of Shakespeare's work they generally did so in institutions that were dedicated to transforming them into cultured members of the middle class, disjoining them, in the process, from their working-class roots; that the incorporation of Shakespeare into the newly emerged university discipline of English literature tended to detach the playwright from popular appreciation, reconfiguring his work as something that required specialist study; that changes in theatre specifically, and in literary culture more generally, effected a bifurcation whereby elite culture (to which Shakespeare was annexed) came to define itself against a popular culture identified as the native province of the working class; and, finally, that this hierarchised distinction was, from the war years forward, confirmed by a government arts policy that concentrated primarily on funding select elite (and largely metropolitan) institutions at the expense of cultivating and encouraging a wider audience for the arts. Putting all of these factors together, we can say that, as the twentieth century progressed, the doorway providing working-class access to Shakespeare progressively narrowed and fewer and fewer members of the working class were likely to find their way to an appreciation of the playwright's work. Having said all of this, it should also be noted that the point of access never, in fact, fully closed, and it is certainly possible to find instances of working-class appreciation of Shakespeare across the twentieth century. Jenny Lee, a Labour MP born in 1904, who became Britain's first Arts minister under Harold Wilson, recalled receiving a complete works of Shakespeare from her coal miner father for her tenth birthday – an experience which had real resonance for her husband, Aneurin Bevan (one of the founding fathers of the British welfare state).[59] Likewise, Jonathan Rose notes the case of Nancy Sharman, born in 1925, whose mother 'a Southampton charwoman, had not time to read until during her last illness, at age fifty-four. Then she devoured the complete works of Shakespeare'. She instructed her daughter that, after her death, she wished to donate her corneas, so that someone else might have the pleasure of reading.[60] Such instances do, however, become increasingly rare as the century progresses.

It is important to note also that to say that access to Shakespeare narrowed in this period is, of course, only part of the story. It might be argued that another reason why Shakespeare began to lose his working-class audience at this time was that there was 'mettle more attractive' available elsewhere. We can gain a sense of this by looking at the results of a study conducted by Arnold Freeman and published under the title *Boy Life and Labour*, in 1914. At the request of the Education Committee of Birmingham Town Council, Freeman had conducted a survey of unskilled boy workers in the city. His sample ran to a total of seventy-one teenagers, ranging from those who were just beginning to learn skilled work, to those he characterised as destined ultimately for long-term unemployment. Freeman described one of the boys he interviewed, identified as 'M. R.', as 'a first-rate young fellow; good at photography and fretwork; fond of Dickens, Robert Louis Stevenson and Bulwer Lytton, and well up in Shakespeare; delightful with the banjo, not over strong, but quite strong enough for normal work'.[61] M. R. could, then, have sat quite happily in the company of the nineteenth century autodidacts we have been tracking in this study, being an enthusiastic reader in his spare time and a lover of Shakespeare. But M. R. is, in fact, exceptional within Freeman's group as a whole. More typical of the general run was a boy who, when Freeman asked him about Shakespeare, responded that he thought he 'was the "head of an army"'.[62] The range of interests identified by this boy was quite characteristic of the bulk of Freeman's sample: 'He is intensely interested in football, horse-racing and boxing ... He reads the *Comics*, *The Gem*, *Butterfly*, *Picture Fun*, *England's Boxing*, the *Sporting Buff* for football and the *Mail* for Police News.'[63] The emphasis on sport here (and on reading about sport) is important. We have noted the professionalisation of various aspects of life during the course of the nineteenth century and a parallel development with the emergence of, for example, the General Medical Council or university English departments, was the increasing professionalisation of sports – most notably football and horse-racing (and, on a smaller scale, cricket). To take the example of soccer: the Football Association (FA) was founded in 1863; by 1880, it had a permanent office, and its secretary was a salaried official by 1886. The number of clubs affiliated with the FA rose from 10 in 1867 to 50 in 1871, 1,000 in 1888 to 10,000 in 1905. With the inception of the FA Cup in 1871 and the national league in 1888, the growth in attendance figures at matches was equally impressive. The first season of the league saw a total attendance across all matches of 602,000, by 1895–6 this had risen to 1,900,000 and by 1905–6 the First Division (the equivalent of the current Premier League) was attracting 5,000,000 spectators. From 1897, the crowd attending the Cup Final routinely exceeded 50,000.[64] The effects of the professionalisation of the game are registered by Edward Brown, who was born in Bromley in 1880:

First class football had started at Plumstead and ... Crystal Palace; and all the junior clubs in our district suffered from its attraction, players who were not very keen being liable to stay away when there was a good League match on at either ground, especially if their own club happened to be playing a friendly game. We had to play short or cancel two or three fixtures from this cause, and I told members I could not continue to act as secretary unless they would carry out the fixtures I arranged.[65]

The great enthusiasm for football was also noted by the railwayman Alfred Williams (1877–1930), in his 1915 autobiography:

Whatever leisure the youngsters have is spent in kicking about something or other amid the dirt and dust; from one week's end to another they are brimful of the fortunes of the local football team. Many a workman boasts that he has denied himself a Sunday dinner in order to find the money necessary for him to attend Saturday's match. Politics, religion, the fates of empires and governments, the interest of life and death itself must all yield to the supreme fascination and excitement of football.[66]

The importance of football was matched only by that of horse-racing. As Robert Roberts noted, 'Betting on horses was about the only way, other than theft, that the worker knew of to get money without earning it. Racing held the rabid interest of millions'.[67] John Eldred, born in Bermondsey in 1885, the son of a stone mason, worked for a time as a messenger boy at the office of a newspaper called *The King*. The paper had been acquired by a Quaker who 'abhorred all gambling' and so refused to print any material concerning horse-racing. The paper quickly folded and Eldred explained that 'the British public demanded racecourse news and pictures, and he was adamant that he would not concede their wishes. So our subscribers said (in effect): "All right, you keep your principles, and we'll keep our sixpences"'.[68]

The professionalisation of sport and the manner in which it became intertwined with developments in journalism serve to indicate the extent to which working-class culture began to change from the latter decades of the nineteenth century. Football, horse-racing and other activities occupied some of the increased leisure time that workers enjoyed as the century drew to a close. As the rate of literacy increased, newspapers began to cater to the emerging need for punters to gain quick access to racing results and for fans who sought news of football fixtures and match reports. Journalism more generally also changed significantly in the period. In an essay written for the *New Review* in 1889, the publisher T. P. O'Connor celebrated the advent of a 'New Journalism', noting that 'To get your ideas through the hurried eyes into the whirling brains that are employed in the reading of a newspaper there must be no mistake about your meaning: to use a somewhat familiar phrase, you must strike your reader right between the eyes'.[69] Aled Jones has noted that 'the New Journalism introduced fresh formats, shorter news items with headlines and cross-heads and more "human interest" stories, particularly by means of the interview'.[70] The newspaper proprietor most closely associated with using the techniques of the New Journalism to cater to the needs of an emerging mass market was, of course, Alfred Harmsworth (Viscount Northcliffe). S. J. Taylor has noted of one of Harmsworth's first titles, the *Evening News*, that 'He adopted a newer and more modern typeface, emphasizing important news with bold headlines. The leaders were cut to the bare bones, the political writing trimmed. Regular features were put in the same place day after day, so the reader could easily find what he wanted.' He also 'laid in maps beside the foreign news – and, in a stroke of pure genius, he introduced the football pools.'[71] In his memoir of Harmsworth, Max Pemberton noted an early conversation with the publisher, in which he observed that 'The Board Schools ... are turning out hundreds of thousands of boys and girls annually who are anxious to read' and that 'they will read anything which is simple and is sufficiently interesting'.[72] Harmsworth sought to capitalise on this new market and, by the end of 1894, his combined stable of publications was achieving sales of 2,000,000 – the largest of any such publishing concern in the world.[73]

It was not just newspapers that changed in this period. There were also significant shifts in publishing more generally. In *Patterns and Trends in British Publishing, 1800–1919*, Simon Eliot demonstrates the degree to which the category of 'Literature' had come to dominate the publishing market by the end of the nineteenth century. Even more striking, from the point of view of the present study, is his finding of the extent to which fiction came gradually to be the most important sector within the literature category. Eliot notes that, between 1814 and 1846, ' "Literature" was composed of, roughly, 68% "Fiction", etc. and 32% "Poetry and Drama" '. By the 1880s, these figures had undergone a very pronounced shift, to 90% 'Fiction' and just 10% 'Poetry and Drama'.[74] A decline in Shakespeare's readership may thus in part be attributable to a more general decline of interest in printed drama. The working class may have been reading Shakespeare less because, quite simply, they were reading other things instead, be it cheap mass-circulation newspapers or fiction. And this was, of course, very much the era specifically of *cheap* fiction, since that traditional stalwart of the publishing trade, the three-decker novel, collapsed after 1894, with the result that the price of new novels (now published in single-volume format) dropped to 6s. (a reduction of about 80% on the previous standard price).[75] *The Spectator*, in 1901, attributed 'the enormous expansion of the reading public' to two principal causes – 'the Education Act of 1870 and the abolition of the three-volume novel'.[76]

By the end of the nineteenth century, then, just as elite culture was beginning to define itself against certain forms of populism, so too was working-class culture beginning to establish its own distinctive parameters, interests and tastes. As Nan Hackett has observed:

Working men and women left the workers' clubs that had middle class sponsors; they preferred the race tracks, music halls, and sing-alongs at the local pub to lectures on Shakespearean tragedy, eighteenth century music, and political deference. The influence of the middle class and its value system which had been perpetuated through self-help clubs, churches, and more conservative political organizations, was rapidly diminishing.[77]

There were other developments which served to accelerate and emphasise the division of cultures. Thomas Burke, who was born in 1886 and who lived much of his young life in Poplar, worked in various jobs, including having a spell of employment at a music hall theatre. Here, he was witness to a conversation between Cosgrove, a successful comedian, and a business entrepreneur, Mr Rosenbaum. Rosenbaum tries to talk the comedian into investing in the 'Pictures', but Cosgrove is sceptical. Rosenbaum argues with him:

'Listen! Let me tell yeh something. The Pictures is going to be a Big Thing.'
 'Big Thing? How?'
 'Listen .... D'you know they're going to build places specially to show 'em in? Going to build picture-theatres and give all-day performances.'

Rosenbaum concludes: 'They're coming in. Coming in fast. America's in it already. It's going to be Big.'[78] Rosenbaum was, of course, entirely correct: the Pictures were Big and one autobiographer – George H. Barber, author of *From Workhouse to Lord Mayor* – made his fortune from them. Barber writes that, as he was struggling to build his first cinema, the 'Jeremiahs of that day were prophesying that George H. Barber was on the brink of ruin, and it was even said by some that he would be a patient in Cheddleton Asylum within six months', but he prospered and built a total of ten cinemas in as many years.[79] The impact of the cinema is registered by many writers. Philip Boswood Ballard, the teacher and school inspector, noted that, when he visited a school in Camberwell, one pupil was picked out for his special attention 'on the ground that the lad was a good actor and had taken the first prize in a competition for the best imitation of Charlie Chaplin'. Ballard himself was unacquainted with Chaplin, but he was quickly informed who the actor was: 'I made further inquiries and found that to every boy in that school of four hundred Charlie Chaplin was as familiar as his own brother. I at once realized that a new force had come into our social life.'[80] In his study of Birmingham working-class teenagers, Arnold Freeman noted that it was 'unquestionable' that the cinema was 'the greatest formative influence at the present time in the life of the average working-boy' and he comments that he gave up asking each individual boy 'if he went to the Cinema, because the response was invariably in the affirmative'.[81] Freeman asked the teenagers in his study to keep diaries of their week's activities and these accounts of their lives invariably include visits to the cinema. One boy, 'H. V.' presents a typical week in which he played football, watched football, talked about football and went to the 'Picture Palace' twice – once to see 'Twix Ambition and Love. Scenery of the Isle of Man. 3 different stages and some more pictures. Spent 3d Entrance Fee, 1d sweets.'[82] Robert Roberts summarised the impact of the cinema by observing that 'in the early years of the century [it] burst like a vision into the underman's existence and, rapidly displacing both concert and theatre, became both his chief source of enjoyment and one of the greatest factors in his cultural development.'[83]

From the early 1920s, cinema was joined by another medium of mass entertainment – the radio. The BBC began broadcasting in 1922 and Roberts, again, notes that, after that year, 'the wireless crystal set spread with phenomenal speed into the lower ranges of the working class, its parts being so cheap to buy and easy to assemble'.[84] In an autobiography published in 1935, the blacksmith Thomas Todd, born in Middleton-in-Teesdale in 1854, looked back on theatrical performances and concerts staged in the local hall by travelling companies and concluded: 'The inhabitants were attracted with such displays to a greater extent than they are nowadays, when most have their wireless, and visit the talkies.'[85] The advance of mass entertainment simply horrified many commentators among the cultural elite, with T. S. Eliot, for example, imagining the dawning of a catastrophic dystopian world 'When every theatre has been replaced by 100 cinemas, when every musical instrument has been replaced by 100 gramophones, when every horse has been replaced by 100 cheap motor-cars, when electrical ingenuity has made it possible for every child to hear its bedtime stories from a loud-speaker'.[86] Eliot was writing in 1932; just a few years after this, the BBC began experimenting with broadcasting television programmes – a project abandoned at the onset of the war, but resumed again, albeit falteringly to begin with, as the conflict was drawing to a close. Michael Collins notes that, in 1950, the *Daily Mirror* warned that 'If you let a television set through your door, life can never be the same again'. Just a year later, the total number of television licences exceeded 1,000,000. Collins observes that 'The working class were early adopters, thanks to hire purchase and TV rentals. A majority of those sets were in the homes of low-income families. Seventy per cent of those with TV licences had not been educated beyond the age of fifteen'.[87] A major turning point for the new medium occurred in 1953, when the coronation of Elizabeth II was broadcast live. The event was watched on television by 20,500,000 people, 56 of the adult population, with a further 11,700,000 listening on radio.[88] As the century progressed, television became ever more central to working-class cultural life. Michael Collins was himself born in the working-class district of Walworth, south-east London, in 1961, and he registers the impact of television within his own family, as he was growing up in the 1960s and 1970s:

Like most of the neighbours, we lived in a home where no one bothered with books. The television had more of an impact on cultural lives than the paperback.

I was named after the actor Michael Landon, who portrayed Little Joe in the TV western *Bonanza*. From her hospital bed, a day after the birth, my mum wrote a note to my brother, informing him of the fact and asking 'did Brownie in *Emergency Ward 10* get better?'[89]

The decline in Shakespeare's popular readership can be regarded, then, from two different perspectives. From one point of view, it is a story of various reconfigurations of culture such that Shakespeare becomes annexed to an elite realm from which the working class are excluded, except when they undergo a form of cultural deracination to become, themselves, middle class. On the other hand, it is also the story of the evolution of working-class interests away from traditional literary culture, with the emergence of professional sports, cheap newspapers and fiction, cinema, radio and television. By the time we reach the second half of the twentieth century, this polarity is particularly marked and Collins' observation that, in common with their neighbours, his family 'lived in a home where no one bothered with books', but where the television was of central importance, is entirely characteristic.[90] In closing this chapter, I, as something of a coda, suggest one final issue which may have played a part in draining away working-class interest in Shakespeare.

We have seen that, in the nineteenth century, working-class education was greatly indebted to the work of the churches, and we have also seen that the instruction provided by the religious bodies was – at least until the mid-century – heavily freighted with religious content. With the advent of the board schools, religious instruction began to lose its place of centrality in the curriculum. J. M. Goldstrom has noted that section VII of the 1870 Act 'restricted religious instruction to certain hours of the day' and he registers that this requirement had the effect of driving religious materials out of the standard class readers – since such material was deemed inappropriate for general instruction. Writing of the nature of education in the period, John Burnett has observed that there was a 'noticeable contrast between the essentially religious basis of Sunday School and Church School education, which often had profound influence on its recipients, and the more secular context in which mass education was spread by the post-1870 Board Schools'.[91]

The secularising of the school curriculum was all of a piece with more general developments in the latter half of the nineteenth century. In 1860, Thomas Huxley – who famously dismissed religion as 'the deadly enemy of science' – defended Darwinian theories of evolution against the views of Samuel Wilberforce, the Bishop of Oxford. This was followed by controversial attempts by the church to censure clergymen involved in two publications, *Essays and Reviews* (a collection by various hands published in 1860) and *The Pentateuch and the Book of Joshua Critically Examined* (written by the Bishop of Natal, William John Colenso, and published in 1862). The former broadly suggested that the Bible should be seen as a historical document rather than as the product of divine inspiration, and the latter 'questioned the literal and inspirational interpretations of the Bible, arguing that they could not account for historical inaccuracies'. Josephine Guy notes that none of these events 'had an immediately disruptive consequence for everyday church-going ... or for the authority of the Church', but she argues that they can be seen as representing 'significant and symbolic moments in the decline of the intellectual prestige and political and social influence of the Christian Church in Britain'.[92] Simon Eliot confirms the general decline in the investment in religion across the period when he logs the progressive reduction in religious publishing over the course of the century. He registers 'the predominance of religion as the subject matter of books published between 1814 and 1846' and charts the decline in religious publishing through to the 1890s, when it had fallen to below 10% of all publishing.[93]

The gradual secularisation of society extended into the working class and Robert Roberts noted that 'In the decade before 1914, whilst organized religion still kept a hold on some from the upper working class (the undermass had defected generations before) a drift was already underway'. Roberts notes that some of those among the upper working class 'salved their conscience by strict insistence on their children's attending Sunday school'.[94] It certainly is true to say that Sunday school attendance did hold up well, at least through the turn of the century, and Rowland Kenney, born in Shelderslow, Yorkshire, in 1883, noted in his autobiography that 'Like all the children in the neighbourhood I went regularly to Sunday school. It was a part of normal life, like eating and drinking'.[95] John Burnett indicates that the Sunday school registers peaked at an impressive 6,179,000 pupils in 1906.[96] As the twentieth century progressed, however, the culture of Sunday school attendance declined among the working class, just as religious observance more generally began to fall away.

To see why the decline of religion matters, from a Shakespearean perspective, it is helpful to return to Mary Ann Hearn (1834–1909). Hearn was a BFSS school teacher; she retired in 1867. In the wake of the 1870 Act, she was approached by the local branch of the Liberal party to stand for membership of the School Board in Northampton. Hearn was ultimately rejected as a candidate because she refused to accept the local association's policy of calling for the Bible to be excluded from the board schools' curricula.[97] Writing of her own experience reading the Bible at both the BFSS school she attended and at her Sunday school, she observes:

> It was a happy thing, for which I have been thankful all my life, that I was able to learn by heart long passages of Scripture. Let no one think that this was ever a hardship. The grand themes, and the stately, beautiful language in which they were told, fed my very life. I think the first I learned was the twenty-third psalm, and there has never been any time when every sentence has not appealed to me.[98]

As Hearn indicates here, a religiously based education meant exposure to the Bible and, specifically, to the *language* of the Bible, including learning passages of the text by heart – a wholly typical experience. The Bible in question, in the case of the great majority of children, would have been the authorised or 'King James' version. So, one very simple point might be made here. The 'King' of the King James Bible was, of course, the same 'King' as that of the King's Men theatre company, of which Shakespeare was a member, namely James VI & I. Thus, for those working-class students who were grounded from an early age in the language of the Renaissance through exposure to the authorised version, the transition from Sunday school and classroom reading of the Bible to private reading of Shakespeare was, linguistically, entirely natural.[99] The language of Shakespeare was already part of their mental make-up.[100] Conversely, the more that working-class culture became secularised, and the less exposure that working-class children had to the language of the Bible, the more alien Shakespeare's language necessarily came to appear. As early as 1921, a government report on *The Teaching of English in England* noted that 'at the present time the Bible is probably less widely read and less directly influential in our life and literature than it has been at any time since the Reformation', while also noting that 'Much of Shakespeare's speech ... is so remote as to be in an unfamiliar tongue ... In many passages Shakespeare is not only difficult, but archaic as well; and thus he seems doubly unsuitable for young readers'.[101] This effect was, of course, accelerated as the twentieth century progressed and everyday language drifted farther and farther away from early-modern English.

We can see the long-term consequences of this linguistic disjunction quite clearly if we move forward to the very end of the twentieth century and the beginning of this century. In Penny Woolcock's *Shakespeare on the Estate*, broadcast on BBC television in 1994 as part of the 'Bard on the Box' season, the theatre director Michael Bogdanov attempts to bring Shakespeare to the

Decline and fall 187

residents of the Ladywood estate in inner-city Birmingham. In a similar programme, entitled *My Shakespeare*, broadcast on the UK's Channel 4 in 2004, the actor Paterson Joseph returns to his native Harlsden, in Northwest London, to assemble a cast of locals with the intention of getting them to stage a performance of *Romeo and Juliet* at one of the theatres of the Royal Academy of Dramatic Arts (RADA).[102] In both cases, the greatest obstacle that the theatre professional faces is getting his working-class amateurs to understand the language of the playwright.

Woolcock's documentary opens with a voice-over from Bogdanov, in which he observes that 'In his time Shakespeare was considered a playwright of the people, but, today, fewer and fewer can afford to see his plays and, for the majority, he's boring and irrelevant'.[103] Bogdanov visits a pub on the Ladywood estate and talks to the overspill crowd, drinking outside, asking them about Shakespeare. One comments: 'Shakespeare: he didn't play football, did he?' Another asks: 'Who was Shakespeare? Who was Shakespeare? Nobody knows. Nobody cares. This is Ladywood. All we want to do is get drunk, get fucked and be merry.' There is a certain amount of playing to the camera here and of having fun at Bogdanov's earnest expense (one man backs out of the doorway of the pub and moons the film crew), but another drinker comments quite seriously – and rather sharply – to the director: 'I'm trying to work out *why* you've come down here talking about Shakespeare when the chances of you meeting anyone round here who's got anything to do with Shakespeare is really nil.' The suspicion of Bogdanov's motives is echoed in the first semi-formal meeting which he has with a group of residents. The director launches into a commentary on how Shakespeare has been appropriated by the elite to support an unequal class structure and he is immediately interrupted by an astute young black resident who tells him:

That's just words. Can anybody repeat anything from what he's said? . . . We don't particularly understand. You're going to have to come a bit clearer than that. You can go on wittering on like that among your other, sort of like, white colleagues, but here and now . . . that's a load of shit, really.

What Bogdanov discovers is that his well-meaning materialist analysis of Shakespearean appropriation has no purchase in the world of the Ladywood residents, many of whom are struggling to get by on social security (though, in their own way, they do actually intuitively understand what he is over-elaborately trying to say). The Shakespeare text itself is even more difficult for them and Bogdanov concludes that 'the language is a real barrier'. It is to the director's credit that he does persevere, and he manages to involve more than eighty residents in performing thirty-four extracts from twelve of the plays. In some cases, he is forced simply to give up on Shakespeare's own language, allowing his performers to rewrite the script in a more modern form. In one of the most interesting pieces included in the documentary, the Romeo–Tybalt fight scene is staged in a local park, with the actor playing Romeo electing to use the original text, but with Tybalt and some of the others modernising the script, thus leading to rather glorious re-writings, such as 'Romeo! You're a *wanker*!' and, from Mercutio, a reconfiguration of 'A plague on both your houses!' as 'Fuck you all!'

In Michael Waldman's *My Shakespeare*, Paterson Joseph characterises his native Harlsden as 'a ghetto ... it's rundown and there's violence and crime and there's all the rest of it.' It is, he says, 'one of the least likeliest places to have Shakespeare, to have this high art ... And I just think: "why not?" why *can't* the people of Harlsden do Shakespeare?'[104] Like Bogdanov, the biggest problem Joseph faces is getting his cast to understand the language of the play. Repeatedly, his volunteer actors are seen stumbling over words like 'chastely', 'tyrannous' ('Do you know what it means?' 'No'), 'fray', and formulations such as 'flesh, flesh, how art thou fishified!' Watching the actor playing Mercutio, the assistant director, Bindu de Stoppani comments that he 'just doesn't understand most of the text. He just doesn't'. The actor himself comments: 'Because it's Shakespeare dialect ... it's ... really, Mr. Shakespeare likes to write like that, doesn't he? He likes to write things in a bit of a funny way.' Like Bogdanov, Joseph persists, and, on the night of the performance, his cast deliver their lines with a real sense of understanding and conviction. Their reward is to be taken to Stratford-on-Avon, to see the Royal Shakespeare Company perform *Romeo and Juliet*. With an admirable sense of tongue-in-cheek glee (and, perhaps, an intuitive eye for cultural reversal), they pronounce the performance to be a real disappointment, in the context of their own efforts at RADA. Leaving the theatre, they comment:

'Our play was much better.'
'There was no *truth* to it.'
'We were better.'
(Embracing the actor who had played Mercutio in the Harlsden production): '*This* is Mercutio. Yeah? Make no doubt about it. This is Mercutio, yeah?'

Bogdanov's and Joseph's initiatives really do achieve something – and they both manage, finally, to get beyond being well-intentioned middle-class attempts to 'bring the bard to the people'.[105] This happens, in part, because 'the people' turn out, in their own way, to be perfectly articulate – and perfectly capable of calling the outsiders to task for being patronisingly well-intentioned. But these initiatives are, of course, infinitesimally small-scale and Michael Bogdanov's conclusion is that 'This has been an exhilarating experience, but I feel angry and upset that all over the country there are communities like Ladywood full of talent and intelligence and [it's] wasted. As Caliban says: "You taught me language and my profit on't is I know how to curse."' Bogdanov is correct in saying that there are intelligent working-class communities right across the country and that the members of those communities are very rarely given the chance to access Shakespeare's work in a meaningful way. But Caliban is an intriguing figure for Bogdanov to light on at the end of the documentary. Why Caliban – and why this specific quotation from Caliban? Is Bogdanov responding to the high level of robust language he has been exposed to during his short period working at Ladywood? Is the director seeing the frank and explicit language of the residents as a betrayal of their Shakespearean linguistic inheritance? Viewed in this light, it is hard not to see Bogdanov's invocation of Caliban as another unconscious example of a rather patronising middle-class attitude to the very people whose 'talent and intelligence' he is seeking to celebrate. In this way, Bogdanov himself becomes a kind of Prospero figure – sailing into the island of the estate to spread a little Shakespearean enlightenment, before returning to his own native realm, ruing the fact that the cultural coloniser – unlike his state or church counterpart – has pitifully limited resources available to him. Such an attitude brings to mind Herbert Beerbohm Tree's 1904 production of the play, in which, in the closing tableau, Caliban mutely reaches out to the departing ship of the Europeans with imploring arms.

But perhaps this is unfair. The politically inflected Shakespeare criticism of the final decades of the twentieth century has taught us to see Caliban as a positive figure, a counter-colonial who makes his own of the coloniser's language and resists domination – 'this island's *mine*'. This counter-colonial Caliban opposes Prospero and, finally, does not need him. Taking this line, one might imagine, as a counterpoint to Beerbohm Tree, a production in which Caliban turns from the shore with settled indifference at the Europeans' departure. But this view of Caliban raises an interesting question for a project such as *Shakespeare on the Estate*: Do the working-class residents of such places as Ladywood, we might ask, really need Michael Bogdanov? And, more to the point, perhaps, do they, when all is said and done, really need William Shakespeare?

NOTES

1 J. E. MacManus, 'In Shakespeare Land', newspaper cutting (source unidentified), dated July 1901, in Lemuel Matthews Griffiths, *Newspaper Cuttings Relating to Shakespeare* at the Birmingham Central Library (hereafter LMG), vol. 1, p. 80.
2 Jonathan Rose, *The Intellectual Life of the British Working Classes* (New Haven: Yale University Press, 2002), p. 124.
3 'Shakespeare for Children', newspaper cutting (source identified as 'M.P.'), dated 7 May 1906, in LMG, vol. 7, p. 35.
4 'Shakespeare and the Schools. Dr. Gollancz and the Teachers', newspaper cutting (source identified as 'P.O.'), dated 11 May 1906, in LMG, as previous endnote.
5 'Shakespeare in the School', newspaper cutting (source identified as the *Standard*), dated 7 May 1906, in LMG, as previous endnote.
6 Rose, *Intellectual Life*, p. 124.
7 See Chapter 1, p. 51.
8 Charles Morley, *Studies in Board Schools* (London: Smith, Elder, & Co., 1897), pp. 91–2.
9 Thomas Wright (originally published under 'The Journeyman Engineer'), *Our New Masters* (New York: Augustus M. Kelley, 1969; originally published London: Strahan & Co., 1873), p. 134.
10 W. E. Adams, *Memoirs of a Social Atom*, 2 vols. (London: Hutchinson, 1903), vol. 1, pp. 581–2.
11 John Burnett (ed. & intro.), *Destiny Obscure: Autobiographies of Childhood, Education and Family from the 1820s to the 1920s* (London: Allen Lane, 1982), p. 168.
12 Alice Foley, *A Bolton Childhood* (Bolton: Bolton Libraries and Arts in co-operation with the Bolton Branch of the Worker's Educational Association, 1990; originally published Manchester: Manchester University Extra-Mural Department and North Western District of the Workers' Educational Association, 1973), p. 11.
13 *Ibid.*, p. 49.
14 Anita Hughes, 'My Autobiography', typescript, Brunel University Library, 1:357, p. 5.
15 Robert Roberts, *The Classic Slum: Salford Life in the First Quarter of the Century* (Harmondsworth: Pelican, 1973; originally published Manchester: Manchester University Press, 1971), p. 145. I have included this text under the autobiographies section of the bibliography, though it is not, strictly speaking, an autobiography. It does, however, contain much information on Roberts' life. Roberts did also publish an autobiography: *A Ragged Schooling: Growing Up in the Classic Slum* (Manchester: Mandolin, nd; originally published Manchester: Manchester University Press, 1976). He was introduced to a Shakespeare by a socialist workmate who lent him various books, including 'a volume in minuscule print of the works of William Shakespeare on which I joyfully ruined my eyes': *Ragged Schooling*, p. 196.

16 Richard Hoggart, *A Local Habitation (Life and Times, Volume I: 1918–1940)* (London: Chatto & Windus, 1988), p. 146.
17 *Ibid.*, p. 29. Born ten years later than Hoggart, in 1928, Alan Sillitoe, like Robert Roberts, failed to secure a scholarship and he notes that the 'unfamiliar puzzles and conundrums I was asked to solve might just as well have been Chinese ideograms, for I had expected to be tested on knowledge rather than intelligence'. A second attempt at the exam also ended in failure: 'A hard try was not enough, however, and my second failure indicated that I was not a fit subject for formal education. Success would in any case have led to all kinds of complications, not least that of leaving my friends and entering a world I was not prepared for': *Life Without Armour: An Autobiography* (London: HarperCollins, 1995), pp. 38–9.
18 V. W. Garratt, *A Man in the Street* (London: Dent, 1939), p. 20.
19 *Ibid.*, pp. 62–3. Garratt served in the army during the First World War and, on being demobbed, gained a place on a journalism course at London University, where he studied with the eminent Shakespearean Sidney Lee. Lee opened to him the possibility of serving as chief steward at the Shakespeare birthplace but, unlike Joseph Skipsey (see Chapter 3, pp. 121–3), he decided to pass on the offer.
20 Hoggart, *Local Habitation*, pp. 168–9.
21 *Ibid.*, p. 29.
22 See Chapter 3, p. 99.
23 Sharon O'Dair makes a similar point in her analysis of Shakespeare and the American educational system, *Class, Critics, and Shakespeare: Bottom Lines on the Culture Wars* (Ann Arbor: University of Michigan Press, 2000): 'formal and higher education offers the vulgar a voice, but principally upon the condition of assimilation into the (upper) middle class, a condition that clearly works to minimize and regulate that voice' (p. 70). Writing more specifically of third-level education, she observes: 'Working-class kids who succeed in the academy or subsequently in the professions are reconstituted and normalized as (upper) middle class. In the academy, working-class identity is not merely not affirmed, but actively erased' (p. 3).
24 Hoggart, *Local Habitation*, p. 156.
25 Raymond Williams, *Border Country* (Cardigan: Parthian, 2006; originally published London: Chatto & Windus, 1960), pp. 99, 275. I have included *Border Country* in the bibliography of autobiographical texts even though it is a novel, since it so closely matches Williams' own biography.
26 As will be clear, my focus in this section of the chapter is on the way in which Shakespeare and other aspects of high culture were experienced by those working-class children who succeeded in gaining entrance to the grammar schools. The teaching of Shakespeare was not, of course, confined to such schools, and there is another story to be told about what happened to Shakespeare in the secondary modern and comprehensive schools. This story lies outside the immediate scope of my argument here, as I am presenting the experience of the scholarship child as one element in a greater mosaic serving

to explain the decline in Shakespeare's working-class popularity. A search through the texts listed in the third volume of Burnett, Vincent and Mayall's *Autobiography of the Working Class* would likely provide a point of entry to the materials necessary for exploring the issue of Shakespeare's role in other kinds of school institutions.

27 My account of developments in secondary education here is, necessarily, highly condensed. A useful starting-point for gaining a more nuanced view of how the school system changed in the period is David Rubinstein and Brian Simon, *The Evolution of the Comprehensive School, 1926–1972* (London: Routledge & Kegan Paul, 1969; 2nd edn, 1973).
28 Brian Jackson and Dennis Marsden, *Education and the Working Class: Some General Themes Raised by a Study of 88 Working-class Children in a Northern Industrial City* (Harmondsworth: Pelican, 1966; originally published London: Routledge & Kegan Paul, 1962), p. 101.
29 *Ibid.*, p. 172.
30 Brian Jackson, *Working-Class Community: Some General Notions Raised by a Series of Studies in Northern England* (Harmondsworth: Penguin, 1972; originally published London: Routledge & Kegan Paul, 1968), p. 153.
31 Jackson and Marsden, *Education*, p. 119.
32 Ray Gosling, *Sum Total* (Hebden Bridge, West Yorkshire: Pomona, 2004; originally published London: Faber & Faber, 1962), pp. 87–8, 88. Gosling worked extensively in TV, radio and print journalism for forty years. Later in life the work dried up and, when his partner died in 1999, he entered a period of crisis, which resulted in his being declared bankrupt. He was rediscovered at this point by the BBC and featured in a series of three documentaries: *Ray Gosling: Bankrupt*, *Ray Gosling: Pensioned Off* and *Ray Gosling: OAP*, all broadcast on BBC 4. Gosling's papers are now held at the library of Nottingham Trent University. The recent documentaries have been issued on DVD by Available Light Productions.
33 Richard Hoggart, *The Uses of Literacy: Aspects of Working-class Life with Special Reference to Publications and Entertainments* (Harmondsworth: Penguin, 1971; originally published London: Chatto & Windus, 1957), p. 249.
34 Gosling, *Sum Total*, p. 164.
35 *Ibid.*, p. 164. In fact, Gosling left the university before the end of his first year.
36 Hoggart, *Local Habitation*, p. 196.
37 Christopher Thomson, *The Autobiography of an Artisan* (London: J. Chapman; Nottingham: J. Shaw and Sons, 1847), p. 101.
38 Julia Swindells, *Victorian Writing and Working Women: The Other Side of Silence* (Cambridge: Polity Press, 1985), p. 16.
39 David Vincent, *Literacy and Popular Culture: England 1750–1914* (Cambridge: Cambridge University Press, 1989), p. 167.
40 David J. Palmer, *The Rise of English Studies: An Account of the Study of English Language and Literature from its Origins to the Making of the Oxford English School* (London: Oxford University Press for the University of Hull, 1965), p. 50.

41 Thomas Dabbs notes that 'the institutional framework, the classroom methods and the lecture-hall philosophy, initially made Shakespeare inaccessible, and while the English education movement sought to democratize the understanding of cultural history, of Shakespeare, for the masses, it had, in the act of intervening on the popular marketplace, de-democratized what had been a popular form of entertainment': 'Shakespeare and the Department of English', *English and American Literature Symposium* (Tuscaloosa: University of Alabama Press, 1993), p. 92.
42 See Chapter 2, pp. 81–6.
43 Vincent, *Literacy*, p. 279.
44 Thomas Frost, *Reminiscences of a Country Journalist* (London: Ward & Downey, 1886), pp. 155, 155–6.
45 Charles James Billson, *Leicester Memories* (Leicester: Edgar Backus, 1924), p. 112.
46 Richard Foulkes, *Performing Shakespeare in the Age of Empire* (Cambridge: Cambridge University Press, 2002), p. 206.
47 Cary DiPietro, *Shakespeare and Modernism* (Cambridge: Cambridge University Press, 2006), p. 91, quoting Edward Gordon Craig, 'A National Theatre: Its Advantages and Disadvantages. An International Symposium', *The Mask*, 2 (July 1909), pp. 81–9, 86–7. Craig's views are further confirmed in a letter he wrote to Israel Gollancz in March 1916, in which he observes: 'If Democracy stands for levelling down, then Art and Democracy can never live in the same country ... It is no doubt true that many other lands are able to boast an equal disrespect and disregard of their natural noblemen, their artists, great and small; but there seems no reason why England should struggle to be first in such a race. While every Englishman must love England, to love this England is not possible': manuscript W.a.79(39) Folger Shakespeare Library.
48 Foulkes, *Performing Shakespeare*, p. 206.
49 Lawrence W. Levine makes a somewhat similar argument regarding cultural divisions in the United States: 'after the turn of the century ... cultural products *had* to be accepted on the terms proffered by those who controlled the cultural institutions. In that sense, while there was never a total monopoly of access, there was a tight control over the terms of access. The taste that now prevailed was that of one segment of the social and economic spectrum which convinced itself and the nation at large that its way of seeing, understanding, and appreciating music, theater, and art was the only legitimate one; that *this* was the way Shakespeare, Beethoven, and Greek sculpture were meant to be experienced': *Highbrow/Lowbrow: The Emergence of Cultural Hierarchy in America* (Cambridge, MA: Harvard University Press, 1988), pp. 230–1.
50 John Carey, *The Intellectuals and the Masses: Pride and Prejudice Among the Literary Intelligentsia, 1880–1939* (London: Faber & Faber, 1992), pp. 16–17. Regenia Gagnier offers something like a parallel argument to this. She observes that the 'social role of "the artist," as well as her subjective identity, that reached its culmination in literary modernism was typified by [the] economy of the resistant self, its privacy, internality, and dream of autonomy from circumstance'

divorced from a commitment to communal identity or politics – *Subjectivities: A History of Self-Representation in Britain, 1832–1920* (Oxford: Oxford University Press, 1991), p. 222.

51 See Hugh Grady, *The Modernist Shakespeare: Critical Texts in a Material World* (Oxford: Clarendon Press, 1991), Richard Halpern, *Shakespeare Among the Moderns* (Ithaca, NY: Yale University Press, 1997) and DiPietro, *Shakespeare and Modernism*.
52 Virginia Woolf, *A Room of One's Own* (Harmondsworth: Penguin, 1945; originally published London: Hogarth Press, 1929), p. 42.
53 *The Teaching of English in England* (London: HMSO, 1921), p. 252.
54 See Chapter 3, p. 99.
55 See Robert Hewison, *Culture and Consensus: England, Arts and Politics since 1940* (London: Methuen, 1995), p. 34. Hewison draws on the memoirs of Mary Glasgow, secretary to CEMA. As will be clear, I am heavily indebted to Hewison's work throughout this section of my study.
56 *Ibid.*, p. 40.
57 *Ibid.*, p. 36.
58 *Ibid.*, p. 80.
59 Details from a conversation with Lee recalled by Sir John Drummond in an interview on *Cultural State*, programme 3 ('Ministers of Taste'), BBC Radio 4, broadcast on 20 September 2004.
60 Rose, *Intellectual Life*, p. 5.
61 Arnold Freeman, *Boy Life and Labour: The Manufacture of Inefficiency* (New York: Garland, 1980 (facsimile reprint); originally published London: P. S. King & Son, 1914), pp. 31–2.
62 *Ibid.*, p. 159.
63 *Ibid.*, p. 158.
64 All of these details are taken from Tony Mason, *Association Football and English Society 1863–1915* (Brighton: Harvester, 1980).
65 Edward Brown, untitled typescript, Brunel University Library, 1:93, p. 37.
66 Alfred Williams, *Life in a Railway Factory* (New York: Garland, 1980; originally published London: Duckworth, 1915), p. 287.
67 Roberts, *Classic Slum*, p. 163.
68 John Eldred, *I Love the Brooks* (London: Skeffington, 1955), p. 94.
69 T. P. O'Connor, 'The New Journalism', *New Review*, 1 (1889), p. 434.
70 Aled Jones, *Powers of the Press: Newspaper, Power and the Public in Nineteenth-century England* (Aldershot: Ashgate, 1996), p. 132.
71 S. J. Taylor, *The Great Outsiders: Northcliffe, Rothermere and the* Daily Mail (London: Phoenix Giant, 1996), pp. 28–9.
72 Max Pemberton, *Lord Northcliffe: A Memoir* (London: Hodder & Stoughton, nd), pp. 29, 29–30.
73 See J. Lee Thompson, *Northcliffe: Press Baron in Politics, 1865–1922* (London: John Murray, 2000), pp. 19–20.
74 Simon Eliot, *Some Patterns and Trends in British Publishing 1800–1919* (London: Bibliographical Society, 1994), p. 50. The balance was slowly

redressed in the following decades, with 'Poetry and Drama' recovering to 12% (1890s), 15% (1900s) and 20% (1910s, though figures for this decade are, of course, distorted somewhat by the general disruption of the publishing industry which occurred because of the First World War).

75 On the decline of the three-decker, see Guinevere L. Griest, *Mudie's Circulating Library and the Victorian Novel* (Newton Abbot, Devon: David & Charles, nd; originally published Indiana University Press, 1970), pp. 168–71. Griest gives the following figures for the number of three volume novels issued in the final years of the format: 1894, 184; 1895, 52; 1896, 25; 1897, 4 (p. 208).
76 'The Manufacture of Novels', *The Spectator*, 3,818 (31 August 1901), p. 278.
77 Nan Hackett, *XIX Century British Working-Class Autobiographies* (New York: AMS, 1985), p. 28.
78 Thomas Burke, *The Wind and the Rain: A Book of Confessions* (London: Thornton Butterworth, 1924), p. 249.
79 George H. Barber, *From Workhouse to Lord Mayor: An Autobiography* (Tunstall: published by the author, 1937), p. 12.
80 Philip Boswood Ballard, *Things I Cannot Forget* (London: University of London Press, 1937), p. 110.
81 Freeman, *Boy Life*, p. 133.
82 *Ibid.*, p. 110.
83 Roberts, *Classic Slum*, p. 175. In a footnote on the same page, Roberts reports that 'In 1912 the governor of Durham gaol was struck by the number of boys in prison who confessed to stealing in order to get money to go to picture palaces'.
84 *Ibid.*, p. 229.
85 Thomas Todd, *My Life as I Have Lived It: Autobiography of Thomas Todd of Middleton-in-Teesdale* (Leeds: printed for Thomas Todd, 1935), p. 124.
86 T. S. Eliot, 'Marie Lloyd', *Selected Essays* (London: Faber & Faber, 1980; first published 1932), p. 459.
87 Michael Collins, *The Likes of Us: A Biography of the White Working Class* (London: Granta, 2004), p. 171.
88 See Hewison, *Culture and Consensus*, pp. 67–8.
89 Collins, *Likes of Us*, pp. 170–1.
90 The decline of interest in reading books is also nicely illustrated by an interview with the Sheffield band the Arctic Monkeys, published in *The Observer* in December 2006. The band, whose members come from broadly working-class backgrounds, has been particularly celebrated for its well-observed lyrics. But when asked by journalist Chris Heath 'What book has changed the way you think about the world?', their answers were as follows:

Jamie Cook (guitar): 'That's a bad question for me. The last book I read, seriously, were *The Fantastic Mr Fox* when I were about 11 . . . I read a lot now – magazines – but I just can't read books at all. I don't know why – everyone reads books around us and that. I get a chapter in and . . . fuck it.'

Nick O'Malley (bass): I don't know if there is one . . . I'm not that big a reader. I haven't read many since school . . .'

Alex Turner (singer/guitarist): Reading's one of those things I think I've got to come. People have tried to get me into it ... But I rarely do love it ...'

Matt Helders (drums): 'I've not read a lot of books, to be honest, but before we've done any tours or anything I read one of the Led Zeppelin books, the one by Richard Cole, the tour manager.'

Chris Heath, 'Cocks of the North', *The Observer Music Monthly*, 40 (December 2006), pp. 32–4. There is a certain irony in the fact that the band's first album takes its title (*Whatever people say I am, that's what I'm not*) from a line in Alan Sillitoe's classic novel of working-class life, *Saturday Night and Sunday Morning* (London: Harper Perennial, 2006; originally published London: W. H. Allen & Co., 1958), where Sillitoe's Arthur Seaton asserts: 'whatever people think I am or say I am, that's what I'm not, because they don't know a bloody thing about me' (p. 138). Significantly, in the current context, the band discovered the line through Karel Reisz's 1960 film, rather than through the book itself.

91 Burnett, *Destiny Obscure*, p. 168.
92 Josephine Guy (ed.), *The Victorian Age: An Anthology of Sources and Documents* (London: Routledge, 2001), pp. 210–11. Philip Boswood Ballard notes in *Things I Cannot Forget* that he followed 'a controversy which was being carried on in *The Nineteenth Century* between Mr. Gladstone and Mr. T. H. Huxley over the First Chapter of Genesis. My sentimental sympathy was with Gladstone, my intellectual sympathy with Huxley. For Huxley, it seemed to me, left the Grand Old Man without a leg to stand on. How empty these controversies seem to us to-day! To find their parallel one must go to the Fundamentalists of Tennessee' (p. 211).
93 Eliot, *Patterns and Trends*, pp. 44, 50–51.
94 Roberts, *Classic Slum*, p. 173.
95 Rowland Kenney, *Westering: An Autobiography* (London: J. M. Dent & Sons, 1939), p. 20.
96 See Burnett, *Destiny Obscure*, p. 141.
97 See Marianne Farningham (pseud. of Mary Anne Hearn), *A Working Woman's Life: An Autobiography* (London: James Clarke, [1907]), pp. 96–8. Hearn was, in fact, elected to the board some years later.
98 *Ibid.*, p. 28.
99 A transition that was helped, it might be said, by the great popularity of *Pilgrim's Progress* (see Chapter 3, p. 101), first published in 1678 and steeped, itself, in the language of the authorised version. Q. D. Leavis' rather haughtily snobbish observation might, in this context, be thought to have a certain relevance: 'it appears axiomatic that one cannot spend Sundays over the Bible and *Pilgrim's Progress* and read the *Windsor Magazine* happily in the week. But if for the Bible and *Pilgrim's Progress* are substituted the *News of the World* and the *Sunday Express*, it will be evident that popular taste is likely to be in some danger': *Fiction and the Reading Public* (London: Chatto & Windus, 1965, first published 1932), p. 117.

100 Having been born in 1928, Alan Sillitoe was somewhat unusual in attending, for a brief period, a school in which the Bible was extensively read in the classroom. In his autobiography, he writes of his teacher that 'She read from her own black leatherbound King James's translation of the Bible whose English, whether or not all parts were immediately understood, entered my soul for life' (*Life Without Armour*, p. 11).
101 *Teaching of English*, pp. 312, 341.
102 For a somewhat similar project in the United States, see Hank Rogerson and Jilann Spitzmiller (prod.), *Shakespeare Behind Bars* (Philomath Films/ITVS/BBC, 2006).
103 Penny Woolcock (dir.), *Shakespeare on the Estate* (BBC, 1994).
104 Michael Waldman (prod. & dir.), *My Shakespeare* (Penguin Television, 2004; broadcast on Channel 4).
105 This is something which happens in the US as much as it does in the UK. See Richard Burt's posting – 'Laura Bush wants to take Shakespeare to US gangland' – on SHAKSPER (SHK 16.0819 Thursday, 28 April 2005). Burt quotes from an AFP report, which includes details of an exchange between Bush and the talkshow host, Jay Leno:

'Will boys really want – Shakespeare, come on,' Leno questioned.

'They actually love it,' Bush replied, saying that she intended to visit a program that uses Shakespeare plays to hook children on reading and acting. 'Think about Shakespeare. It's bloody. All those things that boys might like.'

'See, I couldn't see myself – "Hey, you gang-bangers, come on over here for some Shakespeare"', Leno responded. 'Seems like it would be tricky to do.'

Bush's remarks came as she lamented a lack of worthy male role models, including men teachers, for American youth.

Afterword

So, now, in the twenty-first century, do working-class readers need William Shakespeare? Or, to put it another way, does it matter in any real sense that Shakespeare is no longer so readily embraced or appreciated by a working-class audience? The first thing that we might note in response to this question is that the divisions between elite and popular culture are not – and never have been – quite as clear-cut and rigid as Chapter 5 of this study might appear to suggest. To take the instance of the cinema, it certainly is true that film provided a new kind of entertainment which competed with traditional forms of leisure activity, such as reading and the theatre, but Shakespeare, of course, was very quickly absorbed by the new medium.[1] One of the earliest films to be made in Britain was a condensed version of *King John*, filmed by William Kennedy-Laurie Dickson (an associate of Thomas Edison) at Her Majesty's Theatre in September 1899. It was shown in London for several months and reportedly drew an audience of 170,000.[2] Some 500 silent Shakespeare films (that we know of) were made in the wake of the Dickson *King John*, indicating a ready audience for this particular subgenre of early cinema.

With the advent of sound, Shakespeare continued to have a significant presence in the commercial cinema market, and, in fact, one of the earliest movies to be provided with a synchronised soundtrack was Sam Taylor's *The Taming of the Shrew*, starring Mary Pickford and Douglas Fairbanks, released in 1929 – just two years after *The Jazz Singer*. In 1944, Olivier's *Henry V* proved a genuine popular success and it aimed, specifically, at boosting morale during the final difficult period of the war. The attraction of the film is nicely indicated in Alan Sillitoe's novel of northern working-class life, *Saturday Night and Sunday Morning*, where Arthur Seaton observes of his cinema-going: 'I must have seen thousands of pictures, like everybody else, but I'll bet I can't remember half a dozen. I remember "Henry the Fifth" and I saw it years ago, but that's only because I saw it about six times.'[3] The film strives to forge a unified image of the nation, as emblematised by the 'four captains' scene, in which English, Scottish, Welsh and Irish soldiers work together for the British cause. *Henry V* can, in some respects, be said to be characteristic of a cultural shift which occurred during the course of the war, whereby class divisions were presented as being suspended in the cause of national unity. The four captains scene is thus mirrored in a number of popular wartime films featuring a 'group hero' – a collection of central characters drawn from different levels of society who all pull together for the good of the greater cause.[4]

Through the middle decades of the century, filmed versions of Shakespeare continued to enjoy considerable popular success, with Franco Zeffirelli's *Romeo and Juliet* earning $48,000,000 at the box office (having been made for a budget of $800,000).[5] The most strikingly successful late twentieth-century Shakespeare film was, of course, another version of the same play: Baz Luhrmann's 1996 *Romeo + Juliet*. In Chapter 5, I suggested that one of the greatest barriers to a general appreciation of Shakespeare is the inability of those who have not been schooled in early modern English to understand the actual text of the plays. Luhrmann was given a very strong sense of this problem when he went to pitch the *Romeo + Juliet* project in Hollywood. His executive producer, Peter Rice, gave him one piece of advice before the meeting: 'Don't mention the language. Tell the story; don't mention the language.'[6] The techniques that Luhrmann used to overcome the barrier presented by the text itself are well known, ranging from the rather gimmicky – for example, close-ups of handguns bearing the brand-name 'Sword 9mm' – to more inventive ways of trying to find visual analogies for the text, so that the onscreen image helps to carry the narrative forward, particularly when the audience (and even, some might uncharitably say, some of the actors) do not necessarily understand every word of the dialogue. The addition of a well-chosen soundtrack featuring music by contemporary performers also added to the mass appeal of the film.

It may have been Luhrmann's success that prompted a very particular kind of Shakespearean revival at the turn of the century, with a range of films based on modernised, adapted versions of the plays being released, including, most notably, Gil Junger's *10 Things I Hate About You* (1999; based on *The Taming of the Shrew*), Billy Morrissette's *Scotland, PA* (2001; *Macbeth*), Tim Blake Nelson's *O* (2001; *Othello*), Tommy O'Haver's *Get Over It* (2001; *A Midsummer Night's Dream*) and Andy Fickman's *She's the Man* (2006; *Twelfth Night*). This particular clutch of films is a peculiarly American phenomenon, with all but one of these adaptations being given

US high school settings. But the trend towards drawing on Shakespeare to create new modern narratives can be seen in the UK as well, with the BBC commissioning a series of contemporary interpretations of four Shakespeare plays (*Much Ado About Nothing*, *Macbeth*, *The Taming of the Shrew* and *A Midsummer Night's Dream*), broadcast on BBC One on consecutive weeks in November 2005 (under the series title 'Shakespeare Retold').[7] Likewise, a 2007 episode of the popular British science fiction series *Dr. Who*, entitled *The Shakespeare Code*, relies heavily (though in a rather tongue-in-cheek way) on a popular general knowledge both of the plays and of Shakespeare's life. Reflecting on the impact that Hamnet's death had on him, Shakespeare observes: it 'made me question everything: the futility of this fleeting existence – to be or not to be'. Here, he pauses and comments 'oh, that's quite good', but when the Doctor urges him to write it down, he responds: 'Maybe not. Bit pretentious?' For more hard-core Shakespeareans, the entire plot of the episode centres on a performance of *Love's Labours Won*, the pages of which are irretrievably dispersed in the whirlwind of the story's climax.[8]

What we find here, then, is that Shakespeare's work does have a continuing general presence within popular culture (broadly defined), through the regular appearance of more or less faithful (though, usually, heavily cut) films of the plays and also through the dispersal of Shakespearean narratives into the culture more generally. But, of course, this is not the same thing as having – as Shakespeare crucially did have in the nineteenth century – an audience fully engaged with his work, specifically as readers. There is a big difference, we might say, between watching *She's the Man* at the local multiplex (possibly without ever knowing that it is based on *Twelfth Night*) and engaging in the kind of intense study of the plays that we saw was characteristic of, for example, Thomas Cooper.[9] So, the question still persists: Does it matter that Shakespeare no longer commands that kind of working-class audience?

In one sense, I think the answer to this question is actually 'no, it doesn't'. Shakespeare's status as a centrally important author is guaranteed in a great number of different ways, including through the existence of such institutions as, in the UK, the Shakespeare Institute and the Royal Shakespeare Company and, in the US, the Folger Shakespeare Library. But, it is unrealistic to expect that his work can always remain at the centre of general culture. At the risk of descending into cliché: culture is fluid; it changes over time. New cultural forms emerge, displacing the old, and such new forms are generally resisted at their point of emergence. This was as true of Shakespeare's time as it is of our own. For much of the

Renaissance, stage plays were seen as populist ephemera, not to be ranked with the high literary form of poetry. Philip Sidney observed that 'Our Tragedies, and Comedies . . . not without cause [are] cried out against, . . . obseruing rules neyther of honest ciuilitie nor of skilfull Poetrie' and Thomas Bodley, founder of the Oxford University library that bears his name, famously classified printed plays as 'baggage books', to be excluded from his library.[10] When Ben Jonson's dramas were included in a collected edition of his work published in folio format, it was seen by some as an act of self-aggrandising folly. Moving forward in time, we might note that, while we now regard the novel as an important literary form, at the end of the eighteenth century novels were, like plays before them, the cause of some considerable head-shaking. The *Monthly Review* complained that 'novels spring into existence like insects on the banks of the Nile, and, if we may be indulged in another comparison, cover the shelves of our circulating libraries, as locusts crowd the fields of Asia. Their great and growing number is a serious evil'.[11] By the twentieth century, it was the new medium of sound cinema that was causing alarm. In the *Dialectic of Enlightenment*, Max Horkheimer and Theodor Adorno offered some quite startling observations on the nature of film:

The sound film, far surpassing the theatre of illusion, leaves no room for imagination or reflection on the part of the audience, who is unable to respond within the structure of the film, yet deviate from its precise detail without losing the thread of the story; hence the film forces its victim to equate it directly with reality.[12]

Horkheimer and Adorno found jazz to be an equally alarming cultural development, recruiting Nietzsche to help them oppose the form:

A jazz musician who is playing a piece of serious music, one of Beethoven's simplest minuets, syncopates it involuntarily and will smile superciliously when asked to follow the normal divisions of the beat. This is the 'nature' which, complicated by the ever-present and extravagant demands of the specific medium, constitutes the new style and is a 'system of non-culture, to which one might even concede a certain "unity of style" if it really made any sense to speak of stylized barbarity.'[13]

Moving forward to the beginning of the twenty-first century, we find Sir Peter Maxwell Davies, Master of the Queen's Music, condemning contemporary dance music in even more stark terms, as he observes that 'this music reflects something every bit as disturbing in our collective psyche as communism or fascism at their genocidal worst'.[14]

The rejection of new cultural forms is often accompanied by a nostalgic harking-back to an idyllic past. Thus, when T. S. Eliot, in his essay on

'Marie Lloyd', condemns the age of the cinema, the gramophone and the cheap motor-car, he offers a contrast with the lost era of the music hall – a cultural form condemned as debased in its own day.[15] Richard Hoggart's rejection of the late 1950s' culture of rock and roll and juke-box milk bars in *The Uses of Literacy* adopts much the same strategy: 'Compared even with the pub around the corner, this is all a peculiarly thin and pallid form of dissipation, a sort of spiritual dry-rot amid the odour of boiled milk.'[16] Likewise, when Sir Peter Maxwell Davies links contemporary dance music with the worst excesses of totalitarianism, his point of contrast is the popular music of the early 1960s: 'In [today's] commercial atmosphere, it is hardly astonishing that so little of its kind is produced of Beatles or early Rolling Stones quality.'[17]

Steve Johnson, in *Everything Bad is Good for You*, has delineated a tendency to see culture as being endlessly in decline and he has characterised this analysis as proposing a 'cultural race to the bottom', whereby 'mass culture follows a steadily declining path toward lowest-common-denominator standards, presumably because the "masses" want dumb, simple pleasures and big media companies want to give the masses what they want'.[18] Johnson argues strongly against this view, and he makes a case for the validity and usefulness of contemporary forms such as video games and popular entertainment, suggesting that 'culture is getting more intellectually demanding, not less'.[19] I would not wish to extend Johnson's argument to the point of suggesting that, for example, *Grand Theft Auto: Vice City Stories* or *Need for Speed Carbon* should be seen as exact contemporary equivalents of *Hamlet* (and, in any case, there are significant problems with the criteria of value that Johnson applies in his book).[20] However, I do feel that there is a broader point that can be drawn from Johnson's study. To insist that Shakespeare should have a working-class audience, and to engage in initiatives dedicated to 'bringing Shakespeare to the masses' is surely, in some sense, to fetishise a single particular set of 400-year-old texts and to insist that *this* is what constitutes culture – often at the expense of contemporary forms, many of which emerge, of course, in the first instance precisely from working-class (or other disadvantaged) communities.[21] Viewed from this perspective, to insist that a mass popular audience must always in some way be maintained for Shakespeare is to seek to impose external cultural standards, pushing against the tide of ongoing (and often native working-class) cultural development.

And yet, there is a certain danger in this argument. In his *Characters of Shakespear's Plays*, William Hazlitt famously observed that the 'language of poetry naturally falls in with the language of power'.[22] We might usefully,

I would suggest, in the current context modify Hazlitt's formulation to say that there is a way in which the language of *Shakespeare* naturally falls in with the language of power. In Chapter 5, we noted that Ray Gosling directly linked the appreciation of Shakespeare that was nurtured in him at his grammar school with the greater ethos that the school represented: Shakespeare and the other canonical writers he was introduced to 'were in a package deal with The School and the way up, on to the best possible University, and on to the best possible outlet in teaching or commerce, or what have you'.[23] A knowledge and appreciation of Shakespeare, in this sense, is part and parcel of a culture of success and, ultimately, a culture of power. The significance of this is nicely illustrated by a report entitled *The Educational Backgrounds of Leading Journalists*, published in the UK by the Sutton Trust in June 2006. The report revealed that, while those educated at private schools in the UK account for just 7% of the population, some 54% of leading journalists had attended such schools. Of those journalists holding a university degree, 56% had attended either Oxford or Cambridge (72% attended one of the UK's thirteen leading universities).[24] The report notes that 'the latest new recruits to the national news media are even more likely to come from privileged backgrounds than those from previous generations'.[25] The leading opinion-formers in the UK are, we might say, drawing on Gosling, overwhelmingly products of The School and all that it stands for. If this is true of the media, it is equally true of politics, with those educated at private schools and elite universities being disproportionately represented in both the cabinet and the shadow-cabinet.[26]

Of course, it is hardly fair to blame Shakespeare for all of this. But my point is that adopting an attitude which suggests that the working class should take or leave Shakespeare as they see fit runs the risk of ceding cultural power, which in turn runs the risk of ceding political power. This, surely, was what the Chartists and the earliest Labour activists understood: that cultural power can be as important as political power because, fundamentally, the two are intertwined. From this perspective, then, I would say that the answer to my question 'does it matter that Shakespeare no longer commands a working-class audience?' is actually 'yes, it does'. Shakespeare matters, politically, because his work is bound in with the cultural mechanisms of political power. This is one of the reasons why *The Chartist Circular*, *The Northern Star* and individual Chartist writers adopted Shakespeare's work and re-forged his text to their own ends. For the Chartists and for the first generations of Labour politicians, Shakespeare was a genuine ally, whose words were made to serve progressive political ends. Of course, his work is not in any real sense *necessary* to a progressive politics, and simply reading Shakespeare is not, in isolation, going to change the world – it might turn out to be just a pleasurable end in itself. But, as the apolitical autobiographers encountered in this study have indicated, that, in itself, has its own merits and rewards. And who knows what else it might lead to.

NOTES

1 I take the case of cinema as an exemplary instance here, but one could also discuss popular recyclings of the Shakespeare text in, for example, comicbook and graphic novel renditions, or on the Internet.
2 See Kenneth Rothwell, *A History of Shakespeare on Screen: A Century of Film and Television* (Cambridge: Cambridge University Press, 1999), pp. 1–3. I also draw on Rothwell more generally for the history of Shakespeare on film.
3 Allan Sillitoe, *Saturday Night and Sunday Morning* (London: Harper Perennial, 2006; originally published London: W. H. Allen & Co., 1958), p. 152. Sillitoe relates his own experience of watching the film in *Life Without Armour: An Autobiography* (London: HarperCollins, 1995), pp. 92–3.
4 I owe this point entirely to my colleague Gill Plain and I am very grateful to her for her feedback on the twentieth century section of the book. In her study of *John Mills and British Cinema* (Edinburgh: Edinburgh University Press, 2006), she develops the point: 'The success of the group hero as propaganda ... depends upon difference. It must be, of necessity, heterogeneous, made up of characters divided by class, education and geography, but united by a common purpose. Alongside a number of representatives of middle-class England, the group will usually contain a variety of working-class types, and these characters between them will also embrace further dimensions of region and ethnicity. There will be a Celt, a cockney and/or a northerner, with an optional bookworm or toff thrown in to liven up the oppositional dynamics. The composite hero attempts to represent in microcosm the sum of those who have a stake in the nation at war – at the same time as it works, ideologically, to construct that which it claims to represent' (p. 59).
5 See Rothwell, *Shakespeare on Screen*, p. 134.
6 'Baz Luhrmann tells the story of pitching a modern day Shakespeare to a Hollywood studio', included among the extra material to the DVD of Baz Luhrmann (dir.), *Romeo + Juliet* (Twentieth-Century Fox, 1996).
7 Available on DVD: Laura Mackie and Patrick Spence (exec. prod.), *Shakespeare Retold* (Acorn Video, 2006).
8 Gareth Roberts, *The Shakespeare Code*, dir. Charles Palmer (BBC Wales/Canadian Broadcasting Corporation, 2007). The wittily conceived story is full of such moments. The Doctor's sidekick, Martha Jones, is played by the black actress Freema Agyeman and Shakespeare, enchanted by her, calls her his 'dark lady'. During a seductive exchange between them, the Doctor intervenes, saying impatiently: 'Come on! We can all have a good flirt later', at which Shakespeare archly gazes at him and asks 'Is that a promise, Doctor?',

prompting the Doctor to observe 'Oh, fiftyseven academics just punched the air'. My thanks to Romney Johnstone for drawing my attention to the episode (discussion of the Kingsbarns musical *Macbeth* will, however, have to wait for another occasion).

9 The same might be said of encounters with Shakespeare in other popular cultural forms, for example, *A Bomb-itty of Errors*, 'An ad-rap-tation of Shakespeare's comedy' (see www.bomb-itty.com) or SelfMadeHero's Manga Shakespeare series (see http://comipress.com/press-release/2007/01/16/1337). (Both sites accessed 17 January 2007.)

10 Sir Philip Sidney, *An Apologie for Poetrie* (London: Henry Olney, 1595), I4v; letter from Sir Thomas Bodley to Thomas James, dated 15 January 1612, in G. W. Wheeler, ed., *Letters of Sir Thomas Bodley to Thomas James, First Keeper of the Bodleian Library* (Oxford: Clarendon Press, 1926), p. 222.

11 Review of Helen-Maria Williams' *Julia*, *Monthly Review*, vol. 2 (July 1790), p. 334.

12 Max Horkheimer and Theodor W. Adorno, *Dialect of Enlightenment*, John Cumming (trans.) (New York: Continuum, 1987; original German edition published 1947), p. 126.

13 *Ibid.*, p. 128. The closing quotation is taken (in the original) from Nietzsche, *Unzeitgemässe Betrachtungen*, *Werke*, vol. 1 (Leipzig: Kröner, 1917), p. 187.

14 Quoted in Sean O'Hagan, 'A fine mind poisoned by too much loud Wagner?', *Observer*, 15 April 2007, Review section, p. 11.

15 T. S. Eliot, 'Marie Lloyd', in *Selected Essays* (London: Faber & Faber, 1980; first published 1932), esp. p. 458.

16 Richard Hoggart, *The Uses of Literacy: Aspects of Working-class Life with Special Reference to Publications and Entertainments* (Harmondsworth: Penguin, 1971; originally published London: Chatto & Windus, 1957), p. 24.

17 Quoted in O'Hagan, 'Fine mind', p. 11.

18 Steven Johnson, *Everything Bad is Good for You: How Popular Culture is Making Us Smarter* (London: Allen Lane, 2005), pp. 9, 198.

19 *Ibid.*, p. 9.

20 In many instances, Johnson celebrates what essentially amount to the cognitive benefits to be gained from, for example, playing video games or watching complex television narratives (such as *24* or *The Sopranos*). But, the achievement of, say, better eye–hand co-ordination will, I think, seem a relatively low-level gain in the context of what many people feel is to be had from reading a Shakespeare play, even if the precise benefits of such reading are – as critics such as Terry Eagleton and John Carey have made abundantly clear – notoriously difficult to specify exactly.

21 Popular music is an obvious example here, having its roots in the blues of slave communities, and with notable developments such as punk or rap being carried forward (largely at least) by working-class innovators.

22 William Hazlitt, *Characters of Shakespear's Plays* (London: R. Hunter, C. & J. Ollier, 1817), p. 70.

23 Ray Gosling, *Sum Total* (Hebden Bridge, West Yorkshire: Pomona, 2004; originally published London: Faber & Faber, 1962), p. 88.

24 Identified by Sutton as Birmingham, Bristol, Cambridge, Durham, Edinburgh, Imperial, London School of Economics, Nottingham, Oxford, St Andrews, University College London, Warwick and York.
25 *The Educational Backgrounds of Leading Journalists* (London: Sutton Trust, 2006), p. 4.
26 At the time of writing, both the British Prime Minister and the leader of the opposition have been educated at elite private schools – at (respectively) Fettes and Eton. Both are graduates of Oxford University. More than half the members of the current shadow cabinet have been educated at private schools, with some 20% of them having attended Eton. Of the full Conservative parliamentary party, 57% have attended private schools, with a further 23% having attended grammar schools, giving a total of 80%. See http://politics.guardian.co.uk/conservatives/story/0,,2093552,00.html (accessed 2 June 2007).

Appendix 1: Autobiographers by year of birth

Dates	Name	Place of birth	Father's occupation (and mother's, where applicable)	Principal occupation(s)	Autobiography	DNB
1771–1854	Francis Place	London	Baker and innkeeper	Apprenticed to a leather breeches maker; became a master tailor	Autobiographical texts published in 1972	Yes
b. 1774	John Jones	Clearwell, Forest of Dean	Gardener. Mother kept a small shop	Ploughboy; servant; poet	Short account of his life included in Southey's *Lives of the Uneducated Poets*	No
1774–1860	John Vine Hall	Diss, Norfolk	Had owned property, but lost it. No other details	Apprenticed to a schoolmaster; errand boy; traveller for a wine merchant; ran a bookshop	Published London, 1865	Yes
1775–1846	Allen Davenport	Ewen, Gloucestershire	No details. Mother a hand-loom weaver	Ploughboy; worked at inn; servant; poet	Self-published, London, 1845	Yes
1781–1849	Ebenezer Elliott	Masbrough, Yorkshire	Ironmonger, later a clerk	Worked in foundry; bar iron merchant; poet	Published in *Athenaeum*, 1850, reproduced in *Life, Poetry and Letters*, 1850	Yes
1783–1859	Elizabeth Ham	North Perrot, Somerset	Farmer and brewer	Governess; author	Published London, 1945	Yes
1786–1810	Joseph Blacket	Tunstill, Yorkshire	Labourer	Shoemaker; poet	Included in *Remains of Joseph Blacket*, published London, 1811	Yes
1788–1872	Samuel Bamford	Middleton, Lancashire	Both parents handloom weavers	Weaver; warehouseman	Published in parts, then bound, London, 1848–9. Several further editions, including modern edition, London, 1967	Yes
1789–1860	Betsy Cadwaladyr (published under pseud. Elizabeth Davis)	Pen Rhiw, Merioneth	Shepherd, small-holder, Methodist preacher	Servant; ship's steward; nurse	Published London, 1857, modern edition Cardiff, 1987	Yes
1791–1843	Sarah Martin	Caister, Norfolk	Tradesman (unspecified). Both parents died when she was an infant. Brought up by a grandmother, who was a glove-maker	Dressmaker; teacher at Yarmouth jail	Published Yarmouth, 1844, reissued by Religious Tract Society, 1847	Yes

Dates	Name	Birthplace	Father's occupation	Own occupation	Publication details	
b. 1792	Thomas Carter	Colchester	Husbandman and labourer. Mother a servant	Tailor	Two vols., published London, 1845, 1850	No
1792–1849	Henry Hetherington	Soho, London	Tailor	Compositor; publisher; journalist	Ms fragment at Bishopsgate Institute, London	Yes
b. 1794	Samuel Westcott Tilke	Newton-Poppleford, Devonshire	Baker and vet	Farmworker; baker; physician	Self-published, London, 1840	No
1794–1884	Joseph Livesey	Walton, Lancashire	Handloom cloth manufacturer	Weaver; cheese factor; temperance advocate; publisher of temperance periodicals	Published serially in *Staunch Teetotaller*, 1868, reissued by National Temperance League in 1881 and 1885.	Yes
1796–1859	John Brown	Barnwell, Cambridgeshire	Butcher	Shoemaker; spent some time as an actor and sailor	Self-published, Cambridge, 1858, American edition New York, 1859	No
b. 1797	Robert Skeen	Tweedmouth, Durham	Fisherman	Printer	Privately published (100 copies only), London, 1876	No
1799–1871	Christopher Thomson	Hull	Shipwright and carpenter	Shipwright; actor; housepainter	Published London, 1847	No
1800–77	William Lovett	Newlyn, Cornwall	Captain of small trading vessel (died before Lovett's birth). Mother was a fish-seller	Rope maker; cabinet maker	Published London, 1876. Various subsequent editions, including modern edition, London, 1967	Yes
1802–78	John Wood	Allerton, near Bradford	Handloom weaver	Cotton weaver; schoolmaster	Published by the *Chronicle and Mail* office, Bradford, 1877	No
1804–80	Charles Manby Smith	Tiverton (?), Devonshire	Cabinet maker	Printer	Published serially in *Tait's Edinburgh Magazine*, 1851–2, then London, 1853. Modern edition London, 1967	No
b. 1805	William Heaton	Luddenden, Yorkshire	Tanner	Handloom weaver; poet	'Sketch of the Author's Life' included in collection of poems published London, 1857	No
1805–92	Thomas Cooper	Leicester	Dyer. Died when Cooper was aged four. Mother took up trade of dyer	Shoemaker; teacher; activist; writer; religious lecturer	Published London, 1872, various other editions. Modern edition Leicester, 1971	Yes

Dates	Name	Place of birth	Father's occupation (and mother's, where applicable)	Principal occupation(s)	Autobiography	DNB
1806–75	Joseph Barker	Bramley, Yorkshire	Soldier	Methodist minister; religious controversialist; publisher	Published London, 1880	Yes
1809–63	Robert Lowery	North Shields	Sailor	Worked at a colliery; sailor; apprenticed to tailor; ran a shop and public house	Published serially in *The Weekly Record of the Temperance Movement*, 1856–7. Modern edition London, 1979	Yes
b. 1812	J.A. Leatherland	Kettering	Carpenter	Weaver; poet; newspaper writer	'Autobiographical Memoir' included in *Essays and Poems*, published London, 1862	No
1813–94	Thomas Dunning	Chester	Valet. Mother was a servant	Stableboy; servant; shoemaker; newsagent and bookseller	Published in *Transactions of the Lancashire and Cheshire Antiquarian Society*, 1947. Included in Vincent, *Testaments of Radicalism*, 1977	No
b. 1815	Jane Andrew	Lame Barton, near Plymouth	Farmer	Worked on a farm with her brother	Published London, 1889	No
b. 1816	John James Bezer	Spitalfields, London	Barber. Mother a cotton-spinner	Errand boy; porter	Published serially in *The Christian Socialist*, 1851. Included in Vincent, *Testaments of Radicalism*, 1977	No
1816–99	Joseph Gutteridge	Coventry	Ribbon-weaver	Silk weaver	Published Coventry, 1893. Modern edition London, 1969	Yes
1816–c. 89	Joseph Terry	Not known – lived on a boat for much of early life	Waterman	Waterman; book-keeper at flourmill; ran his own flourmill	Unpublished ts, Brunel University Library. Extract in Burnett, *Destiny Obscure*, 1982	No
1817–1906	George Jacob Holyoake	Birmingham	Whitesmith. Mother made horn buttons	Whitesmith; schoolteacher; public speaker; journalist; printer, publisher	Published London, 1892, two further editions	Yes

Dates	Name	Place	Father's occupation	Own occupation	Publication details	Published?
1817–1906	James Bonwick	Lingfield, Surrey	Carpenter	Teacher; writer of school books; emigrated to Australia and prospected (successfully) for gold	Published London, 1902	Yes
b. 1820	Adam Rushton	Higher Hurdsfield, Macclesfield	Farmer and carter	Worked in silk mill; teacher; Unitarian minister	Published Manchester, 1909	No
1820–84	John Harris	Camborne, Cornwall	Smallholder and copper-miner	Miner; poet	Published London, etc., 1882. Biography by his son, published 1884	Yes
1820–1905	Emmanuel Lovekin	Donnington Wood, Shropshire	Furnaceman	Trapper in coalpit; navvy; colliery manager; mine inspector	Unpublished ms, Brunel University Library. Extract in Burnett, *Useful Toil*	No
b. 1821/2	Thomas Frost	Croydon	Tailor	Printer and journalist	Two volumes, published London, 1880 and 1886	No
1822–80	Thomas Wood	Bingley, Yorkshire	Handloom weaver	Worked in a mill; apprenticed as a mechanic; school attendance officer	Published serially in *Keighley News*, 1956, and reprinted in booklet form	No
1822–89	Mary Smith	Cropredy, Oxfordshire	Boot and shoemaker. Mother a cook	Servant; governess; teacher; poet	Published London and Carlisle, 1892	Yes
1823–1911	John Passmore Edwards	Blackwater, Cornwall	Carpenter, public house keeper	Assisted father; under-clerk to lawyer; journalist; magazine owner; MP (for Salisbury, 1880–5)	Printed for private circulation, 1905. Second edition, London, 1906	Yes
1825–94	Roger Langdon	Chisleborough, Somersetshire	Parish clerk	Farmworker; railwayman	Published London, 1909	No
1825–96	Ben Brierley	Failsworth, near Manchester	Handloom weaver	Handloom weaver; silk wrapper; writer	Published London and Manchester, 1886	Yes
1826–94	John Bedford Leno	Uxbridge, Middlesex	Footman. Mother a needlewoman and dame school teacher	Servant; firework-maker; rope-spinner; postboy; printer; editor; publisher; writer	Published London, 1892	No

Dates	Name	Place of birth	Father's occupation (and mother's, where applicable)	Principal occupation(s)	Autobiography	DNB
1826–1919	Joseph Arch	Barford, Warwickshire	Agricultural labourer. Mother a servant	Agricultural worker; union organiser; MP (for North West Norfolk, 1885–6, 1892–1902)	Published London, 1898. Modern edition London, 1966	Yes
1828–1907	Gerald Massey	Tring, Hertfordshire	Canal boatman	Worked in a mill; clerk; lecturer; poet	Biography by David Shaw, published 1995	Yes
b. 1830	Thomas Oliver	Ludgvan, Cornwall	Mine worker	Miner; shopkeeper	Published Camborne, Cornwall, 1914	No
b. 1831	John Plummer	London	Staymaker	Errand boy; cutter in stay factory; poet	'Autobiographical sketch' included in Songs of Labour, published London and Kettering, 1860	No
1832–1903	Joseph Skipsey	Percy Main, near North Shields	Overman at colliery. Shot during strike when Skipsey was four months old	Coal miner; poet	Biography by Robert Spence Watson, published London, 1909	Yes
1832–1906	W. E. Adams	Cheltenham	Plasterer	Printer; editor; writer	Published London, 1903. Two modern editions, published New York, 1967, 1968	Yes
1832–1906	Charles Shaw	Tunstall, Staffordshire	Painter and gilder	Potter; minister in Methodist New Connexion; worked in cotton-spinning business; partner in mill which failed	Published serially in The Staffordshire Sentinel (1892–3); Published London, 1903; Facsimile reprints, Wakefield, 1969, Firle, 1977	Yes
b. 1833	George Elson	Northampton	Both parents were hawkers	Hawker; chimney-sweep; swimming instructor; masseur	Published London, 1900	No
1833–1910	George Howell	Wrington, Somersetshire	Mason; builder	Shoemaker; bricklayer; journalist; MP (for North East Bethnal Green, 1885–9)	Unpublished ms (6 vols.), Bishopsgate Institute, London	Yes

1834–1909	Mary Anne Hearn (published under pseud. Marianne Farningham)	Farningham, Kent	Postmaster	School teacher; writer; poet	Published London, 1907	Yes
1837–1922	Thomas Burt	Murton Row, near North Shields	Coal hewer	Miner; trade unionist; MP (for Morpeth, 1874–1918)	Published London, 1924	Yes
1840–1911	Henry Broadhurst	Littlemore, near Oxford	Stonemason	Stonemason; trade unionist; MP (for Stoke, 1880–5, Leicester, 1894–1906)	Published London, 1901	Yes
1846–1915	Frederick Rogers	Whitechapel, London	Sailor; draper's assistant; dock labourer	Errand boy; bookbinder; journalist; labour leader	Published London, 1913. Modern edition, Brighton, 1973	Yes
1850–1933	George Edwards	Marsham, Norfolk	Soldier; agricultural labourer. Mother was a handloom weaver	Farm worker; brickmaker; trade unionist; MP (for South Norfolk, 1920–2, 1923–4)	Published London, 1922. Facsimile reprint London, 1957	Yes
1851–1947	C. W. Bowerman	Honiton, Devon	Tinplate worker	Compositor; trade unionist; MP (for Deptford, 1906–31)	Included in the series 'How I got on', *Pearson's Weekly*, 1906	Yes
1852–1921	Will Crooks	Poplar, London	Ship's stoker; watchman. Mother took in washing	Cooper; MP (for Woolwich, 1903–10, 1910–21)	Biography by George Haw (based on conversations with Crooks), published London, 1907	Yes
1852–1922	Henry Jones	Llangernyw, Denbighshire	Shoemaker	Shoemaker; schoolmaster; professor	Published London, 1922	Yes
1852–1933	Tom Barclay	Leicester	Rag and bone man. Mother worked in a shop and hawked firewood	Factory worker	Published Leicester, 1934	No
1852–1935	Thomas Okey	Spitalfields, London	Basket-maker	Basket-maker; Italian scholar; author; professor	Published London, 1930	Yes

Dates	Name	Place of birth	Father's occupation (and mother's, where applicable)	Principal occupation(s)	Autobiography	DNB
b. 1854	Thomas Todd	Middleton-in-Teesdale	Blacksmith	Blacksmith; hotel keeper	Privately printed, Leeds, 1935	No
b. 1855	Mrs Layton	Bethnal Green, London	'Government situation'	Servant; took in washing; nurse and midwife	Included in *Life As We Have Known It*, published London, 1931. Modern edition, London, 1977	No
1855–1930	Joseph Wright	Idle, near Bradford	Weaver; quarryman	Wool-sorter; professor	Biography by Elizabeth Mary Wright, published London, 1932	Yes
1856–1941	Tom Mann	Coventry	Colliery clerk. Mother a servant	Tool maker; trade unionist	Published London, 1923. Modern edition, London, 1967	Yes
b. 1858	Mrs Wrigley	Cefn Mawr	Shoemaker. Mother a seamstress	Servant	Included in *Life As We Have Known It*	No
b. 1860	George Barber	Tunstall, Staffordshire	No details. Mother died when he was five	Worked in coalmine and chemical works; cinema developer	Self-published, Tunstall, 1937	No
1860–1943	Ben Tillett	Bristol	Factory worker	Circus boy; sailor; docker; MP (for North Salford, 1917–24, 1929–31)	Published London, 1931	Yes
1864–1976	Thomas Raymont	Tavistock, Devon	Farrier	School teacher; professor; author	Unpublished ts, Brunel University Library	No
1865–1950	Philip Boswood Ballard	Maesteg, Glamorgan	Employed at tinplate works	Teacher; school inspector	Published London, 1937	Yes
b. 1868	Chester Armstrong	Nenthead, Cumberland	Worked in a smelt-mill	Worked in a coalmine	Published London, 1938	No
1869–1949	J. R. Clynes	Oldham, Lancashire	Farm worker	Worked in a mill; trade unionist; MP (North East Manchester, 1906–31, 1935–45).	Published London, 1937	Yes

Dates	Name	Location	Parents' occupation	Occupation	Publication	
1870–1955	Thomas Jones	Rhymni, Monmouthshire	Manager of grocery shop and farm. Mother a straw-hat maker	Timekeeper at iron company; academic; senior civil servant	*Rhymney Memories*, 1938; *Leeks and Daffodils*, 1942, both published Newtown, Wales. *Rhymney Memories* reissued, Llandysul, 1970	Yes
1871–1934	Joseph Keating	Mountain Ash, South Wales	Dock worker	Miner; novelist; playwright	Published London, 1916	No
1872–1956	Hannah Mitchell	Peak District, Derbyshire	Parents were tenant farmers	Maid; dressmaker's assistant; suffragette	Published London, 1968. Further edition, London, 1977	Yes
1873–1953	Margaret Bondfield	Furnham, Somerset	Foreman lace-maker	Shop assistant; union organiser; MP (for Northampton, 1923–4, Wallsend, 1926–31)	Published London, 1949	Yes
1873–1959	Francis Hughes	Penllyn, Cowbridge	Footman/butler; railway signalman; station master	Clerk, Great Western Railway	Unpublished ts, Brunel University Library	No
1877–1930	Alfred Williams	South Marston, near Swindon	Decorative woodworker	Railwayman; poet	Published London, 1915. New York edition, 1980	Yes
1877–1952	Louise Jermy	Romsey, Hampshire	Stonemason's foreman	Servant; dressmaker	Published Norwich, 1934	Yes
1877–1960	William Margrie	Camberwell, London	Carpenter; builder. Mother a cook	Painter and decorator	Various autobiographical and part-autobiographical texts, with London imprints, some self-published	Yes
1879–1953	Annie Kenney	Springhead, Lancashire	Cotton operative	Factory worker; trade union organiser; suffragette	Published London, 1924	Yes
b. 1880	Harry Alfred West	Upper Stanton, North Somerset	Circus escapologist; clerk	Errand boy; clerk	Unpublished ts, Brunel University Library	No
b. 1880	Edward Brown	Bromley, Kent	Brewery worker	Office boy; clerk	Unpublished ts, Brunel University Library	No
1882–1960	Elizabeth Andrews	Hirwaun, Breconshire	Miner	Dressmaker; political organiser; campaigner for women's rights	Published Ystrad Rhondda, 1949(?)	Yes

Dates	Name	Place of birth	Father's occupation (and mother's, where applicable)	Principal occupation(s)	Autobiography	DNB
b. 1883	Rowland Kenney	Shelderslow, Yorkshire	Cotton operative	Worked in cotton factory; publisher; writer; civil servant	Published London, 1939	No
b. 1885	John Eldred	London	Stonemason	Journalist	Extracts published in *Time and Tide* and *The Outlook*. Published London, 1955	No
b. 1886	Joseph Stamper	St Helens, Lancashire	Iron moulder	Iron moulder; journalist; novelist	Published London, 1960. Further edition, Bath, 1977	No
1886–1945	Thomas Burke	London	Unknown (died when Burke was just a few months old).	Office boy; worked in music hall; writer	Published London, 1924, in limited edition of 110 copies	No
b. 1887	Maud Clarke	Tipton (?)	Plumber; shopkeeper	School teacher	Unpublished ms, Brunel University Library	No
1887–1947	Frank Hodges	Woolaston, Gloucestershire	Agricultural labourer; miner	Miner; trade unionist; MP (for Lichfield, 1923–4)	Published London, 1925	Yes
1889–1965	Howard Spring	Tiger Bay, Cardiff	Gardener. Mother took in washing	Messenger boy at a newspaper office; journalist; novelist	Published London, 1939	Yes
b. 1890	Daisy Cowper	Toxteth Park, Liverpool	Seaman	School teacher	Unpublished ts, Brunel University Library. Extract in Burnett, *Destiny Obscure*	No
1890–1969	Fred Kitchen	Edwinstone, Sherwood Forest	Cowman	Farm worker; navvy, milkman; author	Published London, 1940. Further editions London, 1963, 1982	Yes
1891–1974	Alice Foley	Bolton, Lancashire	Millhand	Factory worker; trade union official	Published Manchester, 1973. Reissued Bolton, 1990	Yes
b. 1892	V. W. Garratt	Birmingham	Glass blower	Factory worker; journalist	Published London, 1939	No

Dates	Name	Birthplace	Father's occupation	Subject's occupation	Publication	
1892–1979	Anita Hughes	Cotesbach, Leicestershire	Gardener	Weaver; worked in a munitions factory during World War I	Unpublished ts, Brunel University Library	No
1905–74	Robert Roberts	Salford, Lancashire	Engineer. Mother ran a corner shop	Served apprenticeship as brass finisher; teacher; writer	Published Manchester, 1976. Second edition published Manchester, nd	Yes
1918–	Richard Hoggart	Leeds	Died when Hoggart was a young child	Academic; assistant director-general, UNESCO; writer	Vol. 1 published London, 1988	N/A
1921–88	Raymond Williams	Pandy, near Abergavenny	Railway signalman	Academic and writer	Autobiographical novel published London, 1960. Several subsequent editions, including Cardigan, Wales, 2006	Yes
1928–	Alan Sillitoe	Nottingham	Mostly unemployed during Sillitoe's childhood	Factory worker; wireless operator in the RAF; writer	Published London, 1995	N/A
1940(?)–	Ray Gosling	Chester	Mechanic. Mother a teacher	Writer and broadcaster	Published London, 1962. Reissued Hebden Bridge, West Yorkshire, 2004	N/A

Appendix 2: Autobiographers listed alphabetically

Name	Year of birth
Adams, W. E.	1832
Andrew, Jane	1815
Andrews, Elizabeth	1882
Arch, Joseph	1826
Armstrong, Chester	1868
Ballard, Philip Boswood	1865
Bamford, Samuel	1788
Barber, George	1865
Barclay, Tom	1852
Barker, Joseph	1806
Bezer, John James	1816
Blacket, Joseph	1786
Bondfield, Margaret	1873
Bonwick, James	1817
Bowerman, C. W.	1851
Brierley, Ben	1825
Broadhurst, Henry	1840
Brown, Edward	1880
Brown, John	1796
Burke, Thomas	1886
Burt, Thomas	1837
Cadwaladyr, Betsy	1789
Carter, Thomas	1792
Clarke, Maud	1887
Clynes, J. R.	1869
Cooper, Thomas	1805
Cowper, Daisy	1890
Crooks, Will	1852
Davenport, Allen	1775
Davis, Elizabeth	see Cadwaladyr, Betsy
Dunning, Thomas	1813
Edwards, George	1850
Edwards, John Passmore	1823
Eldred, John	1885
Elliott, Ebenezer	1781

Name	Year of birth
Elson, George	1833
Farningham, Marianne	see Hearn, Mary Anne
Foley, Alice	1891
Frost, Thomas	1821/2
Garratt, V. W.	1892
Gosling, Ray	1940
Gutteridge, Joseph	1816
Hall, John Vine	1774
Ham, Elizabeth	1783
Harris, John	1820
Hearn, Mary Anne	1834
Heaton, William	1805
Hetherington, Henry	1792
Hodges, Frank	1887
Hoggart, Richard	1918
Holyoake, George Jacob	1817
Howell, George	1833
Hughes, Anita	1892
Hughes, Francis	1873
Jermy, Louise	1877
Jones, Henry	1852
Jones, John	1774
Jones, Thomas	1870
Keating, Joseph	1871
Kenney, Annie	1879
Kenney, Rowland	1883
Kitchen, Fred	1890
Langdon, Roger	1825
Layton, Mrs	1855
Leatherland, J. A.	1812
Leno, John Bedford	1826
Livesey, Joseph	1794
Lovekin, Emmanuel	1820
Lovett, William	1800
Lowery, Robert	1809
Mann, Tom	1856
Margrie, William	1877
Martin, Sarah	1791
Massey, Gerald	1828
Mitchell, Hannah	1872
Okey, Thomas	1852
Oliver, Thomas	1830
Place, Francis	1771
Plummer, John	1831
Raymont, Thomas	1864
Roberts, Robert	1905

Name	Year of birth
Rogers, Frederick	1846
Rushton, Adam	1820
Shaw, Charles	1832
Sillitoe, Alan	1928
Skeen, Robert	1797
Skipsey, Joseph	1832
Smith, Charles Manby	1804
Smith, Mary	1822
Spring, Howard	1889
Stamper, Joseph	1886
Terry, Joseph	1816
Tillett, Ben	1860
Todd, Thomas	1854
West, Harry Alfred	1880
Williams, Alfred	1877
Wood, John	1802
Wood, Thomas	1822
Wright, Joseph	1855
Wrigley, Mrs	1858

Bibliography

AUTOBIOGRAPHICAL (AND BIOGRAPHICAL) TEXTS

MANUSCRIPT

Brown, Edward, untitled ts, Brunel University Library, 1: 93.
Clarke, Maud, untitled ms, Brunel University Library, 1: 156.
Cowper, Daisy, 'De Nobis', ts, Brunel University Library, 1: 182.
[Hetherington, Henry?], Biographical fragment concerning the life of Hetherington, Holyoake Collection, Bishopsgate Institute, London. Original held in the Holyoake Collection, Manchester. Possibly written by Henry Hetherington or by James Watson.
Howell, George, 'The Autobiography of a Toiler', 6 vols. ms, George Howell Collection, Bishopsgate Institute, London.
Hughes, Anita, 'My Autobiography', ts, Brunel University Library, 1: 357.
Hughes, Francis, 'I Remember', ts, Brunel University Library, 1: 359.
Lovekin, Emmanuel, 'Some Notes on My Life', ms, Brunel University Library, 1: 452.
Raymont, Thomas, 'Memoirs of an Octogenarian, 1864–1949', ts, Brunel University Library, 1: 571.
Terry, Joseph, 'Recollections of My Life', ts, Brunel University Library, 1: 693.
West, Harry Alfred, 'The Autobiography of Harry Alfred West: Facts and Comments', ts, Brunel University Library, 1: 745.

PRINT

Adams, William Edwin, *Memoirs of a Social Atom*, 2 vols. (London: Hutchinson, 1903).
Andrew, Jane, *Recorded Mercies: Being the Autobiography of Jane Andrew* (London: E. Wilmhurst; Cranbrook: Miss A. Smart, [1889]).
Andrews, Elizabeth, *A Woman's Work is Never Done* (Ystrad Rhondda: The Cymric Democrat Publishing Society, [1949 (?)]).
Arch, Joseph, *The Autobiography of Joseph Arch*, ed. John Gerald O'Leary (London: MacGibbon & Kee, 1966; originally published London: Hutchinson, 1898).
Armstrong, Chester, *Pilgrimage from Nenthead: An Autobiography* (London: Methuen, 1938).

Ballard, Philip Boswood, *Things I Cannot Forget* (London: University of London Press, 1937).
Bamford, Samuel, *Passages in the Life of a Radical*, in W. H. Chaloner, ed., *The Autobiography of Samuel Bamford*, 2 vols. (London: Frank Cass, 1967).
Barber, George H., *From Workhouse to Lord Mayor: An Autobiography* (Tunstall: published by the author, 1937).
Barclay, Tom, *Memoirs and Medleys: The Autobiography of a Bottle Washer* (Coalville, Leicestershire: Coalville Publishing, 1995; originally published Leicester: Edgar Backus, 1934).
Barker, Joseph, *The Life of Joseph Barker. Written by Himself*, ed. John Thomas Barker (London: Hodder & Stoughton, 1880; originally published London: Chapman Brothers, 1846).
Bezer, John James, 'Autobiography of one of the Chartist Rebels of 1848', in David Vincent, ed., *Testaments of Radicalism: Memoirs of Working Class Politicians, 1790–1885* (London: Europa, 1977): 153–87. Originally published serially in *The Christian Socialist*, 6 September–13 December 1851.
Blacket, Joseph, *The Remains of Joseph Blacket; Consisting of Poems, Dramatic Sketches, 'The Times, An Ode,' and a Memoir of his Life*, 2 vols. (London: Sherwood, Neely, and Jones, 1811).
Bondfield, Margaret, *A Life's Work* (London: Hutchinson, [1949]).
Bonwick, James, *An Octogenarian's Reminiscences* (London: James Nichols, 1902).
Bowerman, Charles William, 'How I got on', *Pearson's Weekly*, 812 (8 February 1906), p. 563.
Brierley, Ben, *Home Memories, and Recollections of a Life* (Manchester: Abel Heywood & Son; London: Simpkin, Marshall, & Co., [1886]).
Broadhurst, Henry, *Henry Broadhurst, M.P.: The Story of his Life from a Stonemason's Bench to the Treasury Bench* (London: Hutchinson, 1901).
Brown, John, *Sixty Years' Gleanings from Life's Harvest. A Genuine Autobiography* (New York: Appleton & Co., 1859; originally published Cambridge: printed for the author, 1858).
Burke, Thomas, *The Wind and the Rain: A Book of Confessions* (London: Thornton Butterworth, 1924).
Burt, Thomas, *Thomas Burt M.P., D.C.L., Pitman & Privy Councillor: An Autobiography* (London: T. Fisher Unwin, 1924).
[Carter, Thomas], *Memoirs of a Working Man* (London: Charles Knight & Co., 1845).
A Continuation of the Memoirs of a Working Man; Illustrated by Some Original Sketches of Character (London: Charles Cox, 1850).
Clynes, John Robert, *Memoirs, 1869–1924* (London: Hutchinson, 1937).
Cooper, Thomas, *The Life of Thomas Cooper* (Leicester: Leicester University Press, 1971; originally published London: Hodder and Stoughton, 1872).
Davenport, Allen, *The Life and Literary Pursuits of Allen Davenport* (New York: Garland, 1986; originally published London: for the author by G. Hancock, 1845).

Davis, Elizabeth (pseud. of Betsy Cadwaladyr), *The Autobiography of Elizabeth Davis*, ed. Jane Williams (Cardiff: Honno, 1987; originally published London: Hurst & Blackett, 1857).

Dunning, Thomas, 'Reminiscences of Thomas Dunning', in David Vincent, ed., *Testaments of Radicalism: Memoirs of Working Class Politicians, 1790–1885* (London: Europa, 1977): 119–46.

Edwards, George, *From Crow-Scaring to Westminster: An Autobiography* (London: National Union of Agricultural Workers, 1957; originally published London: Labour Publishing Company, 1922).

Edwards, J. Passmore, *A Few Footprints* (London: np, 1905).

Eldred, John, *I Love the Brooks* (London: Skeffington, 1955).

Elson, George, *The Last of the Climbing Boys, an Autobiography* (London: John Long, 1900).

Farningham, Marianne (pseud. of Mary Anne Hearn), *A Working Woman's Life: An Autobiography* (London: James Clarke, [1907]).

Foley, Alice, *A Bolton Childhood* (Bolton: Bolton Libraries and Arts in co-operation with the Bolton Branch of the Worker's Educational Association, 1990; originally published Manchester: Manchester University Extra-Mural Department and North Western District of the Workers' Educational Association, 1973).

Frost, Thomas, *Forty Years' Recollections: Literary and Political* (London: Sampson Low, Marston, Searle, and Rivington, 1880).

Reminiscences of a Country Journalist (London: Ward & Downey, 1886).

Garratt, Vero W., *A Man in the Street* (London: Dent, 1939).

Gosling, Ray, *Sum Total* (Hebden Bridge, West Yorkshire: Pomona, 2004; originally published London: Faber & Faber, 1962).

Gutteridge, Joseph, 'The Autobiography of Joseph Gutteridge', in Valerie E. Chancellor, ed. & intro., *Master and Artisan in Victorian England: The Diary of William Andrews and the Autobiography of Joseph Gutteridge* (London: Evelyn, Adams & Mackay, 1969). Originally published as *Lights and Shadows in the Life of an Artisan* (Coventry: Curtis Beamish, 1893).

Hall, John Vine, *Hope for the Hopeless: An Autobiography of John Vine Hall*, ed. Newman Hall (New York: American Tract Society, nd).

Ham, Elizabeth, *Elizabeth Ham by Herself, 1783–1820*, ed. and intro., Eric Gillett (London: Faber & Faber, 1945).

Harris, John, *My Autobiography* (London: Hamilton, Adams & Co., 1822).

Harris, John Howard, *John Harris, the Cornish Poet. The Story of His Life* (London: Partridge, [1884]).

Haw, George, *From Workhouse to Westminster: The Life Story of Will Crooks, M. P.* (London: Cassell & Co., 1907).

Heaton, William, *The Old Soldier; The Wandering Lover; and Other Poems; Together with A Sketch of the Author's Life* (London: Simpkin, Marshall & Co.; Halifax: T. & W. Birtwhistle, 1857).

Hodges, Frank, *My Adventures as a Labour Leader* (London: George Newnes, [1925]).

Hoggart, Richard, *A Local Habitation (Life and Times, Volume I: 1918–1940)* (London: Chatto & Windus, 1988).
Holyoake, George Jacob, *Sixty Years of an Agitator's Life*, 2 vols. (London: T. Fisher Unwin, 1892).
Jermy, Louise, *The Memories of a Working Woman* (Norwich: Goose & Son, 1934).
Jones, John, 'John Jones, an Old Servant: An Account of his Life, Written by Himself', in Robert Southey and J. S. Childers, eds, *The Lives and Works of the Uneducated Poets* (London: Humphrey Milford, 1925).
Jones, Sir Henry, *Old Memories*, ed. Thomas Jones (London: Hodder and Stoughton, [1922]).
Jones, Thomas, *Rhymney Memories* (Newtown: The Welsh Outlook Press, 1938).
Leeks and Daffodils (Newtown: Welsh Outlook Press, 1942).
Keating, Joseph, *My Struggle for Life* (London: Simpkin, Marshall, Hamilton, Kent & Co., 1916).
Kenney, Annie, *Memories of a Militant* (London: Edward Arnold, 1924).
Kenney, Rowland, *Westering: An Autobiography* (London: J. M. Dent & Sons, 1939).
Kitchen, Fred, *Brother to the Ox. The Autobiography of a Farm Labourer* (London: Caliban, 1981; originally published London: J. M. Dent, 1940).
Langdon, Roger, *The Life of Roger Langdon, Told by Himself, with Additions by his Daughter Ellen* (London: Elliot Stock, [1909]).
Mrs. Layton, 'Memories of Seventy Years', in Margaret Llewelyn Davies, ed., *Life as We Have Known It*, Anna Davin (intro.) (London: Virago, 1977; first published London: Hogarth Press, 1931): 1–55.
Leatherland, J. A., *Essays and Poems, with a Brief Autobiographical Memoir* (London: W. Tweedie, 1862).
Leno, John Bedford, *The Aftermath: With Autobiography of the Author* (London: Reeves & Turner, 1892).
Livesey, Joseph, *The Life and Teachings of Joseph Livesey*, ed. John Pearce (London: National Temperance Publication Depot; Preston: Livesey's Temperance Tract Depot, 1887; originally published serially in *The Staunch Teetotaller* in 1867 and 1868).
Lovett, William, *Life and Struggles of William Lovett in his Pursuit of Bread, Knowledge and Freedom* (London: Macgibbon & Kee, 1967; originally published London: np, 1876).
Lowery, Robert, *Robert Lowery: Radical and Chartist*, Brian Harrison and Patricia Hollis (eds) (London: Europa, 1979) (originally published anonymously as a series of 33 articles in the *Weekly Record of the Temperance Movement*. Publication at irregular intervals between 15 April 1856 and 23 May 1857).
Mann, Tom, *Tom Mann's Memoirs* (London: Macgibbon & Kee, 1967; first published London: The Labour Publishing Company, 1923).
Margrie, William, *A Cockney's Pilgrimage in Search of Truth* (London: Watts & Co., 1927).
The Diary of a London Explorer: Forty Years of Vital London Life (London: Watts & Co., [1934]).

My Eighty Years in Camberwell: Highlights – Flashes – Milestones (London: William Margrie, [1958?]).
Martin, Sarah, *A Brief Sketch of the Life of the Late Miss Sarah Martin* (Yarmouth: C. Barber, 1845; originally published Yarmouth, 1844).
Mitchell, Hannah, *The Hard Way Up: The Autobiography of Hannah Mitchell, Suffragette and Rebel*, ed. Geoffrey Mitchell, preface by George Ewart Evans (London: Faber & Faber, 1968).
Okey, Thomas, *A Basketful of Memories: An Autobiographical Sketch* (London: Dent, 1930).
Oliver, Thomas, *Autobiography of a Cornish Miner* (Camborne: Camborne Printing and Stationery Co., 1911).
Place, Francis, *The Autobiography of Francis Place*, ed. Mary Thale (Cambridge: Cambridge University Press, 1972).
Plummer, John, *Songs of Labour, Northamptonshire Rambles, and Other Poems* (London: W. Tweedie; Kettering: Thomas Waddington, 1860).
Roberts, Robert, *The Classic Slum: Salford Life in the First Quarter of the Century* (Harmondsworth: Pelican, 1973; originally published Manchester: Manchester University Press, 1971).
  A Ragged Schooling: Growing Up in the Classic Slum (Manchester: Mandolin, nd; originally published Manchester: Manchester University Press, 1976).
Rogers, Frederick, *Labour, Life and Literature: Some Memories of Sixty Years*, ed. David Rubinstein (Brighton: Harvester, 1973; first published London: Smith, Elder, 1913).
Rushton, Adam, *My Life as Farmer's Boy, Factory Lad, Teacher and Preacher* (Manchester: S. Clarke, 1909).
Shaw, Charles, *When I Was a Child* (Firle, Sussex: Caliban, 1977; originally published serially in *The Staffordshire Sentinel*, December 1892–May 1893, author identified as 'An Old Potter').
Shaw, David, *Gerald Massey: Chartist, Poet, Radical and Freethinker* (London: Buckland, 1995).
Sillitoe, Alan, *Life Without Armour: An Autobiography* (London: HarperCollins, 1995).
Skeen, Robert, *Autobiography of Mr. Robert Skeen, Printer* (London: Wyman & Sons, 1876, for private circulation).
Smith, Charles Manby, *The Working Man's Way in the World* (London: Printing Historical Society, 1967; originally published serially in *Tait's Edinburgh Magazine*, March 1851–May 1852; published in book form London: William and Frederick G. Cash, 1853).
Smith, Mary, *The Autobiography of Mary Smith, Schoolmistress and Nonconformist. A Fragment of a Life* (London: Bemrose & Sons, 1892).
Spring, Howard, *Heaven Lies About Us* (London: Collins, 1956; originally published London: Constable & Co., 1939).
Stamper, Joseph, *So Long Ago . . .* (London: Hutchinson, 1960).
Thomson, Christopher, *The Autobiography of an Artisan* (London: J. Chapman; Nottingham: J. Shaw and Sons, 1847).

Tilke, Samuel Westcott, *An Autobiographical Memoir, with remarks on the various incidents which have occurred during forty-five years of his life, and a full description of his mode of treating diseases, with reasond explanatory of his system* (London: printed for and sold by the author, 1840).
Tillett, Ben, *Memories and Reflections* (London: John Long, 1931).
Todd, Thomas, *My Life as I Have Lived It: Autobiography of Thomas Todd of Middleton-in-Teesdale* (Leeds: printed for Thomas Todd, 1935).
Watkins, John, *Life, Poetry, and Letters of Ebenezer Elliott. The Corn-Law Rhymer. With an Abstract of his Politics* (London: John Mortimer, 1850). Watkins was Elliott's son-in-law. The first chapter of the volume is an autobiographical text written by Elliott himself.
Watson, Robert Spence, *Joseph Skipsey: His Life and Work* (London: T. Fisher Unwin, 1909).
Williams, Alfred, *Life in a Railway Factory* (New York: Garland, 1980; originally published London: Duckworth, 1915).
Williams, Raymond, *Border Country* (Cardigan: Parthian, 2006; originally published London: Chatto & Windus, 1960).
Wood, John, *Autobiography of John Wood, an Old and Well Known Bradfordian, Written in the 75th Year of his Age* (Bradford: *Chronicle and Mail* Office, 1877).
Wood, Thomas, autobiography, published in *Keighley News*, 3, 10, 17, 24 March and 7, 14 April 1956.
Wright, Elizabeth Mary, *The Life of Joseph Wright*, 2 vols. (London: Oxford University Press, 1932).
Mrs. Wrigley, 'A Plate-layer's Wife', in Margaret Llewelyn Davies, ed., *Life as We Have Known It*, Anna Davin (intro.) (London: Virago, 1977; first published London: Hogarth Press, 1931): 56–66.

OTHER SOURCES

Addresses Delivered at the Theatre Royal, Drury Lane, in Aid of the People's Shakspeare Memorial Fund. December 5th, 6th, 8th, 9th, 10th April, 1864 (London: Thomas Hailes Lacy, [1864]).
Advertisement for John Dicks' edition of Shakespeare, *Penny Illustrated Weekly News*, 1:46 (new series), 30 April 1864, p. 726.
Allen, Rose, *The Autobiography of Rose Allen. Edited by a Lady* (London: Longman, Brown, Green, and Longmans, 1847).
Altick, Richard, *The English Common Reader: A Social History of the Mass Reading Public 1800–1900* (Chicago: University of Chicago Press, 1957).
Anderson, Patricia, *The Printed Image and the Transformation of Popular Culture 1790–1860* (Oxford: Clarendon, 1991).
Arnold, Matthew, *Reports on Elementary Schools, 1852–1882*, ed. Francis Sandford (London: Macmillan, 1889).
'Autobiography', *Quarterly Review*, 35 (1827): 148–65.
'Autobiography of Francis Place', *The Times*, 23 December 1835, p. 3.

Bailey, Peter, *Popular Culture and Performance in the Victorian City* (Cambridge: Cambridge University Press, 1998).
Bainbridge, John, letter to J. O. Halliwell-Phillipps, dated September 1864, with Halliwell-Phillipps' reply drafted on verso. University of Edinburgh; James Orchard Halliwell-Phillipps Collection, L.O.A. vol. 7.
Barber, Mary Ann Serrett, *Bread-winning; Or, the Ledger and the Lute. An Autobiography* (London: William Macintosh, [1865]).
Bate, Jonathan, *Shakespearean Constitutions: Politics, Theatre, Criticism 1730–1830* (Oxford: Clarendon Press, 1989).
Beales, Derek, 'Garibaldi in England: The Politics of Italian Enthusiasm', in J. A. Davis and P. Ginsborg, eds, *Society and Politics in the Age of the Risorgimento: Essays in Honour of David Mack Smith* (Cambridge: Cambridge University Press, 1991): 184–216.
Belanger, Terry, 'Tonson, Wellington and the Shakespeare Copyrights', in *Studies in the Book Trade in Honour of Graham Pollard* (Oxford: Bibliographical Society, 1975): 195–209.
Benzie, William, *Dr. F. J. Furnivall: Victorian Scholar Adventurer* (Norman, OK: Pilgrim, 1983).
Bernard, Thomas, *Of the Education of the Poor; Being the first part of a digest of the reports of the society for bettering the condition of the poor: and containing a selection of those articles which have a reference to education* (London: for the Society, 1809).
Billson, Charles James, *Leicester Memories* (Leicester: Edgar Backus, 1924).
Bilton, Charles, *The Class and Standard Series of Reading Books Adapted to the Requirements of the Revised Code* (London: Longmans & Co., 1876–70).
Blayney, Peter, *The First Folio of Shakespeare* (Washington, DC: Folger Shakespeare Library, 1991).
Brougham, Henry, *Practical Observations upon the Education of the People, Addressed to the Working Classes and their Employers* (London: Longman, Hurst, Rees, Orme, Brown and Green, 1825).
'Progress of the People – The Periodical Press', *Edinburgh Review*, 57 (1833): 239–48.
Burke, Edmund, *Reflections on the Revolution in France*, ed. Frank M. Turner (New Haven: Yale University Press, 2003).
Burnett, John, ed. & intro., *Useful Toil: Autobiographies of Working People from the 1820s to the 1920s* (London: Allen Lane, 1974).
Destiny Obscure: Autobiographies of Childhood, Education and Family from the 1820s to the 1920s (London: Allen Lane, 1982).
Burnett, John, David Vincent and David Mayall, *The Autobiography of the Working Class: An Annotated, Critical Bibliography*, 3 vols. (Brighton: Harvester, 1984).
Burt, Richard, 'Laura Bush wants to take Shakespeare to US gangland', SHAKSPER, SHK 16.0819, Thursday 28 April 2005.
Cannadine, David, *Class in Britain* (New Haven: Yale University Press, 1998).
Carey, John, *The Intellectuals and the Masses: Pride and Prejudice among the Literary Intelligentsia, 1880–1939* (London: Faber & Faber, 1992).

What Good Are the Arts? (London: Faber & Faber, 2005).
'Chapman and Hall v. Dicks', *The Times*, 7 August 1882, p. 4.
'Chartism, From Shakespeare', *Northern Star*, 3:128 (25 April 1840); 3:129 (2 May 1840); 3:130 (9 May 1840); 3:132 (23 May 1840); 3:134 (6 June 1840). In all cases the material is included on p. 7.
Clare, John, 'Popularity in Authorship', *European Magazine*, November 1825, reprinted in J. W. and Anne Tibble, eds, *The Prose of John Clare* (London: Routledge & Kegan Paul, [1951]): 256–60.
Cobbett, William, 'To the Editor of the Agricultural Magazine. On the Subject of Potatoes', *Cobbett's Weekly Political Register*, 29:7 (18 November 1815): cols. 193–203.
'Apologies of Milton and Shakspear', *Cobbett's Weekly Political Register*, 29:8 (25 November 1815): cols. 253–5.
Cobbin, Ingram, *The Instructive Reader. Containing Lessons on Religion, Morals, and General Knowledge; in Easy Gradations. Illustrated by Instructive Cuts on an Original Plan; with Questions for Examination, and Elliptical Recapitulations: Designed to Teach Reading, and to Inform and Develop the Powers of the Infant Mind* (London: Frederick Westley and A. H. Davis, 1831).
Collins, Michael, *The Likes of Us: A Biography of the White Working Class* (London: Granta, 2004).
Cooper, Thomas, letters (dated 29 August 1842 and 30 August 1842) to the *Northern Star*, 5:251 (3 September 1842), p. 6.
'Éloge', in George J. Holyoake, ed., *The Life and Character of Henry Hetherington, from the Éloge, by T. Cooper, Author of the 'Purgatory of Suicides:' The Oration at Kensal Green Cemetery, by G. J. Holyoake, Editor of the 'Reasoner:' The Speech of James Watson: A Tribute, by W. J. Linton: With Hetherington's 'Last Will and Testament'* (London: J. Watson, 1849).
Craig, Edward Gordon, letter to Israel Gollancz, dated 15 March 1916, ms W.a.79(30) Folger Shakespeare Library.
Crump, Jeremy, 'The Popular Audience for Shakespeare in Nineteenth-Century Leicester', in Richard Foulkes, ed., *Shakespeare and the Victorian Stage* (Cambridge: Cambridge University Press, 1986): 271–82.
Curwen, Henry, *A History of Booksellers, the Old and the New* (London: Chatto & Windus, 1873).
Dabbs, Thomas, 'Shakespeare and the Department of English', *English and American Literature Symposium* (Tuscaloosa: University of Alabama Press, 1993): 82–98.
Davis, Jim and Victor Emeljanow, 'New Views of Cheap Theatres: Reconstructing the Nineteenth-century Theatre Audience', *Theatre Survey*, 39:2 (November 1998): 53–72.
'Death of Mr. John Thomas Dicks', *Reynolds's Newspaper*, 13 February 1881, p. 1.
DiPietro, Cary, *Shakespeare and Modernism* (Cambridge: Cambridge University Press, 2006).
Donaldson, Alexander, *A catalogue of curious and valuable books, to be disposed of by way of sale (the lowest price being marked at each book), at the shop of Alexander*

Donaldson, *the first fore-stair above the entry to the Royal Bank, Edinburgh* (Edinburgh: Donaldson, 1753).
Drummond, John, interview on 'Ministers of Taste', programme 3 of *Cultural State*, broadcast on BBC Radio 4, 20 September 2004.
Editor, 'Analysis of the Reports of the Committee of the Manchester Statistical Society on the State of Education in the Boroughs of Manchester, Liverpool, Salford, and Bury', Central Society of Education, *Papers*, vol. 1 (London: Taylor and Walton, 1837).
'Editorial', *Comic News*, 7 May 1864, included in Birmingham Central Library Tercentenary Shakespeare Scrapbook, vol. 1, p. 151.
The Educational Backgrounds of Leading Journalists (London: Sutton Trust, 2006).
Eliot, Simon, *Some Patterns and Trends in British Publishing 1800–1919* (London: Bibliographical Society, 1994).
  'Hotten: Rotten: Forgotten? An Apologia for a General Publisher', *Book History* 3 (2000): 61–93.
Eliot, Thomas Stearns, 'Marie Lloyd', in *Selected Essays* (London: Faber & Faber, 1980; first published 1932).
Elliott, Ebenezer, *The Splendid Village: Corn Law Rhymes; and Other Poems*, 2 vols. (London: Benjamin Steill, 1834).
Ellis, Alec, *Books in Victorian Elementary Schools* (Library Association Pamphlet no. 34, 1971).
  Educating Our Masters: Influences on the Growth of Literacy in Victorian Working Class Children (Aldershot: Gower, 1985).
Engels, Frederich, *The Condition of the Working Class in England*, trans. and ed. W. O. Henderson and W. H. Chaloner (Oxford: Blackwell, 1958; first German edition, 1845).
Erskine, Thomas, *The Speeches of the Hon. Thomas Erskine (now Lord Erskine), when at the bar, on subjects connected with the liberty of the press, and against constructive treasons* (London: printed for James Ridgway, 1813; 2nd edn), vol. II.
Eusebius, letter to *The Gentleman's Magazine*, 67 (October 1797): 819–20.
  letter to *The Gentleman's Magazine*, 67 (January 1798): 32–4.
'Festival of the Establishment of Messrs. Reynolds and Dicks', *Reynolds's Newspaper*, 12 July 1868, p. 1.
Foulkes, Richard, 'Shakespeare and Garibaldi on Primrose Hill', *Camden History Review*, 9 (1981): 13–16.
  The Shakespeare Tercentenary of 1864 (London: Society for Theatre Research, 1984).
  Performing Shakespeare in the Age of Empire (Cambridge: Cambridge University Press, 2002).
Freeman, Arnold, *Boy Life and Labour: The Manufacture of Inefficiency* (New York: Garland, 1980 (facsimile reprint); originally published London: P. S. King & Son, 1914).
Gagnier, Regenia, *Subjectivities: A History of Self-Representation in Britain, 1832–1920* (Oxford: Oxford University Press, 1991).
'The Genius of Working Men', *Chartist Circular*, 33 (9 May 1840): 135–6.

Gillies, Leman, 'The Press and the People', *Douglas Jerrold's Shilling Magazine*, 3 (1846): 254.

Goldstrom, Joachin Max, *The Social Content of Education, 1808–70. A Study of the Working-class School Reader in England and Ireland* (Shannon, Ireland: Irish University Press, 1972).

Grady, Hugh, *The Modernist Shakespeare: Critical Texts in a Material World* (Oxford: Clarendon Press, 1991).

Griest, Guinevere L., *Mudie's Circulating Library and the Victorian Novel* (Newton Abbot, Devon: David & Charles, nd; originally published Indiana University Press, 1970).

Guy, Josephine, ed., *The Victorian Age: An Anthology of Sources and Documents* (London: Routledge, 2001).

Habicht, Werner, 'Shakespeare Celebrations in Times of War', *Shakespeare Quarterly*, 52:4 (2001): 441–5.

Hackett, Nan, *XIX Century British Working-Class Autobiographies* (New York: AMS, 1985).

Halliwell[-Phillipps], J. O., letter to the *Athenæum*, 2031, 29 September 1866, p. 404. Correspondence with John Camden Hotten, Edinburgh University Library James Orchard Halliwell-Phillipps collection, L.O.A. 114, 115, 132 (various letters).

Halpern, Richard, *Shakespeare Among the Moderns* (Ithaca, NY: Yale University Press, 1997).

Hardy, Thomas, extract from *Memoir of Thomas Hardy, Founder of, and Secretary to, the London Corresponding Society* ... included in David Vincent, ed., *Testaments of Radicalism. Memoirs of Working Class Politicians 1790–1885* (London: Europa, 1977): 31–102.

Harney, George Julian, obituary for Thomas Cooper, *Newcastle Weekly Chronicle*, 12 July 1892, p. 5.

Harris, John, *Shakspere's Shrine, An Indian Story, Essays, and Poems* (London: Hamilton, Adams, & Co., 1866).

Haywood, Ian, *The Revolution in Popular Literature: Print, Politics and the People, 1790–1860* (Cambridge: Cambridge University Press, 2004).

Hazlitt, William, *Characters of Shakespear's Plays* (London: R. Hunter, C. & J. Ollier, 1817).

Heath, Chris, 'Cocks of the North', *Observer Music Magazine*, 40 (December 2006), pp. 26–43.

Hewison, Robert, *Culture and Consensus: England, Arts and Politics since 1940* (London: Methuen, 1995).

Hoggart, Richard, *The Uses of Literacy: Aspects of Working-class Life with Special Reference to Publications and Entertainments* (Harmondsworth: Penguin, 1971; originally published London: Chatto & Windus, 1957).

Holbrook, Peter, 'Shakespeare, "The Cause of the People", and *The Chartist Circular* 1839–1842', *Textual Practice*, 20:2 (2006): 203–29.

Holyoake, George Jacob, *Public Speaking and Debate* (London: T. Fisher Unwin, nd; first edition probably published in 1849).

Horkheimer, Max and Theodor W. Adorno, *Dialect of Enlightenment*, John Cumming (trans.) (New York: Continuum, 1987; original German edition published 1947).
Hurt, John S., *Elementary Schooling and the Working Classes, 1860–1918* (London: Routledge & Kegan Paul, 1979).
Jackson, Brian, *Working-Class Community: Some General Notions Raised by a Series of Studies in Northern England* (Harmondsworth: Penguin, 1972; originally published London: Routledge & Kegan Paul, 1968).
Jackson, Brian and Dennis Marsden, *Education and the Working Class: Some General Themes Raised by a Study of 88 Working-class Children in a Northern Industrial City* (Harmondsworth: Pelican, 1966; originally published London: Routledge & Keegan Paul, 1962).
James, Henry, 'The Birthplace' in *The Better Sort* (New York: Charles Scribner's Sons, 1903): 245–311.
James, Louis, *Fiction for the Working Man, 1830–1850* (Harmondsworth: Penguin, 1974).
  Print and the People, 1819–1851 (London: Penguin, 1976).
Johnson, Steven, *Everything Bad is Good for You: How Popular Culture is Making Us Smarter* (London: Allen Lane, 2005).
Jones, Aled, *Powers of the Press: Newspaper, Power and the Public in Nineteenth-century England* (Aldershot: Ashgate, 1996).
Joyce, Patrick, *Visions of the People: Industrial England and the Question of Class 1848–1914* (Cambridge: Cambridge University Press, 1991).
Keane, John, *Tom Paine: A Political Life* (London: Bloomsbury, 1995).
Knight, Charles, *The Old Printer and the Modern Press* (London: John Murray, 1854).
  Passages of a Working Life, 3 vols. (London: Bradbury and Evans, 1864–5).
Lackington, James, *Memoirs of the Forty-Five First Years of the Life of James Lackington* (London: For the Author, 1794; originally published 1791).
Lancaster, Joseph, *Improvements in Education*, quoted from an abridged edition lacking a title page, c. 1807, National Library of Scotland shelfmark ABS.2.97.44(16).
Laurie, James Stuart, *Laurie's Graduated Series of Reading Lesson Books* (London: Longmans, Green, & Co., 1866).
Lawson, Joseph, *Letters to the Young on Progress in Pudsey during the Last Sixty Years* (Firle, Sussex: Caliban, 1978; originally published Stanningley: J. W. Birdsall, 1887).
Levine, Lawrence W., *Highbrow/Lowbrow: The Emergence of Cultural Hierarchy in America* (Cambridge, MA: Harvard University Press, 1988).
Linton, William James, *Threescore and Ten Years, 1820–1890, Recollections* (New York: Charles Scribner's Sons, 1894).
Ludlow, George, *The Class Reading Book: Adapted for Schools, and particularly designed to furnish youth with practical information on a variety of interesting subjects* (London: J. W. Parker, 1836).
Ludlow, John Malcolm and Lloyd Jones, *Progress of the Working Class, 1832–1867* (London: Alexander Strahan, 1867).

Luhrmann, Baz (dir.), *Romeo + Juliet* (Twentieth-Century Fox, 1996).
Mackie, Laura and Patrick Spence (exec. prod.), *Shakespeare Retold* (Acorn Video, 2006).
MacManus, J. E., 'In Shakespeare Land', newspaper cutting (source unidentified), dated July 1901, in Lemuel Matthews Griffiths, *Newspaper Cuttings Relating to Shakespeare* at the Birmingham Central Library, vol. 1, p. 80.
Macmillan, Alexander, printed letter to booksellers, dated 15 October 1864.
Macmillan, George, ed., *Letters of Alexander Macmillan* (London: Macmillan, 1908).
'The Manufacture of Novels', *The Spectator*, 3,818 (31 August 1901), pp. 277–8.
Margrie, William, *The Mighty Heart: A Survey of England as It Is and a Vision of What It Might Be* (London: Watts & Co., 1925).
  A Camberwell Man: Being a Record of the Beneficent Activities of Horatio Chucklewit, J. P., Pork Butcher, Orator, Patriot, and Children's Champion (London: Watts & Co., 1926).
  English Grass: Signifying the Soul and Soil of England (London: Watts & Co., 1936).
[Marsh, Herbert], *A Sermon Preached in the Cathedral Church of St. Paul, London: On Thursday, June 7, 1810.* (London: for the Society for Promoting Christian Knowledge, 1810).
Mason, Tony, *Association Football and English Society 1863–1915* (Brighton: Harvester, 1980).
Massey, Gerald, *The Secret Drama of Shakspeare's Sonnets Unfolded, With the Characters Identified* (NP: for subscribers only, 1872).
Mayhew, Henry, *London Labour and the London Poor; a Cyclopædia of the Condition and Earnings of Those that Will Work, Those that Cannot Work, and Those that Will Not Work*, 2 vols. (London: Griffin, Bohn, and Company, 1861–2).
M[ayne], F., 'The Literature of the Working Classes', the *Englishwoman's Magazine and Christian Mother's Miscellany*, N.S., V (October 1850): 619–21.
Moody, Jane, *Illegitimate Theatre in London, 1770–1840* (Cambridge: Cambridge University Press, 2000).
[More, Hannah], *Village Politics. Addressed to All the Mechanics, Journeymen, and Day Labourers, in Great Britain* (Facsimile reprint, Oxford: Woodstock, 1995; originally published London: F. and C. Rivington, 1793).
Morley, Charles, *Studies in Board Schools* (London: Smith, Elder, & Co., 1897).
Morley, Henry, *A First Sketch of English Literature* (London: Cassell & Co., 1896 edition; first published 1873).
Murphy, Andrew, *Shakespeare in Print: A History and Chronology of Shakespeare Publishing* (Cambridge: Cambridge University Press, 2003).
Murphy, Paul Thomas, *Towards a Working-Class Canon: Literary Criticism in British Working-Class Periodicals, 1816–1858* (Columbus: Ohio State University Press, 1994).
Murray, Thomas Boyles, *National Education Promoted. An Account of the Efforts of the Society for Promoting Christian Knowledge, in Behalf of National*

Education: Together with a Notice of the Anniversaries of the Assembled Charity Schools (London: Society for Promoting Christian Knowledge, 1848).
National Society for Promoting the Education of the Poor in the Principles of the Established Church, *A Brief Account of the National Society...* (London: National Society..., 1854).
Neuburg, Victor E., *Popular Literature: A History and Guide from the Beginning of Printing to the Year 1897* (London: Woburn Press, 1977).
'Not Adonis', letter to *T. P.'s Weekly*, vol. 21, June 1911, p. 44.
O'Connor, T. P., 'The New Journalism', *New Review*, 1 (1889): 423–34.
O'Dair, Sharon, *Class, Critics, and Shakespeare: Bottom Lines on the Culture Wars* (Ann Arbor: University of Michigan Press, 2000).
O'Hagan, Sean, 'A fine mind poisoned by too much loud Wagner?', *Observer*, 15 April 2007, Review section, p. 11.
Oldys, Francis [pseud. of George Chalmers], *The Life of Thomas Pain, the Author of Rights of Man. With a Defence of his Writings* (London: John Stockdale, 1791; second edition).
Paine, Thomas, *Rights of Man, Common Sense and Other Political Writings*, ed. Mark Philp (Oxford: Oxford University Press, 1995).
Palmer, David J., *The Rise of English Studies: An Account of the Study of English Language and Literature from its Origins to the Making of the Oxford English School* (London: Oxford University Press for the University of Hull, 1965).
Parker, John, 'On the Literature of the Working Classes' in Viscount Ingestre, ed., *Meliora: or, Better Times to Come. Being the Contributions of Many Men Touching the Present State and Prospects of Society*, 2nd series (London: John W. Parker and Son, 1853).
Patterson, Alfred Temple, *Radical Leicester* (Leicester: University College Leicester, 1954).
Pemberton, Max, *Lord Northcliffe: A Memoir* (London: Hodder & Stoughton, nd).
'Pictorial Penny Shakespeare', *Northern Star*, 9:420 (29 November 1845), p. 3.
Plain, Gill, *John Mills and British Cinema* (Edinburgh: Edinburgh University Press, 2006).
Plant, Marjorie, *The English Book Trade: An Economic History of the Making and Sale of Books* (London: George Allen & Unwin, 1939).
'The Politics of Poets', *Chartist Circular*, 42 (11 July 1840), p. 170.
'Presentation of the Shakspeare Testimonial to Kossuth', *Illustrated London News*, 14 May 1853, page number unknown. Found in Lemuel Matthews Griffiths, *Newspaper Cuttings Relating to Shakespeare*, Birmingham Central Library, vol. II, p. 88.
'Prospectus for the Society', Central Society of Education, *Papers*, vol. 1 (London: Taylor and Walton, 1838).
Report of a Committee of the Manchester Statistical Society on the State of Education in the Borough of Manchester, in 1834 (London: James Ridgway & Son; Manchester: Bancks & Co., 1835)

Report of the British and Foreign School Society, M.DCCC.XV with an Appendix and a List of Subscribers and Benefactors (London: Printed by Richard and Arthur Taylor, 1815).

Report on a performance of *Douglas* by the Shakespearean Chartist Association, *The Leicestershire Mercury*, 7:337 (17 December 1842), p. 3.

Review of Alexander Pope's edition of Shakespeare, *The Weekly Journal or Saturday's Post* (*Mist's Journal*), 20 March 1725, pp. 2075–6 and further comments in the issue of 27 March, p. 2081.

Review of Helen-Maria Williams' *Julia*, *Monthly Review*, 2 (July 1790): 334–5.

Richardson, Alan, *Literature, Education, and Romanticism: Reading as Social Practice, 1780–1832* (Cambridge: Cambridge University Press, 1994).

Roberts, Gareth, *The Shakespeare Code*, dir. Charles Palmer (BBC Wales/Canadian Broadcasting Corporation, 2007).

Rogerson, Hank and Jilann Spitzmiller (prod.), *Shakespeare Behind Bars* (Philomath Films/ITVS/BBC, 2006).

Rose, Jonathan, *The Intellectual Life of the British Working Classes* (New Haven: Yale University Press, 2002).

Rose, Mark, *Authors and Owners: The Invention of Copyright* (Cambridge, MA: Harvard University Press, 1993).

Rothwell, Kenneth, *A History of Shakespeare on Screen: A Century of Film and Television* (Cambridge: Cambridge University Press, 1999).

Rubinstein, David and Brian Simon, *The Evolution of the Comprehensive School, 1926–1972* (London: Routledge & Kegan Paul, 1969; 2nd edn 1973).

St. Clair, William, *The Reading Nation in the Romantic Period* (Cambridge: Cambridge University Press, 2004).

Schoch, Richard W., *Not Shakespeare: Bardolatry and Burlesque in the Nineteenth Century* (Cambridge: Cambridge University Press, 2002).

'Schools for the Industrious Classes', Central Society of Education, *Papers*, vol. 1 (London: Taylor and Walton, 1838).

'The Seven Stages of Whiggery', *Chartist Circular*, 34 (16 May 1840), p. 138.

Shakespeare, William, *King John* (Manchester: J. B. Ledsham; London: Simpkin, Marshall, & Co., 1883).

'Shakespeare and the "Common People"', newspaper cutting (source identified as 'P.O.'), dated 29 December 1905, in Lemuel Matthews Griffiths, *Newspaper Cuttings Relating to Shakespeare* at the Birmingham Central Library, vol. 6, p. 55.

'Shakespeare and the Schools. Dr. Gollancz and the Teachers', newspaper cutting (source identified as 'P.O.'), dated 11 May 1906, in Lemuel Matthews Griffiths, *Newspaper Cuttings Relating to Shakespeare* at the Birmingham Central Library, vol. 7, p. 35.

'Shakespeare for Children', newspaper cutting (source identified as 'M.P.'), dated 7 May 1906, in Lemuel Matthews Griffiths, *Newspaper Cuttings Relating to Shakespeare* at the Birmingham Central Library, vol. 7, p. 35.

'Shakespeare in the School', newspaper cutting (source identified as the *Standard*), dated 7 May 1906, in Lemuel Matthews Griffiths, *Newspaper Cuttings Relating to Shakespeare* at the Birmingham Central Library, vol. 7, p. 35.

'Shakespere's Birthday', *The Leicester Chronicle and Mercury*, 56 (28 April 1866), p. 5.
'The Shaksperian Commemoration – Its Blunders and Its Failures', *Reynolds's Newspaper*, 716 (1 May 1864), p. 4.
'The Shakspeare Tercentenary', *Illustrated London News*, 16 April 1864, included in Lemuel Matthews Griffiths, *Newspaper Cuttings Relating to Shakespeare* at the Birmingham Central Library, vol. 4, p. 24.
Sidney, Philip, *An Apologie for Poetrie* (London: Henry Olney, 1595).
Sillars, Stuart, *Reading Shakespeare, Seeing Shakespeare: The Illustrated Edition, 1709–1860* (Cambridge: Cambridge University Press, 2008).
Sillitoe, Alan, *Saturday Night and Sunday Morning* (London: Harper Perennial, 2006; originally published London: W. H. Allen & Co., 1958).
Silver, Harold, *English Education and the Radicals 1780–1850* (London: Routledge & Kegan Paul, 1975).
Smillie, Robert, *My Life for Labour* (London: Mills & Boon, 1924).
Spater, George, *William Cobbett: The Poor Man's Friend*, 2 vols. (Cambridge: Cambridge University Press, 1982).
Stead, William T., 'The Labour Party and the Books that Helped to Make It', *Review of Reviews*, 33:198 (June 1906): 568–82.
Stephens, William Brewer, *Education, Literacy and Society, 1830–1870* (Manchester: Manchester University Press, 1987).
Stratford Records Office, files ER1/58, ER1/107, DR330.
Summers, Montague, 'John Dicks, Publisher', *Times Literary Supplement*, 7 November 1942, p. 552.
Sutherland, John, *Victorian Novelists and Publishers* (Chicago: University Chicago Press, 1976).
Swindells, Julia, *Victorian Writing and Working Women: The Other Side of Silence* (Cambridge: Polity Press, 1985).
'T.A.', 'The Lounger', *The Pioneer*, no. 364 (30 May 1908), p. 2.
Taylor, Antony, 'Shakespeare and Radicalism: The Uses and Abuses of Shakespeare in Nineteenth-Century Popular Politics', *Historical Journal*, 45:3 (2002): 357–79.
Taylor, Sally J., *The Great Outsiders: Northcliffe, Rothermere and the Daily Mail* (London: Phoenix Giant, 1996).
The Teaching of English in England (London: HMSO, 1921).
'The Tercentenary Celebrations at Dudley', *The Birmingham Daily Post*, 26 April 1864, included in Birmingham Central Library *Tercentenary Shakespeare Scrapbook*, vol. 1, p. 104.
Thompson, Edward Palmer, *The Making of the English Working Class* (Harmondsworth: Penguin, 1980; first published 1963).
Thompson, J. Lee, *Northcliffe: Press Baron in Politics, 1865–1922* (London: John Murray, 2000).
Vicinus, Martha, *The Industrial Muse: A Study of Nineteenth Century British Working-Class Literature* (London: Croom Helm, 1974).
Vincent, David, *Bread, Knowledge and Freedom: A Study of Nineteenth-Century Working Class Autobiography* (London: Methuen, 1981).

Literacy and Popular Culture: England 1750–1914 (Cambridge: Cambridge University Press, 1989).
Vizetelly, Henry, *Glances Back Through Seventy Years: Autobiographical and Other Reminiscences* (London: Kegan Paul, Trench, Trübner & Co., 1893), vol. 1.
Waldman, Michael (prod. & dir.), *My Shakespeare* (Penguin Television, 2004; broadcast on Channel 4).
Webb, Robert Kiefer, *The British Working-class Reader, 1790–1848: Literacy and Social Tension* (London: Allen & Unwin, 1955).
Weedon, Alexis, *Victorian Publishing: The Economics of Book Production for a Mass Market, 1836–1916* (Aldershot: Ashgate, 2003).
Wheeler, George William, ed., *Letters of Sir Thomas Bodley to Thomas James, First Keeper of the Bodleian Library* (Oxford: Clarendon Press, 1926).
'Mr. William Margrie', *The Times*, 12 January 1960, p. 16.
Woolcock, Penny (dir.), *Shakespeare on the Estate* (BBC, 1994).
Woolf, Virginia, *A Room of One's Own* (Harmondsworth: Penguin, 1945; originally published London: Hogarth Press, 1929).
Wordsworth, William, *The Excursion, 1814* (Oxford & New York: Woodstock, 1991; facsimile reprint; originally published London: Longman, Hurst, Rees, Orme, and Brown, 1814).
Working Men's Shakespeare Committee, 'Shakespeare Celebration. Address of the Working Men's Shakespeare Committee', dated 7 June 1864, included in Birmingham Central Library *Tercentenary Shakespeare Scrap Book*, vol. 1, item number 207.
Wright, Thomas [originally published under 'The Journeyman Engineer', all titles], *Some Habits and Customs of the Working Classes* (New York: Augustus M. Kelley, 1967; originally published London: Tinsley Brothers, 1867).
  The Great Unwashed (New York: Augustus M. Kelley, 1970; originally published London: Tinsley Brother, 1868).
  Our New Masters (New York: Augustus M. Kelley, 1969; originally published London: Strahan & Co., 1873).
Wyse, Thomas, 'Education in the United Kingdom, – its Progress and Prospects', Central Society of Education, *Papers*, vol. 1 (London: Taylor and Walton, 1837).
Yearsley, Ann, 'To Mr. R ——, on his Benevolent Scheme for rescuing Poor Children from Vice and Misery, by promoting Sunday Schools', in *Poems on Several Occasions* (London: T. Cadell, 1785).

Index

The main source of evidence for this study is a set of about 100 autobiographical texts. For ease of reference, autobiographers are distinguished in the index by having their names preceded by an asterisk (*).

*Adams, W. E. 18, 56, 79–80, 98, 99, 107–8, 143–9, 152, 165
Adorno, Theodor 201
Allen, Rose 25
Altick, Richard 66, 69
Anderson, Patricia 16, 66, 68
*Andrew, Jane 15
*Andrews, Elizabeth 13
*Arch, Joseph 4, 102, 153–4
Arctic Monkeys 195
*Armstrong, Chester 68
Arnold, Matthew 49, 50
Arts Council of Great Britain 176–7
Autobiographies
   as a source of evidence 5–7
      limitations 10–16
         gender issues 12–15
   confessional tradition of 5–6
   reasons for writing 6
   resistance to working-class autobiography 6–7

Bailey, Peter 7
Bainbridge, John 20
*Ballard, Philip Boswood 18, 41, 182, 196
*Bamford, Samuel 12, 31, 60, 62
*Barber, George H. 182
Barber, M. A. S. 24
*Barclay, Tom 85, 96
*Barker, Joseph 12, 31, 101, 106
Bate, Jonathan 135, 136
Beales, Edmond 151
Bell, Andrew 36–7
Bent's Literary Advertiser 73, 77
Bernard, Thomas 34, 36, 37
Bevan, Aneurin 178
*Bezer, John James 32, 101

Bible 28, 46, 47, 81, 101, 112, 113, 117, 145, 154, 156, 161, 186
   King James version 186
Billson, Charles James 174
Bilton, Charles 49
Black Dwarf 63
*Blacket, Joseph 111
Bloomfield, Robert 23, 71, 104
Bodley, Thomas 201
Bogdanov, Michael 186–9
*Bondfield, Margaret 15
*Bonwick, James 12, 38, 40, 41
The Bookseller 1, 81
bookstalls 72–3
Borough Road school 36, 37, 38, 41
*Bowerman, C. W. 75
*Brierley, Ben 71, 110
British and Foreign School Society 16, 34–40, 46–7, 65, 95
*Broadhurst, Henry 11
Brougham, Henry 65–6, 108
*Brown, Edward 18, 179
*Brown, John 104–5
Bruton, James 20, 137
Bullen, A. H. 125
Burke, Edmund 58, 60, 135–7, 141
*Burke, Thomas 181
Burnett, John 5–6, 7, 10, 12, 14, 32, 37, 42, 165, 185
Burns, John 155
*Burt, Thomas 83, 95, 101, 152, 153
Butler, R. A. 169, 176

*Cadwaladyr, Betsy (Elizabeth Davis) 9, 28, 29
   enthusiasm for Shakespeare 114–16
Cadwaladyr, Dafydd 28
Cannadine, David 8
Carey, John 16, 175

Carlile, Richard 63
*Carter, Thomas 11, 63, 101
Chalmers, George (Francis Oldys) 61
Chaplin, Charlie 182
Chartism 62, 64, 65, 68, 78, 79, 82, 138, 203
  'Chartism from Shakespeare' 141–4
  Shakespearean Chartist Association 144–9
Chartist Circular 137, 139–41
cinema 182–3
Clare, John 17, 23
Clark, Kenneth 176
Clark, William George 81, 173
Clarke, Charles Cowden 119
*Clarke, Maud 55
Class 3
  in twentieth-century education 167–71
  problems of definition 7–10
  Shakespeare imagined as 'working class' 137–8
*Clynes, J. R. 10, 98, 104, 152, 155–7
Cobbett, William 62–3
Cobbin, Ingram 47
Colenso, William John 185
Collier, John Payne 173
Collins, Michael 183–4
Constable, Archibald 70
Cook, Eliza 23
*Cooper, Thomas 10, 64, 65, 72, 144–9
  breakdown 146
  founds Shakespearean Chartist Association 147
  programme of self-improvement 146
  Purgatory of Suicides 148
  stages production of *Hamlet* 147
Council for the Encouragement of Music and Arts 176
*Cowper, Daisy 51, 164–5
Craig, Edward Gordon 174, 193
*Crooks, Will 106
culture
  cost of accepting elite culture 170–1
  elite vs. popular 175–7
  government arts policy 176–7
  politics of 202–4
  shifting cultural forms 200–2

Dabbs, Thomas 193
*Davenport, Allen 28
Davies, Peter Maxwell 201, 202
Davis, Elizabeth – see Cadwaladyr, Betsy
Dicks, John 21, 81–2, 83
DiPietro, Cary 174, 175
Donaldson, Alexander 76
Donaldson v. Beckett 69, 76–7
Dowden, Edward 173
Dr. Who 200

*Dunning, Thomas 38
Dyce, Alexander 173

Education 2, 4, 16–17, 28–51
  Butler's Education Act of 1944 169
  church schools 34–40
    monitorial system 36–8
  class divisions in 167–71
  compulsory school attendance 44–5
  dame schools 29–30, 45–6
  decline of autodidactic impulse 164–5
  decline of religious content in 184–6
  Education Act of 1870 43–4, 163, 164, 184
  elite schools 203
  emergence of primary and secondary sectors 165–7
  expansion towards universal provision 43–5
  government funding of 39–42
    payment by results 41–2, 48
  grammar schools 167–71
  politics of 32–4
  Revised Code 40–2, 48–51
  schoolbooks: availability, contents and pricing 45–51
  Sunday schools 30–2, 185
    curriculum 32
    expansion of 31
*Edwards, George 102
*Edwards, J. Passmore 18, 67, 100
*Eldred, John 180
Eliot, Simon 71, 93, 181, 185
Eliot, T. S. 183, 201
*Elliott, Ebenezer 23, 38, 137
Ellis, Alec 41
*Elson, George 6, 9, 150
Engels, Frederich 35
'Eusebius' 32–3, 43, 58

Farningham, Marianne – see Hearn, Mary Ann
*Foley, Alice 165
football 179
Foulkes, Richard 18, 19, 151, 174–5
Fox, William 30
Freeman, Arnold 178–9, 182
French Revolution 33
Frost, John 143–4
*Frost, Thomas 35, 88, 90, 108, 174
Furnivall, F. J. 108

Gagnier, Regina 193
Garibaldi, Giuseppe 149–51
Garland, A. 137
*Garratt, V. W. 167
Garrick, David 136
The Gentleman's Magazine 32, 33

Geographical limitations of study 16–17
Gillett, Eric 13
Glover, John 81, 173
Goldstrom, J. M. 33, 46, 184
Gollancz, Israel 163
*Gosling, Ray 170–1, 203
Grady, Hugh 175
Griest, Guinevere L. 195
*Gutteridge, Joseph 30, 77
Guy, Josephine 185

Hackett, Nan 13, 181
*Hall, John Vine 86
Halliwell-Phillipps, J. O. 20, 82–3, 173
Halpern, Richard 175
*Ham, Elizabeth 13
Hardy, Thomas 60
Harmsworth, Alfred 180
Harney, George Julian 148, 159
*Harris, John 116–18, 137
  'Tercentenary Ode' 117–18, 137
Haw, George 106
Hawkers Tract Society 61
Haywood, Ian 62, 68
Hazlitt, William 202
*Hearn, Mary Ann (Marianne Farningham) 13, 35, 46, 95–6, 97, 116, 185
*Heaton, William 129
*Hetherington, Henry 29, 64–5
Hewison, Robert 176–7
*Hodges, Frank 107, 121
*Hoggart, Richard 166–8, 171–2, 202
*Holyoake, George Jacob 63, 67, 158
Horkheimer, Max 201
horse racing 180
Hotten, John Camden 82–3
*Howell, George 150
*Hughes, Anita 166
*Hughes, Francis 94
Hurt, J. S. 43, 54
Huxley, Thomas 184

Ireland 25
Irving, Henry 18, 125

Jackson, Brian 169–70
James, Henry 133
James, Louis 59
*Jermy, Louise 56
Johnson, John 154
Johnson, Steve 202
Jones, Aled 180
*Jones, Henry 10, 98, 99
*Jones, John 103
Jones, Lloyd 9

*Jones, Thomas 41, 44, 99, 176
Jonson, Ben 201
Joseph, Patterson 187, 188
journalism 180–1
Joyce, Patrick 7, 8

Kean, Charles 174
Kean, Edmund 18
Keane, John 59
*Keating, Joseph 57
Kemble, Charles 105, 115–16
Kemble, John Philip 111, 145
*Kenney, Annie 154
*Kenney, Rowland 185
Keynes, John Maynard 176
Kimmins, C. W. 163
King, T. C. 18, 125
King's College London 108
*Kitchen, Fred 102
Knight, Charles 11, 66, 70, 173
Knowles, Rosina Jane 119
Kossuth, Louis 149

Labour Party 154–7
Labour Representation League 152
Lackington, James 31
Lancaster, Joseph 36–7, 46
*Langdon, Roger 160
language 184–8
Lawson, Joseph 43
*Layton, Mrs. 103
*Leatherland, J. A. 101, 159
Leavis, Q. D. 196
Lee, Jenny 178
Lee, Sidney 124, 191
*Leno, John Bedford 10, 38, 119, 150
Levine, Lawrence W. 193
libraries 72, 85, 102
Linton, W. J. 148
*Livesey, Joseph 106
London Shakespeare League 126
*Lovekin, Emmanuel 100
Lowe, Robert 40
*Lowery, Robert 6, 16, 65, 69, 102, 108, 138, 141
Luard, H. R. 173
Ludlow, J. M. 9
Ludlow, George 48
Luhrmann, Baz 199

MacManus, J. E. 162
Macmillan, Alexander 81
Macready, William Charles 18
Malone, Edmond 173
*Mann, Tom 105–6, 111
*Margrie, William 125–7

Marriott, Alice 18, 123
Marsden, Dennis 169–70
Marsh, Herbert 33–4, 58
*Martin, Sarah 12
Marx, Karl 8
*Massey, Gerald 118–21
  theory of the origins of the sonnets 119–20
Mathias, T. J. 59
Maurice, F. D. 108
Mayall, David 5–6, 12, 14
Mayhew, Henry 73
mechanics institutes 107–10
  see also mutual improvement societies, university extension lectures
Milton, John 62
Mitchell, Geoffrey 14
*Mitchell, Hannah 6, 14, 103
modernism 175
More, Hannah 61, 65, 77, 112
Morley, Charles 50, 163
Morley, Henry 120, 172
mutual improvement societies 71, 110–11, 119
  see also mechanics institutes
My Shakespeare 187, 188

National Society for the Education of the Poor in the Principles of the Established Church 16, 34–40, 47–8
Neuburg, Victor E. 92
Newcastle Commission (on education) 40
Northern Star 79
  'Chartism from Shakespeare' 141–4

O'Connor, Feargus 78
O'Connor, T. P. 180
O'Dair, Sharon 191
O'Neill, Eliza 114
Odger, George 152
*Okey, Thomas 42, 85
Oldys, Francis – see George Chalmers
*Oliver, Thomas 132
Olivier, Laurence 198–9

Paine, Thomas 33, 58–61, 62, 77, 104, 136–7, 141
  Rights of Man 58–9, 136
Palmer, David J. 108, 172
Parker, John 75
Patterson, Alfred Temple 147
Pemberton, Max 180
Penny Magazine 66–8
Phelps, Samuel 18, 151, 174
Pilgrim's Progress 101, 196
*Place, Francis 6, 9, 38, 60, 98–9
Plain, Gill 204
*Plummer, John 67, 96

Poel, William 125
political journals 62–9
  attempted suppression of 63–5
  Political Register (Cobbett's) 41, 62–3
  Political Register (Sherwin's) 63
  Poor Man's Guardian 64–5
  response to the launching of *Penny Magazine* 67
  Publishers' Circular 48, 80, 81, 83
Publishing 58–86
  commercial models deployed in 70–1
  and contemporary politics 58–69
  – see also political journals
  cost of books 69–71, 75
  editions published by parts 78–81
  patterns and trends in 181, 185

radio 183
Raikes, Robert 30
*Raymont, Thomas 43
reading
  difficulties of 95–102
    family objections to 96–7, 103
    isolation from community 99–100
    pitfalls of undirected reading 100–2
    problems in the workplace 98–9
    religious objections to 97
  support for 102–11
    in the workplace 103–7
    within the family 102–3
Reform League 151
Religious Tract Society 61
Republican 63, 64
Reynolds, G. M. W. 68, 81, 85
Reynolds's Miscellany 68
Reynolds's Newspaper 1, 68, 82
Richardson, Alan 110
*Roberts, Robert 166, 180, 182, 185
Robertson, Forbes 18, 125
*Rogers, Frederick 18, 43, 100
  enthusiasm for Shakespeare 123–5
Rose, Jonathan 5, 54, 162, 163, 178
Rowlands, James 154
Royal Lancastrian Society 36, 65
*Rushton, Adam 71, 97, 104

St. Clair, William 58, 69, 76–7
Sawyer, William 21
Schoch, Richard 26
Scotland 16–17
Shakespeare, William
  and cinema 198–200
  Cobbett's view of 62
  editions
    Boswell-Malone 77
    Cambridge 173

Cassells 80
Chalmers 78
Dicks 81–6, 153, 173
Edinburgh 76
First Folio 76
Globe 81, 82
Hotten 82–3
Johnson-Steevens-Reed 77
Charles Knight 149
J. C. Moore's 'Penny' 79–80
Alexander Pope 76
Rivingtons' 'Stereotype' 78
Steevens 77
Stratford Town 125
Robert Tyas' 'Peoples' 78–9
Robert Walker 76
Ward & Lock 'Sixpenny' 85
Willoughby 'for the million' 80
edition prices 3, 76–86
  reduction in prices 4–5, 77–86
editions published by part 78–81
extracts of his work used in school books 49–50
imagined as being of humble origins 137–8
incorporation into school requirements 50–1
in the workplace 104–6, 107
likelihood of children reading him at school 50
individual works
  Antony and Cleopatra 142
  As You Like It 51, 141
  Coriolanus 142
  Hamlet 11, 12, 17, 18, 105, 106, 114, 115, 123, 125, 127, 139, 146, 147
  1 Henry IV 12, 139–41
  2 Henry IV 143
  Henry V 50, 83, 164, 198–9
  2 Henry VI 144, 156
  3 Henry VI 139–41
  Henry VIII 18, 49
  Julius Caesar 49, 112, 142, 155, 156
  King John 18, 50, 142, 198
  King Lear 137, 146, 154
  Macbeth 17, 110, 115, 135, 136, 139, 171
  Merchant of Venice 49, 51, 105, 138
  A Midsummer Night's Dream 174
  Much Ado About Nothing 156
  Othello 17, 111, 114, 136
  Richard II 49
  Richard III 105, 111
  Romeo and Juliet 17, 18, 114, 116, 187, 188, 199
  Sonnets 49, 119–20
  The Taming of the Shrew 198
  The Tempest 174
  Timon of Athens 18
  Titus Andronicus 153
  Twelfth Night 155

Venus and Adonis 107
A Winter's Tale 163, 174
professionalisation of Shakespeare studies 171–4
sale of his work at street stalls 73
schoolchildren's negative experience of 162–4
Tercentenary celebrations of his birth 1–3, 15, 20–1, 80–1, 83, 117–18, 150–1
work deployed for political ends 138–57
Shakespearean Chartist Association 144–9
Shakespearean Chartist Hymnbook 144
Shakespeare on the Estate 186–8
Sharman, Nancy 178
*Shaw, Charles ('An Old Potter') 30, 95, 100
Shaw, David 119
Sherwin, William T. 63
Siddons, Sarah 114, 136, 145
Sidney, Philip 201
Sillars, Stuart 93
*Sillitoe, Alan 191, 196, 197, 198
Six Acts 63–5
*Skeen, Robert 72
*Skipsey, Joseph 23
  custodianship of Shakespeare birthplace 122–3
  enthusiasm for Shakespeare 121–3
Smiles, Samuel 112
Smillie, Robert 161
*Smith, Charles Manby 6, 59, 110
*Smith, Mary 15, 30, 72, 96, 137
soccer – see football
Society for Promoting Christian Knowledge 34, 47, 66
Society for the Diffusion of Useful Knowledge 66–8, 78
Spectator 101, 181
sport 179–80
*Spring, Howard 75
*Stamper, Joseph 44–5
Stead, William T. 154
Steadman, W. C. 154
Steevens, George 173
Stratford-on-Avon 1, 11, 24, 102, 116, 117, 125, 149, 154, 162, 167, 188
  birthplace property 122–3, 191
Sullivan, Barry 18, 125
Sunday School Society 16, 30
Sutherland, John 70
Sutton Trust 203
Swindells, Julia 14, 172

Taylor, Antony 137, 154
Taylor, S. J. 180
television 183–4
*Terry, Joseph 13, 30, 98
Theatre 17–19, 24, 105, 110, 113–16, 123, 125
  elite vs. popular 174–5

Thompson, E. P. 7, 8, 87
Thomson, Christopher 18, 31, 39, 63, 95, 97, 102, 172
Tilke, Samuel Westcott 112–14
*Tillett, Ben 105
*Todd, Thomas 183
Tonson cartel 76
Tree, Herbert Beerbohm 18, 189
Tyas, Robert 78–9

university extension lectures 124
University of St. Andrews 10
unstamped periodicals 63–5

Vicinus, Martha 139, 148
Vincent, David 5–6, 12, 14, 50, 172, 173
Vincent, Henry 143
Vizetelly, Henry 64

Walsh, Stephen 154
Watson, Robert Spence 122
Weedon, Alexis 75

*West, Harry Alfred 101
Wilberforce, Samuel 184
*Williams, Alfred 179
Williams, Raymond 168
Williams, W. E. 177
*Wood, John 100
*Wood, Thomas 46
Wooler, Thomas 63
Woolf, Virginia 175
Wordsworth, William 37
working men's clubs 123–4
working men's colleges – see mechanics institutes
Working Men's Committee 1, 20–1, 151, 152
*Wright, Joseph 96
Wright, Thomas ('The Journeyman Engineer') 4, 9, 10, 90, 165
Wright, William Aldis 81, 173
*Wrigley, Mrs. 44

Yearsley, Ann 30

Lightning Source UK Ltd.
Milton Keynes UK
UKHW01f2022130718
325706UK00001B/21/P